DAVE BRUBECK'S *TIME OUT*

OXFORD STUDIES IN RECORDED JAZZ

Series Editor JEREMY BARHAM

DAVE BRUBECK'S
TIME OUT

STEPHEN A. CRIST

OXFORD
UNIVERSITY PRESS

Oxford University Press is a department of the University of Oxford. It furthers
the University's objective of excellence in research, scholarship, and education
by publishing worldwide. Oxford is a registered trade mark of Oxford University
Press in the UK and certain other countries.

Published in the United States of America by Oxford University Press
198 Madison Avenue, New York, NY 10016, United States of America.

CIP data is on file at the Library of Congress
ISBN 978–0–19–021772–3 (pbk.)
ISBN 978–0–19–021771–6 (hbk.)

9 8 7 6 5 4 3 2 1

Paperback printed by Marquis, Canada
Hardback printed by Bridgeport National Bindery, Inc., United States of America

FOR DONALD RALPH CRIST (1928-2014)

CONTENTS

ILLUSTRATIONS

TABLES

MUSIC EXAMPLES

3/c Paul Townsend, "Takes two," excerpt from the saxophone chorus in the performance by Mitchison on March 10, 1990 with allusion to Rodgers and Hammerstein duetting, 196

3/d Paul Dawson, "The Rose," excerpt from the saxophone chorus in the performance by Mitchison on March 10, 1990, with allusion to "The Hawaiian theme," 196

3/e Hammond Saxonance from Rhododendron Garden, 197

3/f Paul Hammond, "July Rose," excerpt from the saxophone chorus in the performance by Mitchison on March 10, 1990, with allusion to "The Song to Marching," 197

3/g Rhododendron & Fisher Garden, p.n. 162, 199

PREFACE

SOME YEARS AGO, walking through the streets of Padua, Italy, on a weekday morning, I heard in the open air the distant strains of an alto saxophone playing "Take Five." The music startled me, not only because of its unexpected venue but also because I had heard the Dave Brubeck Quartet perform the same tune as recently as the previous month, at a concert in Atlanta. I was struck by the ubiquity of this jazz standard, which itself had originated more than forty years earlier, and, by extension, the album on which it first appeared—resonating both in the modern city of Dr. Martin Luther King Jr., and across the Atlantic in the centuries-old town of Galileo Galilei.

This book tells the story of *Time Out,* one of the best-selling albums in the history of jazz. As I worked on this project, dozens of people from all walks of life told me that they, or their parents, owned a copy and they grew up with its familiar sounds. This is true of not only aficionados but also those less experienced in jazz. Indeed, even if one possesses only a small jazz collection, it is likely to include *Time Out* and Miles Davis's *Kind of Blue.* Both were recorded in 1959 at the legendary 30th Street Studio of Columbia Records, with Teo Macero as producer or co-producer.[1] Davis's album achieved critical acclaim second to none. *Kind of Blue* is the top-ranking jazz album (#12) on the *Rolling Stone* list of "500 Greatest Albums of All

---

1 Macero served as a co-producer with Irving Townsend for Davis's album, and as producer for Brubeck's.

Time,"[2] and in 2008 the Recording Industry Association of America certified it as quadruple platinum (sales of more than four million copies). But Brubeck's *Time Out* isn't far behind. It achieved platinum status in 1997, along with *Kind of Blue,* and it reached double platinum in 2011.[3] Moreover, *Time Out* was added to the Library of Congress's National Recording Registry for 2005 and inducted into the Grammy Hall of Fame in 2009.[4]

The secondary literature on Davis's *Kind of Blue* encompasses numerous monographs and journal articles. There is, however, no comparable body of critical discourse concerning *Time Out.* Indeed, scholarly investigation of Brubeck and his music is still in its infancy,[5] and the best overall treatment is Ted Gioia's chapter on "Dave Brubeck and Modern Jazz in San Francisco," which dates back twenty years at this point.[6]

---

2 "500 Greatest Albums of All Time," *Rolling Stone* (May 31, 2012). http://www.rollingstone. com/music/lists/500-greatest-albums-of-all-time-20120531 (accessed January 2, 2018).

3 "Gold & Platinum—RIAA" https://www.riaa.com/gold-platinum/ (accessed January 2, 2018); "Dave Brubeck's 1959 Jazz Masterpiece Time Out Certified Double Platinum by RIAA" (December 6, 2011) http://www.prnewswire.com/news-releases/dave-brubecks-1959-jazz-masterpiece-time-out-certified-double-platinum-by-riaa-135117793.html (accessed January 2, 2018).

4 "2005—National Recording Preservation Board" (Library of Congress) https://www.loc. gov/programs/national-recording-preservation-board/recording-registry/registry-by-induction-years/2005/ (accessed January 2, 2018); "GRAMMY Hall of Fame" https://www. grammy.com/grammys/awards/hall-of-fame#t (accessed January 2, 2018). "Take Five" had previously been inducted as a single in 1996, when Brubeck himself was awarded The Recording Academy's Lifetime Achievement Award. See https://www.grammy.com/ grammys/videos/dave-brubeck-lifetime-achievement-award-acceptance (accessed January 2, 2018).

5 There are at present only two books devoted exclusively to Brubeck. Ilse Storb's *Dave Brubeck: Improvisations and Compositions—The Idea of Cultural Exchange* (New York: Peter Lang, 1994) aspires to scholarly examination of its subject but is marred by inaccuracies and infelicities of all kinds. Fred M. Hall's *It's about Time: The Dave Brubeck Story* (Fayetteville: University of Arkansas Press, 1996) is pleasant but short, and intended for a general readership, with no footnotes, bibliography, or serious evaluative pretensions. Kelsey Klotz's "Racial Ideologies in 1950s Cool Jazz" (PhD diss., Washington University in St. Louis, 2016) is an important study of the Modern Jazz Quartet, the Dave Brubeck Quartet, and Miles Davis. Her forthcoming book focuses on Brubeck.

6 Ted Gioia, *West Coast Jazz: Modern Jazz in California, 1945–1960* (Berkeley: University of California Press, 1998), 60–85. Significant recent studies include Stephen A. Crist, "Jazz as Democracy? Dave Brubeck and Cold War Politics," *Journal of Musicology* 26 (2009): 133–174; Mark McFarland, "Dave Brubeck and Polytonal Jazz," *Jazz Perspectives* 3 (2009): 153–176; Andy Birtwistle, "Marking Time and Sounding Difference: Brubeck, Temporality and Modernity," *Popular Music* 29 (2010): 351–371; and Michael Spencer, "'Jazz-mad

A drawback of most previous studies is that only a few take into account the vast archival resources of the Brubeck Collection in Holt-Atherton Special Collections at the University of the Pacific Library in Stockton, California. One of the largest and most comprehensive archives of its kind, it includes an enormous number of music manuscripts, photographs, recordings, personal and business correspondence, and other items from the entire span of Brubeck's life. The period of the "classic" Dave Brubeck Quartet, which toured and recorded from 1951 to 1967, is documented quite thoroughly in the collections, and the materials frequently shed light on aspects of Brubeck's career—including *Time Out*—that are otherwise hidden from view.

In addition to primary sources in the Brubeck Collection, which I examined in a series of research trips beginning in 2004, my work here is informed by contact with and cooperation from several individuals. These include Dave Brubeck himself, whom I interviewed on numerous occasions during the fifteen-year period from 1997 until his passing in December 2012, and his wife Iola, with whom I corresponded for many years, until shortly before her own death in March 2014. I also interviewed the Brubecks' daughter Catherine—dedicatee of "Kathy's Waltz," the fifth cut on *Time Out*—in New Haven, Connecticut, in November 2013. Catherine delivered to me a copy of her eldest brother Darius's master's thesis on "Jazz 1959: The Beginning of Beyond" (University of Nottingham, 2002), which he kindly brought over for me during a visit from England.[7] Dave Brubeck's long-time manager, Russell Gloyd, and personal attorney, Richard Jeweler—both affiliated with the organization since the 1970s—provided invaluable information and assistance as well.

Finally, I have drawn upon two additional archival resources at the New York Public Library, the Teo Macero Collection and the George Avakian Papers. Macero was the producer of *Time Out*, and indeed of most of Dave Brubeck's other recordings for Columbia. The Macero Collection includes folders of correspondence, datasheets, and

---

Collegiennes': Dave Brubeck, Cultural Convergence, and the College Jazz Renaissance in California," *Jazz Perspectives* 6 (2012): 337–353. The latter is an outgrowth of Michael T. Spencer, "Pacific Standard Time: Modernism and the Making of West Coast Jazz" (PhD diss., Michigan State University, 2011). Another substantial contribution is the chapter "Brubeck! Jazz Goes to College" in Kevin Starr, *Golden Dreams: California in an Age of Abundance, 1950–1963* (New York: Oxford University Press, 2009), 381–410.

7 This thesis forms the basis for Darius Brubeck, "1959: The Beginning of Beyond," in *The Cambridge Companion to Jazz*, ed. Mervyn Cooke and David Horn (Cambridge: Cambridge University Press, 2002), 177–201, 351–352.

promotional materials concerning *Time Out* and other projects. George Avakian was the executive who signed Brubeck to Columbia Records in 1954 and produced some of his first projects there. Avakian's Brubeck materials provide valuable clues about Dave's early years as a Columbia recording artist.

The core of the book consists of six chapters, each chapter examining the album's seven cuts from a particular point of view. Three historical and contextual chapters precede these core discussions, and one follows, treating key events, issues, and projects connected with the album's genesis and reception. Though focused on *Time Out*, this study ultimately also sketches the contours of the entire life cycle of the Dave Brubeck Quartet, from its formation in 1951 until its dissolution in 1967. It capitalizes on the marvelous coincidence that *Time Out*, the album that arguably defined Brubeck's career and legacy, came into being at the exact midpoint of the "classic" Quartet's sixteen-year tenure.

The music of *Time Out* is well known, and the album has spawned countless back stories. Someone once asked me what more could possibly be said about such a familiar item in the jazz discography. I believe this book is a potent demonstration that there is indeed much more here to say. This recording represents both the literal and figurative centerpiece of a crucial chapter in American cultural history. The story of *Time Out* is about the expansion of jazz to encompass new time signatures and rhythms, and simultaneously to include among its admirers many first-time listeners and people who thought they didn't like jazz. It is fundamentally a tale about the popularization of this art form, against all odds, in astonishing and unexpected ways.

ACKNOWLEDGMENTS

THIS BOOK OWES its existence to Suzanne Ryan, my editor at Oxford University Press. I wasn't thinking of writing a study of *Time Out* until she asked a few key questions. Then one thing led to another, and here is the result. I'm grateful for her patience and encouragement along the way. I'm indebted as well to Jeremy Barham, and delighted for the opportunity to contribute to the distinguished series for which he serves as general editor.

One of the great and unexpected pleasures of my life has been the chance to get to know Dave Brubeck and his wonderful family during the past two decades. I first met Dave and his wife Iola in April 1998 at their home in Wilton, Connecticut. We spent a pleasant half-day conversing about our mutual affection for the music of J. S. Bach, which formed the basis for my chapter in an edited volume on *Bach in America*. I never imagined that my acquaintance with the Brubecks, or my research on Dave's role in jazz history, would continue into the future. But my initial excursion in this area was so satisfying that I've been glad to return on several occasions, interleaved with my continuing work on Bach and his contemporaries. Dave and Iola were always extremely generous about providing information to facilitate my research, and they welcomed the challenging and probing questions I sent their way. Since their passing a few years ago, their eldest son, Darius Brubeck, has graciously fielded a number of my queries. I appreciated the opportunity to read Darius's master's thesis about jazz in 1959, which involved a coordinated family effort, since the University of Nottingham was unwilling to ship their copy overseas. The Brubecks' daughter, Catherine Brubeck Yaghzisian, for whom Dave composed "Kathy's Waltz," has been very interested in this book's progress. She also was enormously encouraging and helpful, for which I'm deeply grateful.

I'm indebted to several other individuals with close ties to the Brubecks. I appreciate the assistance of Richard Jeweler, who handles permissions and other business matters. Russell Gloyd—Dave's manager, conductor, and right hand for nearly forty years—has been unfailingly responsive to my questions over the years. His steel-trap mind and prodigious memory have helped to solve many a research conundrum.

It is a great pleasure to acknowledge with thanks the invaluable assistance of the staff at Holt-Atherton Special Collections of the University of the Pacific Library, Stockton, California, where the archives of Dave Brubeck are held, especially Mike Wurtz, Head of Special Collections, and Nicole Grady, Special Collections Librarian, but also their predecessors, Shan Sutton and Trish Richards. I appreciate as well the cooperation of the staff at the New York Public Library for the Performing Arts, where the papers of Teo Macero and George Avakian are preserved, especially George Boziwick, chief of the Music Division, and his successor, Jonathan Hiam. This book has also been enriched and informed by materials held in the Sony Music Archives Library (New York). My thanks to its director, Tom Tierney, and former manager, the late Michael Panico, for their kind assistance, and to Toby Silver, who handled the permissions.

Among many colleagues who have shown great interest in this project, and who have helped in tangible ways, I wish to mention in particular Keith Hatschek, Kelsey Klotz, and John Salmon. At Emory, I thank especially Dwight Andrews, Kevin Karnes, and Gary Motley, for many stimulating conversations concerning this material. I'm grateful as well to Emory College of Arts and Sciences for a research leave that kickstarted an early stage of the writing process.

Finally, my deepest thanks go to my family—Caitlin, Michael, Alexander, Hannah, and especially my wife, Susan. But above all, I wish to thank my father, Don Crist, for his encouragement throughout my scholarly career. He died of brain cancer just as this project was getting off the ground. One of my fondest memories of his final days was letting him know that this book would be dedicated to him. Though the writing took longer than anticipated, the happy outcome is that I'm able to pen these words on what would have been his ninetieth birthday.

Atlanta, Georgia
March 15, 2018

ACKNOWLEDGMENTS

DAVE BRUBECK'S *TIME OUT*

CHAPTER I

TIME AND *BRUBECK TIME*

THE SEEDS OF Dave Brubeck's success with the *Time Out* album in 1959 were sown throughout the decade of the 1950s—and even earlier during his years as an undergraduate, his service in the US Army toward the end of World War II, and his graduate studies that followed. Brubeck had always been quite intentional about his efforts to achieve jazz stardom, and his student and journeyman days in the 1940s were essential to his musical development. Yet the roots of the *Time Out* project are primarily entangled with three important events that led to the formation of the Dave Brubeck Quartet and its rise to fame through the early months of 1955: Brubeck's contract with Columbia Records, beginning in 1954; his appearance on the cover of *Time* magazine later that year; and the release of *Brubeck Time*, his first studio album for Columbia, at the beginning of the following year.

Although *Time Out* was Brubeck's first project to be devoted single-mindedly to the use of time signatures uncommon in jazz, it was hardly his first foray into this territory. In a 1961 television show hosted by Ralph J. Gleason—the prominent San Francisco jazz critic with whom he had something of a "love-hate" relationship—Brubeck said that the two things to which he had devoted the most effort during the previous decade were polytonality and polyrhythm. He pursued the latter because "jazz was much too tame." The specific method he described was that "the drummer would be playing one rhythm, the bass player another rhythm, and Paul [Desmond on the alto saxophone] and I could play in either of those rhythms, or a new rhythm." He expressed satisfaction that the Quartet had improved in its ability to combine multiple rhythms, and that this approach was finding public acceptance. He also noted, "*Time Out* was the first album where we took a whole series of time signatures different than we're used to playing in."[1]

It is hard to pinpoint exactly when Brubeck first became interested in polyrhythms. In 1990, when he was nearly seventy years old, he said that he "had been experimenting with odd time signatures since [he] was a kid."[2] Many years earlier—before *Time Out*, in fact—he told Gleason that it started when he was eighteen years old.[3] It must have been even sooner, though, probably before he entered college in 1938. Brubeck often told the story of growing up on a 45,000-acre ranch in northern California and the formative influence of the sounds around him:

My dad was a champion roper. . . . In the summer I would ride with my dad. You can't imagine how many miles long the ranch was. He might send me to start the pump so the cattle had water. I had to ride there and start it, and the pump had great rhythm. I'd lie down and the pump on the two-by-fours would make vibrations. And when the

---

1 "Ralph J. Gleason's Jazz Casual: Dave Brubeck, Featuring Paul Desmond." Los Angeles: Rhino Home Video, 2003. Originally aired on KQED, San Francisco, on October 17, 1961. Thirty-five years later, Brubeck said something similar, that what he "tried to do from the beginning was to play polyrhythmically and polytonally." Rosemary Hallum, "The Best of Times for Dave Brubeck," *Clavier* 35, no. 4 (April 1996): 8. Like many jazz musicians, Brubeck used terms such as "rhythm," "time signatures" (denoting meter), and "tempo" more or less interchangeably to signify the temporal aspects of music.

2 Howard Reich, "Brubeck: Going Full Tilt at 70, He Still Likes to Take Five," *Chicago Tribune*, March 25, 1990.

3 Ralph J. Gleason, "'They Said I Was Too Far Out,'" *Down Beat* 24, no. 16 (August 8, 1957): 18.

horse would walk or trot or gallop, it would put rhythms in my head, polyrhythms in my head. Same way with the pump.[4]

Doug Ramsey referred to these sounds as "rhythms of the range." Brubeck's imagination was sparked not only by the horse's gait and the gasoline engine that drove the water pump, but also by the "sound permutations of anvils in the blacksmith shop" and "machinery in the hay fields."[5]

Brubeck said that from the beginning of his career he wanted to pursue unusual approaches to meter and rhythm. He apparently began incorporating these techniques into his compositions even before he graduated from college.[6] He claimed explicitly that the ideas that germinated in *Time Out* so many years later "started in the early forties."[7] In an interview for Radio Free Europe in the mid-1960s, he said that he began playing "a more polyrhythmic, more polytonal jazz" in 1942, and he noted presciently, "if I live to be an old man [he died in 2012, one day before his ninety-second birthday], I'll never exhaust the polyrhythmic, polytonal possibilities."[8]

The year 1942 was especially eventful. It was when Brubeck graduated from the College of the Pacific in Stockton, California. This was not as straightforward a matter as one might expect. Brubeck had matriculated with the intention of majoring in veterinary medicine but switched to music during his second year. When he was a senior, his struggles with musical notation (apparently a form of dyslexia) came to light and caused a dispute between a group of faculty members who recognized his extraordinary aural skills and imagination, and others who felt it would be a disgrace to award a degree to a student who couldn't read music.[9]

4 Barbara Isenberg, *State of the Arts: California Artists Talk about Their Work* (New York: William Morrow, 2000), 9.

5 Doug Ramsey, "Dave Brubeck: A Life in American Music," in booklet for four-CD compilation, *Dave Brubeck: Time Signatures: A Career Retrospective* (New York: Columbia/Legacy, 1992), 28.

6 Elyse Mach, "With Dave Brubeck the Music Never Stops," *Clavier* 40, no. 5 (May 2001): 7.

7 Paul Zollo, *Songwriters on Songwriting*, 4th ed. (Cambridge, MA: Da Capo Press, 2003), 55. Zollo's interview with Brubeck was conducted in 1995.

8 Horst Petzall, "A Visit with Dave Brubeck" (interview), Radio Free Europe, New York, News Department, June 16, 1965. Brubeck Collection, Holt-Atherton Special Collections, University of the Pacific Library, MSS 004 (hereafter "Brubeck Collection"). An article published the following year specified a slightly later date. Brubeck was quoted as saying, "Even as far back as 1945, I was thinking along these lines." Bob Houston, "Dave Brubeck: Such a Long Time over This Matter of Time," *Melody Maker* (November 5, 1966): 8.

9 Regarding Brubeck's "musical dyslexia," see John Salmon, "What Brubeck Got from Milhaud," *American Music Teacher* 41, no. 4 (February–March 1992): 26.

In September 1942, Brubeck married Iola Whitlock, who remained his closest companion for seventy years and with whom he raised six children. Meanwhile, he had joined the army and was stationed at Camp Haan, about sixty miles east of Los Angeles. During his stateside time of military service, Brubeck took the opportunity to compose a piece titled *Prayer of the Conquered* for Stan Kenton's band. Kenton told him it was too avant-garde and he should come back a decade later. Brubeck also made brief contact with the eminent classical composer, Arnold Schoenberg, who at that time was teaching at UCLA. But the two didn't see eye to eye, so their association ended after just one lesson.[10]

A much more fruitful period of compositional tutelage took place when Brubeck returned from his European tour of duty after the end of World War II. With the support of the GI Bill, Brubeck enrolled in 1946 as a graduate student at Mills College in Oakland, California. His mentor was Darius Milhaud, a member of the group of French modernist composers known as *Les Six,* which also included Arthur Honegger and Francis Poulenc. Milhaud encouraged Brubeck's abiding interest in polyrhythms and challenged him to explore advanced compositional techniques within the context of the jazz idiom.[11]

Around the same time, Brubeck was deeply impressed by a set of recordings of indigenous music that were made in central Africa in the mid-1930s. One of the concrete compositional results of this influence was an alternative version of "Pick Up Sticks" (the last cut on *Time Out*), known as "Watusi Drums."[12] More broadly, however, the complex patterns of this music provided additional fuel for Brubeck's polyrhythmic experimentation.

TIME EXPERIMENTS OF THE DAVE BRUBECK OCTET AND TRIO

The Quartet was by far the best known of Dave Brubeck's groups, but it was preceded by two others. The group that eventually recorded as the Dave Brubeck Octet was originally constituted in 1946 as the Jazz Workshop Ensemble. Most of the musicians—on saxophones, clarinet, trumpet, and trombone, in addition to the rhythm section, with Brubeck

---

10 Fred Hall, *It's about Time: The Dave Brubeck Story* (Fayetteville: University of Arkansas, 1996), 14–24.

11 Salmon, "What Brubeck Got from Milhaud," 26–29, 76.

12 The transformation of "Watusi Drums" into "Pick Up Sticks" will be discussed in Chapter 6.

himself at the piano—were studying with Milhaud at Mills, and its initial purpose was to provide a performance medium for their compositions. The repertoire of the Octet included a considerable amount of metrical and rhythmic exploration.[13] One of the freshest examples is Bill Smith's version of the Cole Porter standard "What Is This Thing Called Love?" Smith enjoyed a long and distinguished dual career as a jazz musician and classical clarinetist who specialized in multiphonics and other extended techniques.[14] His arrangement begins with an ominous passage (see Example 1.1), thirty seconds in length, in which an ostinato in 5/4 (piano and bass) is pitted against a dissonant harmonization of the opening phrases of the tune (clarinet, saxophones, muted trumpet). This opening is followed by a complete change of mood, taking off into a swinging big-band style for the balance of the cut.[15]

After discovering through hard experience that the Octet wasn't financially viable—on account of its unconventional musical style as well as its relatively large number of members—Brubeck extracted the group's rhythm section to form the Dave Brubeck Trio with Cal Tjader (vibes, drums, bongos) and Ron Crotty (bass). In retrospective discussions of Brubeck's early time experiments, by Dave himself and others who were well acquainted with his music, one of the most frequently mentioned examples is the Trio's recording of "Singin' in the Rain." The arrangement begins in standard 4/4 meter. After four sixteen-bar strains, it shifts at 1:46 to a double-time feel. But there is a simultaneous change to compound meter (6/8), which alternates with up-tempo 4/4 until the end (see Example 1.2).

13 Brubeck said that some of what the Octet played was so avant-garde it was never released on disc. Gudrun Endress and Ulrich Roth, "Zwischen Jazzclub und Kirche: Dave Brubeck," *Jazz Podium* 39 (February 1990): 6.

14 See Kathryn Hallgrimson Suther, "Two Sides of William O. 'Bill' Smith," *Clarinet* 24, no. 4 (July–August 1997): 40–45; 25, no. 1 (November–December 1997): 42–48. Smith was also an important pedagogue at the University of Washington, and his faculty webpage is similarly bifurcated to reflect the diverse activities of "Bill Smith" on the one hand and "William O. Smith" on the other.

15 After sixty-four bars of quadruple meter (the last two of which are regrouped as 3+3+2), there is a shift to jazz-waltz style at 2:11. Ten bars of triple meter are followed by one measure in 2/4 and six in 4/4, before concluding with four more in 3/4. Frank Tirro has called attention to the pathbreaking nature of the metrical patterns in Smith's arrangements, comparing them with Gerry Mulligan's use of changing meters in "Jeru" for the *Birth of the Cool* band. Frank Tirro, *"The Birth of the Cool" of Miles Davis and His Associates* (Hillsdale, NY: Pendragon, 2009), 35–36.

BRUBECK'S AMBITIONS AND THE FORMATION OF THE QUARTET

The Dave Brubeck Quartet came into being during summer 1951, but not without some stress and strain. The group's formation was, in fact, the result of its leader's attempt to make the best of a difficult situation.

EXAMPLE 1.2. Arthur Freed and Nacio Herb Brown, "Singin' in the Rain," arranged by Dave Brubeck, transcription.

Brubeck had long set his sights on a successful career as a jazz musician. As early as 1946, he told Iola that he felt he could be "one of the outstanding pianists in the country," if he was in New York or some place where he could be heard.[16] By the last quarter of 1950, he was at a crossroads. In a highly informative letter to his booking agent in Hollywood, Brubeck laid his cards on the table:

> I do not wish to make jazz my career unless I see the possibilities of becoming a top name in the country. . . . If the national future of the trio does not look too promising, I intend to return to San Francisco, teach in some college and be a "local boy who almost made good.". . . I feel at present I am equipped with a library and the musicians to become a top name in American jazz with my octet and trio, if handled correctly.[17]

Brubeck's dream of becoming a "top name" is especially poignant in view of what was happening behind the scenes at home. In an intimate letter to a close friend, only three weeks after Dave's note to his agent, Iola wrote frankly about their dire financial straits and requested repayment of $30.00: "I'm sorry to bring up an unpleasant subject like money—but, I don't know what else to do, in the predicament I'm in now. . . . As it stands now I'm having to figure every penny."[18] A few months later, in April 1951, the Brubeck family left for what was supposed to have been a three-month engagement in Hawaii.[19] Dave later recalled they were so

16 Ralph J. Gleason, "'They Said I Was Too Far Out,'" *Down Beat* 24, no. 16 (August 8, 1957): 39.

17 Dave Brubeck to Cliff Aranson (Associated Booking Corporation, Hollywood), November 15, 1950 (Brubeck Collection).

18 Iola Brubeck to Mary Jeanne Marbury, December 5, 1950 (Brubeck Collection).

19 Their commitment was set to begin on April 16. Iola Brubeck to Mary Jeanne Marbury, March 21, 1951 (Brubeck Collection).

poor at that time, they "bought a footlocker full of baby food that had been in a fire and took it with us all the way to Honolulu."[20]

Once they had reached their destination, Brubeck unfortunately added injury to their already precarious circumstances. On the afternoon of May 1, while swimming at the beach with his family, he dived in a shallow spot, hit his head, and dislocated two vertebrae in his neck. Instead of playing music at Waikiki's Zebra Room, he spent the next three weeks in traction at the hospital.[21] The Trio then met its end when his drummer (Tjader) and bass player (Jack Weeks, who had replaced Crotty) both returned to the mainland.

During his convalescence, Brubeck contacted the alto saxophonist Paul Desmond, with whom he had played from time to time since the early 1940s. He recruited Desmond to join as the fourth member of his group, along with a new bass player and drummer. In one of a remarkable set of letters from the Brubecks to Desmond dating from May 1951, Iola implored Paul, "Write immediately. Dave can't rest until he hears from you." She then provided another rare window into their private hopes and fears: "This may sound sentimental, but for two days we weren't sure whether Dave would ever play piano again—or even walk again. During that time Dave kept thinking—'if I'm through, now, I've had to quit before I've begun.' All the compromises seemed so futile—so unnecessary—so ridiculous."[22]

Brubeck and Desmond were the constants in the Dave Brubeck Quartet from its inception, through the period of *Time Out* and its sequels, until the group's dissolution at the end of 1967. Early on, Brubeck enlisted Desmond's assistance in securing drummers and bass players. The occupants of these two slots shifted, sometimes rather frequently, until Joe Morello became the drummer in 1956 and Eugene Wright the bass player in 1958. Some years later, in answer to a query from a college student, Brubeck said the original members of the Quartet included Herb Barman on drums and Wyatt Ruther on bass.[23] In a letter that probably dates from May 1951, while he was still in Hawaii, Brubeck wrote to Desmond about Barman: "Would Herb Barman do for Seattle? You

20 Carol Montparker, "Taking Five with Dave Brubeck," *Clavier* 26, no. 2 (February 1987): 10.

21 Robert Rice, "The Cleanup Man," *New Yorker* 37, no. 16 (June 3, 1961): 74, 77.

22 Iola Brubeck to Paul Desmond, May 11, 1951. Paul Desmond Papers, Holt-Atherton Department of Special Collections, University of the Pacific Library (hereafter "Desmond Papers").

23 S. Charmian Slade (Brubeck's secretary) to J. Ann Herbst, November 11, 1964 (Brubeck Collection).

are working with him, so would you recommend him? I jammed with him once and he swung like a bastard, but was loud. Personally, I think him a bit, shall we say, strange."[24] Desmond's response isn't reflected in the historical record, but Barman's name appears in Brubeck's payroll ledger for the first year, from July 10, 1951 until June 29, 1952, when he was replaced by Lloyd Davis. Ruther, whose nickname was "Bull," didn't join the Quartet until the end of October 1951. He was preceded by three other bass players: Roger Nichols (July 10–August 29), Fred Dutton (September 7–28), and Gene England (September 28–October 26).[25]

Though Dutton's tenure with the Quartet was brief, the fact that he doubled on the bassoon—not a usual jazz instrument—was a definite selling point. Brubeck asked Desmond to "scout him in every possible phrase" and suggested they could "do a couple of numbers a night that feature him on bassoon as a gimmick." He felt they "either have to copy the old trio or get something uniquely different." And he favored "getting far removed from it, if we can do something *well*."[26] The novelty of Dutton's "hot bassoon" figured prominently in a contemporary account of the debut of the "new Brubeck quartet." The writer characterized it as "something the like of which has not been heard before," noting that Dutton's playing "on introductions, endings, and the few things they had put together seemed to make everybody very happy."[27] A fascinating artifact of this fleeting phase of the early Quartet can be heard in the August 1951 recordings of "Crazy Chris," "A Foggy Day," and "Somebody Loves Me" (Fantasy 3-5), widely available on YouTube and elsewhere.

RISE TO FAME

The Dave Brubeck Quartet moved from strength to strength in 1952 and 1953. One index of the group's popularity was its placement in national polls. The Quartet ranked second in *Metronome* magazine's "Small Group" category in 1952, and it advanced to first place the following year.[28] Moreover, the periodical selected the Quartet as its Editors' Choice in

---

24 Dave Brubeck to Paul Desmond, undated (Desmond Papers).
25 Cash Book, 1948–1954 (Brubeck Collection).
26 Dave Brubeck (in Iola's hand) to Paul Desmond, May 25, 1951 (Desmond Papers).
27 Hal Holly, "New Dave Brubeck Combo Scores Solid Hit in L.A.," *Down Beat* 18, no. 21 (October 19, 1951): 9. See also Ralph J. Gleason, "Brubeck Adds a Bassoonist," *Down Beat* 18, no. 19 (September 21, 1951): 13.
28 Lee Cummings (*Metronome*, New York) to Dave Brubeck, December 10, 1956 (Brubeck Collection).

1952.[29]

The editors in question were the editor-in-chief George T. Simon, the eminent jazz journalist Leonard Feather, and Barry Ulanov, a professor in the English department at Princeton University (1951–1953) and at Barnard College (1953–1988), who wrote extensively about jazz.[30] Both Dave and Iola Brubeck acknowledged Ulanov as an early supporter of Dave's work, especially as contrasted with Ralph Gleason. In a personal letter whose primary purpose was to approve an article for publication in *Down Beat*, Dave noted, "Barry Ulanov visited San Francisco in 1950 [*recte:* 1949[31]] and his subsequent critical reviews of my trio records finally made us known outside of our hometown."[32] Similarly, Iola told the editor of *Down Beat*, "It is still my belief that the first recognition of [the octet's] talents and potential contribution to jazz came from Barry Ulanov after his visit to San Francisco," and she expressed her displeasure that the group's "three years of writing and experimentation [1946–1949] ... was unnoticed by the only jazz reporter in our area [Gleason]."[33]

Ulanov spoke admiringly of the "inner tension" between Brubeck's classical training and jazz practice, and cast him in the role of a pioneer who "knows better than most musicians where we are in jazz, approximately where we can go next, and with what means."[34] Gleason, for his part, usually tempered his distaste in public. But his contempt and insensitivity is evident in the liner notes for a 1952 Dave Brubeck Trio LP. In the page proof, Gleason's narration of the trio's itinerary included an insult, which was edited out of the final version (italicized in the following): "With several return engagements at the Blackhawk [nightclub in San Francisco] the trio made trips to Salt Lake City, Portland, Ore.,

29 Kevin Starr, *Golden Dreams: California in an Age of Abundance, 1950–1963* (New York: Oxford University Press, 2009), 404.

30 Ben Ratliff, "Barry Ulanov, 82, a Scholar of Jazz, Art, and Catholicism" [obituary], *New York Times*, May 7, 2000.

31 Ulanov's recollection, less than three years after the fact, is quite precise: "I first heard Dave in the KNBC studios in San Francisco. He was running down tunes with his trio for Jimmy Lyons' early evening radio show. Then—August, 1949—and in all his recording activity for two years, the keynote of Dave's sound was a rhythmic brilliance produced by Ron Crotty's bass, Cal Tjader's drums and vibes, and his own vigorous left piano hand." Barry Ulanov, "Dave Brubeck," *Metronome* 68, no. 3 (March 1952): 17.

32 Dave Brubeck to Donald Freeman (Radio-TV Editor, *San Francisco Union*), June 25, 1955 (Brubeck Collection). See Don Freeman, "Dave Brubeck Answers His Critics," *Down Beat* 22, no. 16 (August 10, 1955): 7.

33 Iola Brubeck to editor, *Down Beat*, August 18, 1956 (Brubeck Collection).

34 Barry Ulanov, "A Talk with Dave Brubeck," *Metronome* 69, no. 4 (April 1953): 29–30.

Seattle, Los Angeles, Chicago and Honolulu, *where Dave, the stupid shit, almost broke his neck.*[35]

By the time Brubeck signed with Columbia Records in 1954, his quartet was inextricably associated with the performance of jazz concerts on college campuses. The very first album issued by Columbia was, in fact, titled *Jazz Goes to College* (Columbia CL 566), and it was recorded live at the University of Michigan, the University of Cincinnati, and Oberlin College. The so-called college circuit was an important factor in Brubeck's growing popularity, and its origins can be traced to the early 1950s. The vision for this enterprise must be credited to Iola Brubeck, and she provided much of the elbow grease as well. As Iola explained in an interview at the Library of Congress, she and her husband discovered that the best audiences for his music were young students who could grasp its new vocabulary. She recalled deciding that "the best way to spread the word would be to try to get the quartet to perform in as many schools as possible," and described it as "kitchen table work." She "sat down and wrote to every college up and down the West Coast that . . . was in driving distance of where we lived in San Francisco, and offered their services." The Quartet proposed to work for union scale, and they would split with the organizers any amount that was made over that fee. The scheme worked extremely well and turned out to be "the very thing that . . . set Dave apart from the others at that particular time."[36]

The most famous campus concert took place on March 2, 1953 at Oberlin College, and several selections from that occasion were released on *Jazz at Oberlin* (Fantasy 3-11). Brubeck's promotional letter ("Dear Friend" on Fantasy Records letterhead) reveals that he considered this moment to be a personal high-water mark: "Frankly, this LP is one that we are all proud of and one that we think comes nearer to expressing the musical potential of the group than anything we have issued before." Its excellence was surprising because "when we played that concert at Oberlin we were tired, sick and harassed and were hardly speaking to each other." But after they reviewed the tapes, the Quartet members (Brubeck and Desmond, with Ron Crotty on bass and Lloyd Davis on drums) "were all convinced it was the best thing we've ever done."[37]

---

35 Page proof, Ralph J. Gleason, liner notes, *The Dave Brubeck Trio* (Fantasy 3-4) (Brubeck Collection).

36 Denise Gallo, "Lyricist Iola Brubeck" (April 10, 2008 interview, 39 minutes). The relevant segment begins around 27:00. http://www.loc.gov/today/cyberlc/feature_wdesc.php?rec=4797 (accessed January 18, 2018).

37 Dave Brubeck, undated (Brubeck Collection).

The Oberlin concert was important not only because the group played so well but also on account of its venue. According to the student who organized the event, the venerable Conservatory of Music at Oberlin had never "seen fit to include jazz in its curriculum," and there was little support for jazz on campus—as opposed to classical music. As a result of Brubeck's performance, jazz "found itself firmly and comfortably at home in surroundings, where, in the past, it had been met only with apathy and misunderstanding."[38] Fifty years later, the chair of Oberlin's jazz studies department hailed it as "the watershed event that signaled the change of performance space for jazz from the nightclub to the concert hall."[39]

Just a few weeks before the concert at Oberlin, the editor of *Down Beat*, the most important jazz periodical of the time, predicted meteoric success in the near future: "It should be a large next couple of years for [Brubeck]. . . . Begin preparations to hail the new king. He'll be crowned any time now."[40] The accuracy of these prescient remarks became evident already in the late summer, when the Quartet was named winner in the combo division of a poll of jazz critics conducted by *Down Beat*, and Brubeck appeared on the magazine's cover along with Duke Ellington.[41] Amazingly, just four months later, the Quartet was honored again, this time as best instrumental group in *Down Beat*'s annual readers poll.[42]

Brubeck's rise to fame played into larger trends and issues that have been discussed by jazz critics and scholars. For instance, Steven Elworth called attention to an "increased intellectualization" in the 1950s, connected with the "conviction that jazz was an art." He pointed to Dave Brubeck as a figure who aspired to acceptance of jazz "in the same public sphere as classical music," and noted that "Brubeck was extremely popular on the white college circuit, where his image was seen as that of an exemplary white jazz musician who was also an artist and intellectual."[43]

---

38 James Newman, liner notes, *Jazz at Oberlin*.

39 Jonah Berman, "Legendary Brubeck Album *Jazz at Oberlin* Marks 50 Years," *Oberlin Conservatory Magazine* (2003). http://www2.oberlin.edu/con/connews/2003/ofnote.html#9 (accessed March 16, 2018).

40 Jack [Tracy], "Coronation Ceremonies Nearing for Brubeck," *Down Beat* 20, no. 3 (February 11, 1953): 3.

41 *Down Beat* 20, no. 17 (August 26, 1953). The July 26 telegram informing Brubeck of this achievement was sent by Tracy, the editor who had predicted his ascendancy (Brubeck Collection).

42 *Down Beat* 20, no. 25 (December 16, 1953). Tracy was again the bearer of this good news, in a telegram to Brubeck on November 24 (Brubeck Collection).

43 Steven B. Elworth, "Jazz in Crisis, 1948–1958: Ideology and Representation," in *Jazz among the Discourses*, ed. Krin Gabbard (Durham, NC: Duke University Press, 1995), 65.

Likewise, Francis Davis observed in an article that originally appeared in *The Atlantic Monthly* (February 2000), "In the mid-1950s a taste for 'progressive' jazz, as exemplified by Stan Kenton and Dave Brubeck . . . was virtually a rite of passage for a certain type of male college student with horn-rimmed glasses and intellectual aspirations."[44] Along similar lines, the sociologist Paul Lopes viewed the Dave Brubeck Quartet as the personification of "a new legitimacy for jazz music as the jazz art world successfully pursued the college market as a new source of income and prestige."[45] Brubeck's increasing commercial success and broad appeal— to those experienced in jazz as well as to those who had not previously given it a chance—set the stage for two career highlights that will be examined in the following sections.

COLUMBIA RECORDS CONTRACT

The year 1954 was when Dave Brubeck's ship came in. His best-known achievement from that time was his appearance on the cover of *Time* magazine. But that was preceded by the signing of a multiyear contract with Columbia Records. Both of these milestones are well known. But the story of their connection to each other, and to the production of Brubeck's first studio album for Columbia, has lain dormant until now.

By the last quarter of 1953 Brubeck was reevaluating his recording options. His earliest records—with the Trio and Octet, then the Quartet— appeared on Fantasy, the label he had founded with the brothers Sol and Max Weiss for a few hundred dollars.[46] As late as October Brubeck expressed his willingness to "sign as many years as Fantasy wishes me to sign" under new terms.[47] But six weeks later George Avakian of Columbia Records sent Brubeck a query, noting simply, "Have heard you are free of Fantasy record contract. Please let me know."[48] Shortly after the first of the year Brubeck's manager, Joe Glaser, weighed in: "I personally think that you should definitely and positively have some sort of understanding with Fantasy." One important question concerned "how

---

44 Francis Davis, *Like Young: Jazz and Pop, Youth and Middle Age* (Cambridge, MA: Da Capo Press, 2001), 142.

45 Paul Lopes, *The Rise of a Jazz Art World* (Cambridge: Cambridge University Press, 2002), 235.

46 Hall, *It's about Time*, 51.

47 Dave Brubeck to "Cy" (Cyrus King, Brubeck's tax attorney), October 26, 1953 (Brubeck Collection).

48 George Avakian to Dave Brubeck, telegram, December 7, 1953 (Brubeck Collection).

long you are going to remain with Fantasy." He offered to meet in person, to "try to help you decide as to what you are going to do about your recording situation in the future."[49]

The principal players in negotiating Brubeck's contract with Columbia Records, then, were Avakian and Glaser. More than a half-century later, when Brubeck was selected as a Kennedy Center Honoree in 2009, Avakian recounted the story of their early acquaintance in a written tribute for the commemorative program that was distributed to the guests. After World War II Avakian married Anahid Ajemian, a prize-winning violinist who had graduated from Juilliard, and Anahid's sister, Maro, a pianist, wedded a man from San Francisco. The sisters rehearsed together in the summertime in Berkeley, and Avakian had the opportunity to hear the Dave Brubeck Quartet in the Bay Area many times during that period. In 1953, when the partnership with Fantasy foundered and "Dave was eased out," Avakian proposed that he sign with Columbia. Brubeck was attracted by the fact that Avakian had delved deeply into jazz but was also invested in the music of composers such as Debussy, Stravinsky, the "super-modernist" Edgard Varèse, John Cage, and Alan Hovhaness. Because of Avakian's broad musical background, Brubeck felt he would be assured of the freedom to pursue his own vision.[50]

For his part, there is evidence that Glaser brokered the deal. A letter to Brubeck from one of the Weiss brothers in California mentions a recent phone call from a distributor in New York, who told him, "Joe Glaser has got you [Brubeck] a recording contract with a large label."[51] In a letter dating from early April 1954 and addressed jokingly to "The Honorable

---

49 Joe Glaser to Dave Brubeck, January 8, 1954 (Brubeck Collection). Ralph Gleason later reported that, around the beginning of 1954, "Brubeck was bombarded with offers to depart from Fantasy." Gleason, "'They Said I Was Too Far Out,'" 39. Glaser's letter mentions some of them by name, speaking of "the situation pertaining to Norman Granz and the recording contract he wanted to give you and the situation pertaining to Eddie Mesner and contracts that were offered to you by two or three other companies."

50 George Avakian, typescript of tribute to Dave Brubeck for commemorative program, Kennedy Center Honors, November 28, 2009. George Avakian and Anahid Ajemian Papers, Music Division, New York Public Library, JPB 14–28 (hereafter "Avakian Papers"), box 18, folder 18. This account is corroborated by an email message from Dave and Iola Brubeck on the occasion of Avakian's eighty-seventh birthday. They sent their congratulations on March 15, 2006, from Berkeley, where Dave was performing, and "which takes my mind back to meeting you and Anahid, Anahid's sister, Maro and her husband, in Berkeley over 50 years ago. We were celebrating. You had just signed me with Columbia" (Avakian Papers).

51 Max Weiss to Dave Brubeck, undated (presumably early 1954) (Brubeck Collection).

Dave Brubeck," Glaser said he had just called Avakian and "advised him to make up the contract."[52]

Shortly thereafter, the director of Columbia's press department was in touch with Brubeck with regard to photographs for an album cover, and she mentioned that they had previously met in person, even though his contract was not yet finalized.[53] Then, less than three weeks later, Avakian's secretary told Brubeck that a photographer for *Life* magazine would very likely visit him, in connection with "a color photograph layout depicting some leading musicians in such a way that the musicians' personalities emerge in terms of the color photograph."[54]

Even with all this activity, the Columbia deal could easily have fallen apart. RCA Victor, for one, was still hot on Brubeck's trail around the date he was to have signed with Columbia.[55] Moreover, an extensive body of correspondence reveals that Brubeck delayed in signing his contract until the end of May, when the details were finally ironed out to his satisfaction. From the start, Brubeck drove a hard bargain, to the point that Columbia's attorney complained, "We are somewhat chagrined at this point that our proposed contract has not been promptly signed and the deal put to bed." He noted further that Brubeck had "already obtained from us a contract with more concessions than we think any other major company would have bothered to negotiate and grant."[56] When Brubeck notified Avakian that he was ready to sign, he asked him to tell the attorney, "All is forgiven. . . . I look forward to a long, happy association without hassles at Columbia Records. I hope this letter and the signing of the contracts will clear all matters of doubt since the last time I saw you."[57]

52 Joe Glaser to Dave Brubeck, April 6, 1954 (Brubeck Collection).

53 Debbie Ishlon to Dave Brubeck, April 9, 1954 (Brubeck Collection).

54 Millicent Smith to Dave Brubeck, April 27, 1954 (Brubeck Collection). The photographic essay appeared early the next year. Eliot Elisofon, "New Life for U.S. Jazz," *Life* 38, no. 3 (January 17, 1955): 42–49.

55 Jack Lewis (Artists and Repertoire, RCA Victor) to Dave Brubeck, telegram, April 14, 1954: "Have you definitely signed with Columbia Records? Please advise immediately." More than a year earlier, one of the editors of *Metronome* magazine apparently had arranged a meeting with another representative at RCA Victor (Dave Kapp) to discuss a possible record deal. George T. Simon to Dave Brubeck, February 18, 1953 (Brubeck Collection).

56 Alfred B. Lorber to Joe Glaser, May 3, 1954 (Brubeck Collection).

57 Dave Brubeck to George Avakian, May 24, 1954 (Brubeck Collection). The contract was not fully executed until mid-June. Joe Glaser to Dave Brubeck, June 16, 1954 (Brubeck Collection).

Shortly after Brubeck signed with Columbia, he hired a public relations man.[58] This individual served for a relatively short period of time.[59] His signal accomplishment appears to have been the organization of a cocktail party at Zardi's in Hollywood to celebrate Brubeck's association with Columbia. The guest list included prominent musicians and celebrities such as Stan Kenton, Shelly Manne, Shorty Rogers, Debbie Reynolds, Peggy Lee, Rosemary Clooney, Janet Leigh, Tony Curtis, Shelley Winters, Vic Damone, and Clint Eastwood—"all the top young actors and actresses in town."[60]

More important, however, was the high-level publicity Columbia was able to generate. In his 2009 tribute, mentioned earlier, Avakian noted that Brubeck's first Columbia album, *Jazz Goes to College,* sold so well that it earned back the advance and began producing royalties within just a few weeks. This extraordinary commercial success enabled Avakian to initiate the conversations that led to Brubeck's greatest public relations coup: "So great was the excitement it generated that Henry Grunwald, managing editor of *Time* magazine, agreed over a vodka martini to do a cover story on Dave."[61]

Avakian's martini lunch with Grunwald must have taken place during the summer. At all events, the plan was evidently under consideration by early August, three months before the article appeared, when Columbia's publicist wrote to Brubeck, "Still have all my fingers crossed about *Time.* Who knows?"[62] Two months later, when she wrote again to request "some material for the *Time* story," it was clearly a done deal.[63]

The article was a collaborative effort, involving writer Carter Harman, Dorothea Bourne of *Time*'s research staff, and chief correspondent

---

58 Jay Thompson to Dave Brubeck, July 19, 1954, outlining his duties; Dave Brubeck to Jay Thompson, July 19, 1954, signed contract (Brubeck Collection).

59 Thompson's contract specified the period of one year, and a ledger entry shows that he was paid for the last five months of 1954, at least (Brubeck Collection).

60 Jay Thompson to "Pablo" (Mort Lewis, Brubeck's manager), undated; typed "tentative guest list" (Brubeck Collection).

61 Avakian, "Dave Brubeck," typescript, November 28, 2009 (Avakian Papers). Grunwald didn't become managing editor until 1968. His position in 1954 was senior editor, and Roy Alexander was serving as managing editor. Grunwald was, however, the key figure in shaping the "Back of the Book"—i.e., the magazine's cultural sections, including music. See Norberto Angeletti and Alberto Oliva, *"TIME": The Illustrated History of the World's Most Influential Magazine* (New York: Rizzoli, 2010), 130–136.

62 Debbie Ishlon to Dave Brubeck, August 2, 1954 (Brubeck Collection).

63 Debbie Ishlon to Iola Brubeck, October 2, 1954 (Brubeck Collection).

T. George Harris.[64] It has frequently been claimed that Brubeck was "the first jazz musician to be featured on the cover of *Time* magazine."[65] But this is incorrect, as Louis Armstrong had previously appeared there in February 1949.[66] The widespread belief that a white musician had first garnered this "signal honor reserved for the great and near-great" reflects the racial politics associated with this article and its reception. As Grover Sales observed many years ago, "Brubeck's *Time* cover fanned the long-smoldering resentment within the black jazz community against the commercial dominance of white 'cool' and its genteel restraint. . . . Feeling *Time* should have honored Ellington, among others, black musicians were put out because they held Brubeck to be peripheral to important developments, outside the mainstream of modern jazz, a founder of no schools, and an inspirer of few disciples."[67] According to Eric Porter's trenchant analysis, the content of the piece was offensive because it "employed a discourse of respectability as it celebrated Brubeck and his contemporaries while marginalizing the contributions and experiences of black musicians. The article associated blackness and immorality in jazz and saw the new 'mainstream' jazz as a step forward from an unhealthy past."[68] Ingrid Monson noted similarly, "The *Time* magazine article was racially coded. . . . Brubeck's popularity with college students across the country seemed to promise a jazz that would be more upscale, less interested in social protest, and whiter."[69]

Brubeck was nearing the end of a twenty-five-day tour for Norman Granz's Jazz at the Philharmonic, with Duke Ellington and Gerry Mulligan, when the *Time* cover story appeared. One version of this oft-told tale runs as follows:

64 A thank-you note after the story went to press mentions "all the time you gave Carter [Harman] and me—and T. George Harris." Dorothea Bourne to Dave Brubeck, "Sunday night" [October 31, 1954] (Brubeck Collection). "The Man on Cloud No. 7," *Time* 64, no. 19 (November 8, 1954): 67–76. Two years earlier, nearly to the day, Harman had first introduced the relatively unknown Brubeck to the magazine's readership, in "Subconscious Pianist," *Time* 60, no. 20 (November 10, 1952): 94. See also Suzanne Swick (editorial assistant, *Time* magazine) to Dave Brubeck, November 6, 1952 (Brubeck Collection).

65 Ingrid Monson, *Freedom Sounds: Civil Rights Call Out to Jazz and Africa* (New York: Oxford University Press, 2007), 93.

66 "Louis the First," *Time* 53, no. 8 (February 21, 1949): 54–59.

67 Grover Sales, *Jazz: America's Classical Music* (1984; repr., New York: Da Capo Press, 1992), 168–169.

68 Eric Porter, *What Is This Thing Called Jazz? African American Musicians as Artists, Critics, and Activists* (Berkeley: University of California Press, 2002), 119–120.

69 Monson, *Freedom Sounds*, 94.

"Duke [Ellington] and I were on tour together across the country and this night, we were in Denver," Brubeck told correspondent Hedrick Smith. "And at seven o'clock in the morning, there was a knock on my door, and I opened the door, and there's Duke, and he said, 'You're on the cover of *Time*.' And he handed me *Time* magazine. It was the worst and the best moment possible, all mixed up, because I didn't want to have my story come first. I was so hoping that they would do Duke first, because I idolized him. He was so much more important than I was . . . he deserved to be first."[70]

The core elements of this narrative—Denver, the early-morning hour, and Brubeck's embarrassment—are present in most accounts and comport with other evidence. The itinerary for Granz's tour (in the Brubeck Collection) shows that they played Denver's City Auditorium on Wednesday night, November 3, 1954. So presumably Ellington's knock on the door took place first thing the next morning, on Thursday, November 4.

It is not difficult to understand why Brubeck would have been chagrined when Duke Ellington, of all people, showed him the magazine. He consistently identified Ellington as his "favorite composer-arranger-bandleader." Even though they toured together, Ellington was more than two decades his senior, and Brubeck had idolized him for years. When they met for the first time, in the early 1940s, Brubeck was dumbstruck. His friend, the bassist Junior Raglin, had recently joined the Duke Ellington Orchestra, so Brubeck asked if he would make the introduction. According to Brubeck, Raglin "pointed at Duke's dressing room and suggested I go in and say hello. I went in, Duke looked up at me, and I couldn't open my mouth! I didn't say a word and had to turn around and walk out."[71]

One of Brubeck's most famous compositions was a tribute to Duke Ellington, titled "The Duke." There is reason to think it originated in the glow of anticipation of touring with the great master. In 1957 the tune was arranged by Gil Evans for big band and recorded by Miles Davis on *Miles Ahead* (Columbia CL 1041). But it was written in

70 "PBS: Rediscovering Dave Brubeck | The Man | With Hedrick Smith," originally broadcast on December 16, 2001. http://www.pbs.org/brubeck/theMan/classicBrubeckQuartet.htm (accessed January 18, 2018).

    Ellington's cover story came nearly two years later, in Carter Harman, "Mood Indigo & Beyond," *Time* 68, no. 8 (August 20, 1956): 56–63.

71 Scott Yanow, "Dave Brubeck: A 75th Birthday Celebration," *Coda* 264 (November 1995): 20.

1954.[72] Brubeck said the idea came to him when he was in the car, taking his son Chris to nursery school.[73] He recorded it for the first time on October 13, 1954, just two days before the inception of the tour.[74]

A few weeks after the *Time* article appeared, the author thanked Iola Brubeck for her "good letter" and reported that response from the readership had been brisk. The magazine had received almost a hundred letters, "about three times as many as Billy Graham and almost ten times as many as some of our political cover stories." About seventy were positive, "happy that *Time* saw fit to do a jazz story, happy that it was about modern jazz, and happy that it was Dave's group that we featured." The others were negative reactions from "die-hard Dixieland fans who, predictably, thought we were nuts to see anything in that kind of music." He expressed his hope that the story would have "constructive results."[75] As it happened, Brubeck's fortune was a double-edged sword that led some of his former supporters to turn against him. There may have been some solace in the fact that a longtime friend, an executive in the music publishing industry, had forecasted a downside. Nearly as soon as the ink was dry, he wrote to Iola, "Perverse as it may seem, general publicity of the *Time* nature has potential thorns in it for Dave. . . . I am confident that you and Dave will 'survive' all the good fortune and good press that is bound to come your way."[76]

BRUBECK TIME

The link between the *Time* magazine article and Brubeck's musical projects was the portrait that appeared on the cover. It was painted by Boris Artzybasheff (1899–1965), an artist who was born in Ukraine and emigrated to New York around the age of twenty. He created a large

---

72 That is the year given in a list of Brubeck's compositions in a brochure published by Broadcast Music, Incorporated (BMI) in New York in 1961 (Brubeck Collection).

73 Song by song commentary by Dave Brubeck, taken from interviews with Howard Mandel, in booklet for *Dave Brubeck: Time Signatures*, 6.

74 Klaus-Gotthard Fischer, "Discography," in Ilse Storb and Klaus-Gotthard Fischer, *Dave Brubeck, Improvisations and Compositions: The Idea of Cultural Exchange*, trans. Bert Thompson (New York: Peter Lang, 1994), 205. The 1954 recording was apparently not released. Brubeck recorded it again with the Quartet in 1955 (*Jazz: Red Hot and Cool*, Columbia CL 699) and as a piano solo in 1956 (*Brubeck Plays Brubeck*, Columbia CL 878). See Fischer, "Discography," 207–210.

75 Carter Harman to Iola Brubeck, December 5, 1954 (Brubeck Collection).

76 Ernie Farmer (Shawnee Press) to Iola Brubeck, November 12, 1954 (Brubeck Collection).

number of magazine covers, including more than 200 for *Time*.[77] As of 2010, his painting was hanging in the Brubeck home.[78]

Brubeck's first studio album for Columbia was recorded October 12–14 and November 10, 1954—i.e., all but one of the recording sessions had already taken place before the November 8 *Time* cover.[79] Two letters from George Avakian around this time provide important documentary evidence about its origins. The first concerns his attempt to finalize the album's content by the firm deadline of November 10. The most valuable nugget here is confirmation that its tentative title was *Hi-Fi Brubeck*, referring to the high-fidelity audio technology that was all the rage in the 1950s. The letter also reveals the extent to which recordings were edited at this early date. Avakian mentioned "adding room noise" to create the illusion of performance before a live audience, and splicing segments as minute as "one note by Paul [Desmond] in bar 31" that "can be patched in from somewhere else."[80] Just a few days later, Avakian told Brubeck that Columbia was "negotiating with *Time* to use the cover painting for your *Hi-Fi* album," and that the title would change, should this permission be received. The clunky formulations that were initially under consideration—*In Time with Dave Brubeck* or *Makin' Time with Dave Brubeck*—both included the magazine's name.[81]

By the time the record was released, in February 1955, they had settled on a sleeker title, *Brubeck Time* (Columbia CL 622), which elegantly unites the names of the musician and the magazine—a brilliant marketing strategy. The liner notes were presented in the guise of letters from Avakian to Brubeck (dated January 4, 1955) and from Brubeck to Avakian (January 10). This exchange of correspondence is not preserved elsewhere in Brubeck's or Avakian's archives, and it may have been concocted—complete with a cover memo, dated January 14, to the producer Irving Townsend—in order to create the aura of an insider's view. In any case, the notes include a good deal of relevant information.

77 R. John Williams, "'I Like Machines': Boris Artzybasheff's Machine Aesthetic and the Ends of Cyborg Culture," *Interdisciplinary Humanities* 24 (2007): 120–142, esp. 127, 140 n. 32.

78 Marc Myers, "Ranching's Loss, Jazz's Gain," *Wall Street Journal*, December 1, 2010. A search of the Boris Artzybasheff Papers in the Special Collections Research Center at Syracuse University Libraries unfortunately brought to light no materials relevant to Brubeck or the portrait. I am grateful to Anna Chovanec, a reference assistant there, for investigating this matter.

79 Fischer, "Discography," 204–206.

80 George Avakian to Dave Brubeck, October 29, 1954 (Brubeck Collection).

81 George Avakian to Dave Brubeck, November 4, 1954 (Brubeck Collection).

Brubeck's letter mentions, for instance, the Quartet's initial reluctance to do a formal studio session, because "we all felt that our group performs better before a live audience." He then commends Avakian's technical expertise, noting that "it was 'hi-time' for a really 'hi-fi' record from us," a veiled reference to the album's original title. The bulk of Brubeck's narration is devoted to the story of "Stompin' for Mili," an original whose title was coined by Avakian. In brief, George Avakian's brother, Aram ("Al"), had convinced the eminent Albanian-American photographer Gjon Mili (1904–1984) to make a short film of the Quartet. It was a sequel to *Jammin' the Blues* (1944), which featured the famous saxophonist Lester Young. At one point during the filming, Mili insulted the group. As Brubeck recalled, "My blood began to boil," and he characterized the tune as a "musical expression of rage and frustration."

The other cut from *Brubeck Time* that was included in the first half of Mili's film was "a minor blues in a quiet vein," which served "to counterbalance the raucous 'Stompin' for Mili.'" Its title was "Audrey," because in an attempt to evoke the mood he wanted, Mili had said, "I would like to see Audrey Hepburn come walking through the woods" (to which Paul Desmond replied, "Gee, so would I").[82] Nearly forty years later, in 1993, the Dave Brubeck Quartet played "Audrey" at a memorial tribute to Audrey Hepburn at the United Nations, in recognition of "her dedicated voluntary service to the world's children" through her UNICEF missions.[83] Brubeck later recalled that her husband told him after the program, "Audrey sang that every night before she went to bed, or walking through her garden."[84]

In view of the earlier time experiments on the Octet and Trio recordings, it is significant that all eight selections on *Brubeck Time* were in 4/4 meter. This goes for the two originals as well as for the other six jazz standards ("Jeepers Creepers," "Pennies from Heaven," "Why Do I Love You," "Keepin' Out of Mischief Now," "A Fine Romance," "Brother,

---

82 Mili's nine-minute black-and-white film is beautifully shot and well worth viewing, though it was commercially unsuccessful. It was reviewed in Scott Yanow, *Jazz on Film: The Complete Story of the Musicians & Music Onscreen* (San Francisco: Backbeat Books, 2004), 257.

83 Richard Reid (Director, Division of Public Affairs) to "all UNICEF staff," April 21, 1993. http://www.unicef.org/about/history/trim/audrey_hepburn_materials/doc/doc401423. PDF (accessed January 18, 2018).
   According to this internal memo, the tribute took place on April 30.

84 Dave Brubeck, "A Long Partnership in Life and Music," an oral history conducted in 1999 and 2001 by Caroline C. Crawford, Regional Oral History Office, The Bancroft Library, University of California, Berkeley, 2006, p. 57 (February 17, 1999).

Can you Spare a Dime"), which Avakian referred to in his liner notes as "'oldie but goodie' tunes." When Columbia settled on the title *Brubeck Time*, then, this was purely a promotional tactic—designed to tie the album to the *Time* magazine cover—and it implied nothing about the temporal aspects of its music. The experimental meter signatures of *Time Out* were still five years in the future.

CHAPTER 2

ONTO THE WORLD STAGE

BY THE FIRST quarter of 1955, nearly everyone in the United States had heard of Brubeck, through the cover story in *Time* magazine, his first three albums for Columbia Records (*Brubeck Time* was preceded by *Jazz Goes to College* and *Dave Brubeck at Storyville: 1954*, both of which were recorded live), and his frequent appearances in other print and broadcast media. But his group had not yet traveled overseas. Serious discussion of the possibility of international travel threaded its way through the next few years. It finally happened during the first half of 1958, the year before *Time Out*, and it yielded some fascinating musical results.

By the end of 1958, the Quartet's personnel finally reached a steady state, after a series of different bass players and drummers. The "classic" Quartet (Dave Brubeck, Paul Desmond, Eugene Wright, and Joe Morello) was the group of musicians who recorded *Time Out* the next year. Around the same time, Brubeck became increasingly involved with issues of civil rights, but he also spent a lot of time and energy in defending his reputation and managing his image. And the Quartet made history in the late 1950s by performing jazz in the relatively unaccustomed venue of the concert hall, in addition to college campuses. Throughout this period, beginning in 1956, Dave and Iola Brubeck devoted themselves tirelessly to the creation and promotion of *The Real Ambassadors,* a musical that was borne of their experiences at home and abroad and that they hoped would be produced on Broadway.

JAZZ: RED HOT AND COOL

Brubeck's next album for Columbia after *Brubeck Time* was *Jazz: Red Hot and Cool* (CL 699). It is remembered above all for the provocative photo on the cover, featuring a sultry brunette in a revealing red dress and matching lipstick, reclining on the piano and gazing into the pianist's eyes. In the lower left corner, this image is credited to the eminent fashion photographer Richard Avedon, who was working on behalf of a special promotional effort that paired Brubeck's music with a new lipstick from Helena Rubinstein, which had the same name as the album.[1]

In an important retrospective piece for the *Village Voice,* Gary Giddins noted that the album, recorded live in October 1954 and July 1955 at Basin Street in New York, "serves as a fascinating transition to the time-code Brubeck." The first cut ("Lover"), in particular, pits Brubeck in "waltz time" against the drummer Joe Dodge in "an insistent four-beat," creating the pattern of three against four. But Giddins calls out George Avakian, who contributed the liner notes, for claiming that this was "something very new." He cites Louis Armstrong's scat vocal on "Hotter Than That" (1927) as a significant predecessor, nearly thirty years earlier.[2]

*THE LONG AND WINDING ROAD
TO INTERNATIONALIZATION*

Even before Brubeck hit the big time, there were preliminary discussions about international travel. For instance, in 1952 a radio and record company executive said he had "written to Sweden about a possible tour." Evidently the sticking point was the confluence of the high cost of

---

1 "Col Rampant with Every Type of Jazz," *Billboard* (September 10, 1955): 19, 24.
2 "A Quartet of Five (Dave Brubeck)," in Gary Giddins, *Weather Bird: Jazz at the Dawn of Its Second Century* (New York: Oxford University Press, 2004), 335. Originally published in *Village Voice* (May 15, 2001).

airline tickets for the whole group and Brubeck's unwillingness to travel alone.[3] About three years later, just over a year after the *Time* cover story, Brubeck's agent said, "I hope to book you in Europe in the very near future."[4] Although he had previously told Brubeck that he was trying to work out "a very good deal" for a tour in Australia similar to those he had negotiated in the past on behalf of Gene Krupa, Louis Armstrong, and Buddy DeFranco, apparently nothing came of those efforts.[5] Indeed, it wasn't until 1957 that he spoke again of trying to make arrangements to send the Quartet to "Japan or Australia or South America"—and this was evidently in response to Brubeck's own urging.[6]

Brubeck himself was much more proactive than his booking agent. In May 1956 he had floated the idea of touring the Soviet Union and was told it was unlikely, because "the Russians just do not care for jazz." The regional manager for the Belgian airline Sabena, with whom he corresponded, was, however, "only too happy to sit down and discuss" a European tour. Iola Brubeck's handwritten note indicates that she and Dave intended to pursue this matter with their agent.[7]

Things finally began to heat up as 1957 wore on. A letter from Brubeck's manager to an official at Broadcast Music, Inc. (BMI) mentioned the imminent release of *Jazz Impressions of the U.S.A.* (Columbia CL 984).[8] Despite the reference in the album's title to Brubeck's own country, this project inaugurated a series that included two albums of international scope: *Jazz Impressions of Eurasia* (Columbia CL 1251), which will be discussed later in this chapter, and *Jazz Impressions of Japan* (Columbia CL 2212).[9]

---

3 Claes Dahlgren to Dave Brubeck, November 25, 1952 (Brubeck Collection).

4 Joe Glaser (President, Associated Booking Corporation) to Dave Brubeck, December 6, 1955 (Brubeck Collection).

5 Joe Glaser to Dave Brubeck, April 22, 1955 (Brubeck Collection).

6 Joe Glaser to Dave Brubeck, January 8, 1957 (Brubeck Collection).

7 Andrew C. Myser (Regional Manager, Sabena) to Dave Brubeck, May 18, 1956 (Brubeck Collection).

8 Mort Lewis to Theodora Zavin, April 28, 1957 (Brubeck Collection).

9 The fourth and final member of this series was *Jazz Impressions of New York* (Columbia CL 2275). Brubeck's four "jazz impressions" releases formed part of a vogue in the late 1950s and 1960s for albums inspired by specific places, movies, theatrical productions, and the like. Another Bay Area jazz pianist, Vince Guaraldi, made several such recordings with his trio: *Jazz Impressions of Black Orpheus* (Fantasy 3337/8089), *Jazz Impressions of "A Boy Named Charlie Brown"* (Fantasy 5017), and *Jazz Impressions* (Fantasy 3359/8359). Similar projects included *Jazz Impressions of Pal Joey* by the Kenny Drew Trio (Riverside RLP 12–249), *Jazz Impressions of Lawrence of Arabia* by the Walt Dickerson Quartet (Dauntless DS

Shortly thereafter Brubeck's manager asked one of their booking agents, "Did anything develop from that inquiry about our going to Japan?"[10] He was told that it was still in the works.[11] It wasn't until seven years later, however, in 1964, that the Quartet finally made it to Japan.

By the midpoint of 1957, though, discussions were under way that would lead to an international tour of nearly unprecedented proportions during the first half of 1958. I have published elsewhere a fine-grained account of that journey, which need not be repeated here.[12] Its contours involved a three-month trip to the United Kingdom, western Europe (Germany, the Netherlands, Belgium, Sweden, and Denmark), Poland, Turkey, India, Sri Lanka, Bangladesh, Pakistan, Afghanistan, Iran, and Iraq—the latter two-thirds (from Poland onward) under the auspices of the US State Department. The negotiations apparently began early in 1957, for the general manager of the organization charged with administering cultural exchange programs of this type was able to report by mid-April that the Quartet was available for this purpose.[13]

The planning for this trip—which commenced in London on February 8, 1958, and concluded in Baghdad on May 9—occupied the second half of 1957. As late as December, the assistant to the president of Brubeck's booking agency was still "working on Italy," having "had no luck whatsoever in France or North Africa," because his records were relatively unknown there.[14] Ultimately, Italy didn't work out either, and some portions of the itinerary even evolved while the group was on the road. In short, the 1958 tour "did not advance in an orderly and self-evident manner," but "was an extremely contingent enterprise . . . and frequently teetered on the brink of chaos."[15]

6313), *Jazz Impressions of Oliver!* by Bobby Hackett and His Sextet (Epic BA 17037), and *Jazz Impressions of Folk Music* by the Harold Land Quintet (Imperial LP 12247).

10 Mort Lewis to Bobby Phillips (Associated Booking Corporation, Hollywood), May 4, 1957 (Brubeck Collection).

11 Bob Phillips to Mort Lewis, May 6, 1957 (Brubeck Collection).

12 Stephen A. Crist, "Jazz as Democracy? Dave Brubeck and Cold War Politics," *Journal of Musicology* 26 (2009): 133–162. See also Penny M. Von Eschen, *Satchmo Blows Up the World: Jazz Ambassadors Play the Cold War* (Cambridge, MA: Harvard University Press, 2004); Keith Hatschek, "The Impact of American Jazz Diplomacy in Poland during the Cold War Era," *Jazz Perspectives* 4 (2010): 253–300; and Danielle Fosler-Lussier, *Music in America's Cold War Diplomacy* (Oakland: University of California Press, 2015).

13 Crist, "Jazz as Democracy," 139.

14 Frances Church to Mort Lewis, December 2, 1957 (Brubeck Collection).

15 Crist, "Jazz as Democracy," 137.

Given the all-consuming nature of the logistics for Brubeck's first international expedition, it is hard to imagine how anyone could have had the energy to conceive another major venture at the same time. But an extensive thread of correspondence reveals that that is exactly what was happening. The principal correspondents were Brubeck's manager, Mort Lewis, and an Australian promoter by the name of Art Thurston. Thurston reported to Lewis in June 1957 that, according to Coronet Records, Brubeck was already quite popular in Australia: "The Dave Brubeck Quartet is very hot. . . . There is a craze among the high school kids at the moment, where it is considered the 'most' to carry a Brubeck record, and to dig Brubeck is a must with them."[16] The company's general manager expressed it more cautiously. He acknowledged that "the name of Brubeck and an appreciation of his work is very widespread, particularly in Sydney, Melbourne and Adelaide," but noted that "the sales of Brubeck records thus far in Australia have not been too exciting." There was, however, reason to believe that a tour would be "both successful and profitable," on account of cooperation from the record company, disc jockeys, and radio stations.[17]

This initial burst of enthusiasm continued through the summer.[18] Brubeck himself maintained high hopes even into the fall. For instance, he told a disc jockey in Melbourne that the Quartet was "hoping to appear in your country someday soon."[19] Similarly, he wrote to a fan in New Zealand, "We have not as yet set a definite date for an appearance 'down under' but I hope it will be soon."[20] It wasn't until more than two years later, however, that the Dave Brubeck Quartet finally made it to the other side of the world. They toured Australia and New Zealand for the first time in March 1960, just a few weeks after the release of *Time Out*.

16 Art Thurston to Mort Lewis, June 10, [1957] (Brubeck Collection).
17 J. H. Argent (General Manager, Coronet Records) to Mort Lewis, June 14, 1957 (Brubeck Collection).
18 See, for instance, Lewis's July 2, 1957 reply to Argent, which mentions that the tour is "still in the planning stage." Similarly, George Avakian (Columbia Records) told P. K. Macker (public relations man in San Francisco) on July 11 that "none of this is beyond the discussion stage," but voiced his support for an album with "a cover photograph of the Quartet boarding a Qantas plane," for promotional purposes. All of these documents, plus three additional letters from Mort Lewis to Art Thurston (July 2, July 15, August 2), are preserved in the Brubeck Collection.
19 Dave Brubeck to Myke Dyer, October 30, 1957 (Brubeck Collection).
20 Dave Brubeck to Rena McDonald, November 18, 1957 (Brubeck Collection).

During the first five years of the Quartet's existence, until Joe Morello became the mainstay in 1956, its drummers included Herb Barman, Lloyd Davis, and Joe Dodge. An even longer list of bass players preceded Gene Wright's tenure, which began in 1958. These included Fred Dutton, Wyatt "Bull" Ruther, Ron Crotty, Bob Bates, and Norman Bates (Bob's brother). Once Morello and Wright were in place, along with Brubeck and Desmond, the "classic" Quartet remained intact for ten years, from the beginning of 1958 until its dissolution on December 26, 1967. This longevity was nearly unparalleled in the volatile jazz world.

The addition of Morello to the Quartet was of crucial importance to the eventual creation of *Time Out*. The biographical sketch in the group's program book for 1959 traces Morello's rags-to-riches story. He is said to have "struggled in New York trying to land his first important professional job." He initially worked with the Jimmy Smith Quintet and the Stan Kenton Orchestra before settling down for "a three-year engagement with the Marian McPartland Trio." He then joined Brubeck in October 1956 and "has since become recognized as one of the outstanding drummers in the country."[21]

McPartland herself, a fellow pianist and great friend of Brubeck for many years, observed that Morello was "probably the one drummer who has made it possible for Dave to do things with the group that he would have had difficulty accomplishing otherwise. Joe's technique, ideas, *ability to play multiple rhythms and unusual time signatures,* humor, and unflagging zest for playing are a combination of attributes few other drummers have."[22] And Brubeck himself readily acknowledged Morello's pivotal role in the pursuit of his creative agenda, which blossomed in *Time Out* and the other four albums organized around experimentation with the temporal aspects of music: "The character of the group changed when he became our drummer. Before that, I'd never had a rhythm section that allowed me to do what I wanted. Joe is the best drummer in the world for rhythms. And I think that rhythmic experimentation is the way that jazz has to go. Melodically and harmonically, classical

---

21 *The Dave Brubeck Quartet* ([San Francisco:] Derry Music Company, 1959), 7 (Brubeck Collection).

22 "Joe Morello: With a Light Touch," in Marian McPartland, *Marian McPartland's Jazz World: All in Good Time* (Urbana and Chicago: University of Illinois Press, 2003), 43 (emphasis added). This essay originally appeared in 1965.

composers have done everything there is to do, so you have to challenge an audience rhythmically."[23]

Morello came to the Quartet on Desmond's recommendation. Desmond had heard him at the Hickory House in New York with McPartland's trio. When Joe Dodge was ready to call it quits in the fall of 1956, Desmond put in a good word for Morello.[24] Morello was reluctant to join the Quartet at first, because he "didn't want to be a service drummer." Brubeck told him he was looking for "a new image," and that he would let Morello play as much as he wanted. What attracted Morello the most was "the rhythm things"—i.e., the opportunity to play in more than one meter at a time. When he used to jam with saxophonist Phil Woods, guitarist Sal Salvador, and bassist Chuck Andrus in his hometown of Springfield, Massachusetts, Morello was "into doing polyrhythms, superimposing five on top of four." He recalled, "The guys would look at me and say, 'What the hell are you doing?' I used to get a kick out of it because I knew where I was." So he welcomed the chance to develop this aspect of his artistry with Brubeck.[25]

A telegram from Brubeck confirmed the hiring of Morello's services for a trial period, "starting approximately October 12th, ending definitely November 26th, 1956."[26] By year's end he offered Morello a contract for "$1,350 per month, beginning December 31, 1956." This was an excellent salary—approximately $148,000 in today's dollars—but it came with a caveat. Brubeck told Morello candidly, "I don't see any hope of being able to better this salary very soon without giving up the slack time which means more to me than any amount of money."[27]

Morello's musical contributions to the Quartet were evident straightaway. For instance, *Billboard*'s brief review of *Jazz Impressions of the U.S.A.* singled him out for special recognition: "The drumming of recently acquired Joe Morello gives the group a rhythmic solidity, unity and tastefulness it never has enjoyed before."[28] When Columbia reissued six

23 This quotation dates from 1963. Mort Goode, liner notes, *Dave Brubeck's All-Time Greatest Hits* (Columbia KG 32761, 1974), typescript. Teo Macero Collection, Music Division, New York Public Library, JPB 00–8 (hereafter "Macero Collection"), box 4, folder 8.

24 Doug Ramsey, *Take Five: The Public and Private Lives of Paul Desmond* (Seattle: Parkside Publications, 2005), 185–187.

25 Arnold Jay Smith, "The Dave Brubeck Quartet: A Quarter of a Century Young," *Down Beat* 43, no. 6 (March 25, 1976): 46.

26 Dave Brubeck to Joe Morello, telegram, September 17, 1956 (Brubeck Collection).

27 Dave Brubeck to Joe Morello, December 17, 1956 (Brubeck Collection).

28 *Billboard* 60, no. 21 (May 20, 1957): 115.

recordings as "The Dave Brubeck Collection" in 1998, another reviewer recognized that Morello had enabled a renaissance, of sorts, in Brubeck's creativity: "Morello's technical brilliance allowed Brubeck to indulge in rhythmic experiments that had lain dormant since Cal Tjader, his original drummer in California, went his own way in 1951."[29] Shortly after Morello's debut with the Quartet, Desmond began to resent the attention his colleague was receiving and he threatened to resign, saying, "Either he goes or I go." Brubeck defended Morello and asserted his importance for the group's future trajectory: "He's not going, Paul. He's the drummer I need to do what I've been thinking about with time signatures."[30]

EUGENE WRIGHT AND ISSUES OF RACE

It is ironic, but unfortunately not very surprising, that the addition of Eugene Wright to the Quartet engendered conflict. He was a fine bass player and, by all accounts, a gentle soul. But the content of his character (and music making) was less important to many people, especially in the South, than the color of his skin.

Brubeck's group had been intermittently interracial since the early 1950s, when Frank Butler sat in on drums and "Bull" Ruther on bass. But it was all white during the half-decade when it rose to fame (1953–1957), so it was a shock in some quarters to see a black musician on stage with three white colleagues. And this was, in fact, considered to be illegal in regions where Jim Crow laws were in effect.

This was in many ways a fraught moment in the evolution of the Dave Brubeck Quartet.[31] The key point is that the group encountered opposition almost immediately. After several uneventful dates in New Jersey, Massachusetts, and Pennsylvania, they were scheduled to perform at East Carolina College in Greenville, North Carolina, on February 5, 1958, the night before they left for the three-month international tour described above. The administration

was not aware that Brubeck's quartet was racially mixed. They were not allowed to go on stage because this was prohibited by Jim Crow laws. After refusing to play without Wright, Brubeck told the college's

---

29 Jack Chambers, "Bravo, Brubeck!" [Review of *The Dave Brubeck Collection* on Columbia] *Coda* 285 (May 1999): 31.

30 "The Dave Brubeck-Columbia Records Story," insert with reissue of *Time Out* (Columbia/Legacy CK 65122, 1997).

31 Crist, "Jazz as Democracy," 148–150.

president that they would be departing for Europe the next day and "I hated to leave my country thinking that we couldn't appear here but that we could go behind the Iron Curtain." The president called the governor, who said to let them play, remarking that "we don't want another Little Rock." Brubeck was instructed to keep Wright in the background. But instead he told Wright that his microphone was broken and he would have to use one at the front of the stage. Wright did so and, according to Brubeck, "we integrated that school in nothing flat."[32]

This sad episode encountered by the Quartet is only one of many. And it wasn't the first time that Brubeck had become involved in issues of civil rights. One of the flashpoints of the Civil Rights Movement had taken place just a few months earlier. At the beginning of September 1957 Governor Orval Faubus summoned the National Guard to prevent the integration of Central High School in Little Rock, Arkansas.[33] A few weeks later President Dwight D. Eisenhower ordered Faubus to remove the troops. Shortly thereafter the president federalized the National Guard and sent in the 101st Airborne Division, which escorted the Little Rock Nine during their first full day of classes.

As this scenario unfolded, the eminent Louis Armstrong uncharacteristically entered the fray. During a concert tour that took him to Grand Forks, North Dakota, he said he had given up plans for a government-sponsored trip to the Soviet Union because "the way they are treating my people in the South, the Government can go to hell." He characterized Eisenhower as "two-faced" and Faubus as an "uneducated plow boy."[34] A week later, from Davenport, Iowa, Armstrong expressed his approval of Eisenhower's subsequent action and sent the president a telegram with the message, "If you decide to walk into the school with the little colored kids, take me along, daddy. God bless you."[35]

32 Crist, "Jazz as Democracy," 149.
33 This cowardly and misguided act was immortalized and roundly satirized in "Fables of Faubus" on Charles Mingus's album *Mingus Ah Um* (Columbia CL 1370, 1959), which was recorded shortly before *Time Out* in the same studio (30th Street) and under the supervision of the same producer (Teo Macero).
34 "Louis Armstrong, Barring Soviet Tour, Denounces Eisenhower and Gov. Faubus," *New York Times*, September 19, 1957.
35 "Musician Backs Move: Armstrong Lauds Eisenhower for Little Rock Action," *New York Times*, September 26, 1957.

This story is relatively well known. What has been hidden from view, however, is the fact that Armstrong was apparently following his colleague Dave Brubeck's advice in softening his tone. A letter from Joe Glaser at exactly this time included some coded language. Glaser was especially close to this situation because he served as booking agent for both Armstrong and Brubeck. He wrote to Dave, "I appreciate the way you express yourself about Louis and I assure you, Dave, that Louis has already done exactly what you say he should, as no doubt you have heard the various stories on the air and seen the press stories—in fact you will find enclosed some information on what he just did—in sending President Eisenhower a personal wire, and I assure you I am going along with the thoughts that you have expressed." And he included on a separate page the text of Armstrong's telegram to Eisenhower, with the patronizing comment, "It was all done in very good taste, the way Louis expressed himself, and the wire is on [the] front page of the Chicago paper today."[36]

It is difficult to know what to make of this. On the one hand, it is disappointing to witness a white jazz musician counseling moderation instead of outrage in the wake of the Little Rock debacle. On the other hand, there is every reason to think that Brubeck's motives for offering this advice were as pure as possible, under the circumstances. Brubeck held Armstrong in the highest esteem. He apparently wished to protect his colleague's reputation from the potential consequences of his understandably angry outburst. Above all, Brubeck seems to have been interested in helping to forge a constructive method of engagement with this tense situation. Armstrong's own further thoughts on this matter have not been preserved, so far as I am aware. But a couple of weeks later, Glaser told Iola Brubeck, "I am very happy at how you and Dave feel about Louis," and he included a copy of a piece about Armstrong by the syndicated newspaper columnist Drew Pearson.[37]

BRUBECK AND THE CRITICS AFTER THE TIME COVER STORY

Ernie Farmer's prediction of "potential thorns" for Brubeck that accompanied his congratulations for the cover story in *Time* magazine turned out to be prescient. Indeed, about a half-year later Brubeck revealed his angst to a journalist who had drafted an article about him for *Down Beat* magazine: "I feel that I am particularly vulnerable to attack at this time

36 Joe Glaser to Dave Brubeck, September 25, 1957 (Brubeck Collection).
37 Joe Glaser to Iola Brubeck, October 9, 1957 (Brubeck Collection).

and almost anything I might say or be quoted as saying would most likely be misconstrued."[38] He was weighing the potential costs of pushing back against critics who were not in his corner.

Brubeck had always been a controversial figure. But the rhetoric about him intensified after his success in 1954. This is not the place for a comprehensive analysis of the vagaries and complexities of Brubeck's reception in the 1950s. But several selected examples will suffice to illustrate what was at stake.

Ralph J. Gleason's column in an April 1955 issue of *Down Beat* may well have been the catalyst for Brubeck's misgivings. Gleason began with the following provocative statement: "Quite possibly the most unfortunate thing that ever happened to Dave Brubeck was to get his picture on the cover of *Time* magazine and to have such a laudatory story inside." On the one hand, "it made him a national figure." But at the same time, "it crystalized the resentment of thousands of jazz musicians and fans." Gleason took this opportunity to point out the conflicting opinions, citing a recent pro-Brubeck column by Nat Hentoff versus more critical pieces by Leonard Feather and Jack Tracy. He then went on to declare that he himself had been "an unbeliever" since 1948, when he first heard Brubeck, and that Brubeck "has made remarkably little contribution for such a well-publicized artist."[39]

A later column by Gleason, which appeared in *Down Beat* in August 1956, so angered Iola Brubeck that she lodged a formal complaint with the editor:

I have read many articles about my husband that have not pleased me. This is the first time I have ever felt compelled to write a protest. Indisputably a writer is entitled to state his opinions if he confines himself to an evaluation of music. There is always the music itself to stand as the final arbiter if a reader chooses to draw his own conclusions. However, in the August 8 column Ralph Gleason chose to attack the personal integrity of a man who has a great respect for truth. I cannot allow his statements to stand unchallenged.

Beyond what she perceived to be an ad hominem attack, what especially galled Iola was Gleason's assertion that he had never favored her husband's music. She pointed out that he had contributed liner notes,

---

38 Dave Brubeck to Donald Freeman (*San Diego Union*), June 25, 1955 (Brubeck Collection).
39 Ralph J. Gleason, "Perspectives," *Down Beat* 22, no. 7 (April 6, 1955): 18.

which is "tantamount to an endorsement."[40] She apparently didn't notice, however, that Gleason had cagily avoided stating his own opinion in these notes by quoting liberally from remarks by John Hammond and Barry Ulanov. And she was probably unaware of Gleason's expunged characterization of her husband as a "stupid shit."

Ultimately, though, the joke was on Gleason. When Gleason was making preparations for an extensive three-part profile that appeared in *Down Beat* during summer 1957, Brubeck went behind his back. Before he consented to another interview with Gleason, Brubeck arranged privately with the magazine for "the opportunity to approve or reject the article" before it was published.[41]

Shortly before Gleason's piece appeared, though, another prominent jazz personality published an essay about Brubeck in *Down Beat*. John Mehegan was a pianist, who was best known as a pedagogue at the Juilliard School (1947–1964) and author of a four-volume textbook on jazz improvisation. His snarky commentary is typical of the invective that was heaped upon Brubeck by his detractors. Although Mehegan characterized Brubeck himself as "sincere and serious," the article included the following zingers concerning his brand of jazz:

- "Musicians have been fairly unanimous in putting down the quartet as a dull, unswinging group."
- ". . . the inescapable ennui which settles upon the listener after a little bit . . . of the Brubeck quartet."
- "Dave is not by jazz standards a good pianist."
- "There is not one swinging moment on the entire record" (*Brubeck Plays Brubeck*).
- ". . . the rather senile romanticism of Dave's playing."
- ". . . the rampant success he enjoys with fringe jazz audiences."
- "Dave's particular concepts of jazz piano" are "an arid desert for young swinging ideas.".

40 Ralph J. Gleason, "Perspectives," *Down Beat* 23, no. 16 (August 8, 1956): 39. Iola Brubeck to editor, *Down Beat*, August 18, 1956 (Brubeck Collection). Iola's letter was apparently not published.

41 "Draft of possible letter to 'Downbeat.'" June 7, 1957 (Brubeck Collection). This document was evidently prepared by Mort Lewis. The profile appeared as Ralph J. Gleason, "Brubeck: For the First Time, Read How Dave Thinks, Works, Believes, and How He Reacts to Critics," *Down Beat* 24, no. 15 (July 25, 1957): 13–14, 54; Gleason, "'They Said I Was Too Far Out,'" *Down Beat* 24, no. 16 (August 8, 1957): 17–19, 39; Gleason, "Brubeck: 'I Did Do Some Things First,'" *Down Beat* 24, no. 18 (September 5, 1957): 14–16, 35.

Mehegan concluded that popular acceptance was "the worst thing that could [have happened] to Dave and his quartet," and charged that Brubeck "contributed little or nothing . . . to the [resurgent West Coast] movement" in jazz.[42]

Typical, too, of the duplicitous stance of many of Brubeck's critics is a request for endorsement of Mehegan's book, which came after the appearance of the unflattering essay. Leighton Guptill, president of Watson-Guptill Publications, told Brubeck in 1960 that he would "personally drop by to see you tonight [at Basin Street East] . . . and also listen to you play." He then added the following postscript, whose sentiments are strikingly at odds with the comments just listed: "John Mehegan and his daughter—*both of whom are enthusiastic followers of yours*—will also be stopping by to say hello and listen to you play within a day or two."[43]

BRUBECK AND THE CRITICS IN ENGLAND

The reception of Brubeck's music in England was at least as important as its critical evaluation in the United States—and perhaps even more so for the *Time Out* project, since its liner notes were penned by a Brit (Steve Race, whose connections with Brubeck and this album will be examined in Chapter 3). A pair of essays in the British *Jazz Journal* illustrates the attempt to achieve an evenhanded appraisal, over against the carping of Gleason, Mehegan, and other American critics. Brian Nicholls took the hullaballoo over Brubeck's appearance on the cover of *Time* as his point of departure. In September 1956 he noted soberly and hopefully, "Now that much of the dust of battle has settled and the fierce divisions over the merits of Dave Brubeck have become more mellowed with time and familiarity, it may well be rewarding to examine his contributions to the jazz scene and attempt an assessment of his place in the jazz world." According to Nicholls's commonsensical view, "the hostile elements who deny that [Brubeck's] music is indeed jazz at all can probably be discounted completely in view of . . . the evidence of one's own ears." In other words, if not jazz, what else could this music possibly be? Brubeck's main contribution was expansion of the limits of true jazz: "In the final analysis, Brubeck will rank amongst the pioneers in what is always a growing and acquisitive art form."[44]

---

42 John Mehegan, "Jazz Pianists: 2," *Down Beat* 24, no. 13 (June 27, 1957): 17.
43 Leighton Guptill to Dave Brubeck, February 18, 1960 (Brubeck Collection); emphasis added.
44 Brian Nicholls, "Dave Brubeck," *Jazz Journal* 9, no. 9 (September 1956): 1, 4.

A similar piece by Stanley White, focusing on "Brubeck the pianist," appeared about a year and a half later, timed to coincide with Brubeck's first tour in the United Kingdom. White envisioned his project as an "honest attempt to present Brubeck in his true light, to examine his more obvious drawbacks, to assess his relative merits." His opinions were nearly opposite those of Mehegan the previous year. White declared that Brubeck "can play with tremendous swing." Moreover, he viewed Brubeck as "one of the jazz world's more intellectual musicians" and found "in Brubeck's more inspired moments a positive creative genius." White's conclusion—that "Brubeck is neither an outstandingly good jazz artist, nor an inadequate one"—was disappointingly banal. But his inclination to view the abundance of "abusive criticism" that Brubeck had endured as "a sign of his startling originality and modern approach" was a refreshing antidote to the venom spewed by other critics.[45]

The most substantial evaluation of Brubeck in the British press in the late 1950s was by Raymond Horricks. A revised version of his essay, an informative and exceptionally literate piece, was published as a book chapter in 1959, the year of *Time Out,* but it had originated two years earlier.[46] The essence of Horricks' stance was that he had initially been enthusiastic about Brubeck's "ambitious approach," but he had experienced "growing disillusion" over Brubeck's contribution to jazz.[47] So far as he was concerned, the apex of Brubeck's creativity was reached in the December 1953 live recording of the Jerome Kern standard, "All the Things You Are," on *Jazz at the College of the Pacific* (Fantasy 3-223). Since the Columbia recording contract and *Time* magazine profile ("the ultimate in American acceptance") in 1954, the Quartet "has been well recompensed to maintain an unvarying musical style." As a result, "its performances . . . have tended to be semi-mechanical relays of the stylistic mannerisms long associated with the Quartet." Moreover, "all the previous spirit of adventure . . . is missing from them."[48] Horricks' vigorous call to arms is worth quoting at length:

45 Stanley H. White, "Dave Brubeck," *Jazz Journal* 11, no. 2 (February 1958): 3–4.
46 Raymond Horricks, "Dave Brubeck—A Two-Part Appraisal," *Jazz Monthly* 3, no. 3 (May 1957): 7–9; "Dave Brubeck—An Appraisal, Pt. 2," *Jazz Monthly* 3, no. 5 (July 1957): 5–7, 31. Reprinted together as "Dave Brubeck: A Formula and a Dilemma," in Raymond Horricks et al., *These Jazzmen of Our Time* (London: Victor Gollancz, 1959), 161–175.
47 Horricks, "Brubeck: Formula and Dilemma," 161–162.
48 Horricks, "Brubeck: Formula and Dilemma," 170–173.

If Brubeck is to be in any way a potent force in jazz within the next few years, then it is certain that his group will have to undergo a thorough rejuvenation, possibly with a change of instrumentation or at the very least a resharpening of the existing unit's mental and emotional faculties so that its genuinely individual style becomes once more coloured by a sincere desire to feel and innovate. The Quartet must get away from merely reiterating its well-tried ideas and the sooner the better.[49]

These words proved to be prophetic, for by the time they were reprinted in 1959, Brubeck had enacted a "thorough rejuvenation" of his group by means of the *Time Out* project.

JAZZ IN THE CONCERT HALL

A broad-ranging piece by Nat Hentoff in a 1958 issue of *Harper's Magazine* considered "What's Happening to Jazz." One of the main things that was happening, according to the opening caption, involved a significant change of venue: "Over the sound of clinking glasses and cash registers, the musicians are fighting to be heard . . . to get jazz out of the night clubs and into the concert hall." Hentoff identified the Dave Brubeck Quartet as a leader in this trend, and he noted the restorative results of performing in more congenial circumstances: "The presence of an audience that has come primarily to listen, and the knowledge that the two or two-and-a-half hours involved will not be followed by several more the same night, can have remarkably energizing and satisfying effects on many modern groups."[50]

Hentoff also called attention to a new venture of the impresario George Wein, who had organized the legendary Newport Jazz Festival in the summers, beginning in 1954. Wein had recently begun booking jazz musicians, including the Dave Brubeck Quartet, for full-length concerts in venues such as Boston's Symphony Hall, which had traditionally been the exclusive preserve of classical music.[51] Wein himself proclaimed the uniqueness of this endeavor. A March 1957 performance was "unique in the sense that it is the first time that a jazz group of this size has been presented in solo concert at Symphony Hall." Moreover, he claimed that Brubeck was "the single most important figure in the recent surge of interest in jazz as an American art form." Brubeck initiated the appeal

49 Horricks, "Brubeck: Formula and Dilemma," 174.
50 Nat Hentoff, "What's Happening to Jazz," *Harper's Magazine* 216, no. 1295 (April 1958): 25, 29.
51 Hentoff, "What's Happening," 29–30.

of modern jazz to "the intellectuals," and his classical background "has made him the object of much interest in the classical music world."[52]

The importance of jazz's migration from clubs to concerts halls in the late 1950s for the germination of an experimental project such as *Time Out* cannot be overstated. According to a perceptive recent analysis,

> [j]azz began turning into an art music, no longer an accompaniment for dancing and drinking, but rather a music people listened to attentively in . . . the concert hall, supported by the synergistic sale of recordings and tickets, where people came to hear the groups they had learned to appreciate from recordings. . . . In university concert halls, Brubeck could play music people couldn't easily dance to, like his experiments with unconventional (for jazz) time signatures like 5/4 ("Take Five"). The quartet could play as they felt like, as long as they liked, and experiment with forms of expression the public had never heard before. The ticket buyers had come to hear them do just that. The place—the concert hall—created the musical opportunity.[53]

THREE INTERNATIONAL PROJECTS

Sometime in 1956, Dave and Iola Brubeck got it into their heads that they wanted to write a musical together.[54] Iola was to contribute the lyrics and Dave would compose the music. In the end, it was called *The Real Ambassadors*, but its original title was *World Take a Holiday*. By late in 1957, about eight weeks before the Quartet left for their first international tour, the Brubecks had made significant progress on their show, but it was "still in the beginning stages."[55] A year later, they were "working night and day on it" and had rewritten it.[56] The contours of the show were reshaped profoundly as a result of the Quartet's own experiences

---

52 George Wein, "Unique Concert by Brubeck at Symphony Hall March 10," *Boston Sunday Herald*, February 24, 1957.

53 Robert R. Faulkner and Howard S. Becker, *"Do You Know . . . ?" The Jazz Repertoire in Action* (Chicago: University of Chicago Press, 2009), 95.

54 Milan Schijatschky to Iola Brubeck, January 13, 1964 (Brubeck Collection). This broadcaster for Swiss Radio was planning a show about *The Real Ambassadors*. On the portion of his questionnaire concerning its origins, Iola Brubeck entered the year 1956.

55 Dave Brubeck to George Avakian, December 13, 1957 (Brubeck Collection).

56 Dave Brubeck to Joe Glaser, November 20, 1958 (Brubeck Collection).

overseas, and more importantly, the opening song—"Everybody's Comin'"—was recast as "Everybody's Jumpin'," the penultimate cut on *Time Out*.

The other two projects were albums that came out in 1958. The Quartet's *In Europe* (Columbia CL 1168) could just as well have been titled *In Denmark*, or even *In Copenhagen*, because it was recorded live in that city in early March 1958, the night before the group ventured behind the Iron Curtain into Poland.[57] The album played a pivotal role in the group's history, since it was the first to be recorded outside North America and also the first to feature the rhythm section of the "classic" Quartet (Morello on drums, Wright on bass). Not surprisingly, the first cut is their rendition of "Wonderful Copenhagen," a song by Frank Loesser from the 1952 Hollywood film *Hans Christian Andersen*, starring Danny Kaye. Brubeck's spoken introduction links it to their later (and previous) time experiments, when he tells the audience, "We'll do it in 3/4 and 4/4 at the same time." The album's final cut, "Watusi Drums," an alternative version of "Pick Up Sticks," is even more closely connected with *Time Out*.

On *Jazz Impressions of Eurasia* (Columbia CL 1251), Joe Benjamin sat in on bass while Eugene Wright was completing his contractual obligations with the singer Carmen McRae.[58] As its title implies, the six originals that comprise the album were inspired by the Quartet's recent travels overseas. In addition to compositions connected with Afghanistan, Germany, Poland, England, and India, the third cut ("The Golden Horn") alludes to the geography, language, and music of Turkey—and accordingly it

---

57 The European title was undoubtedly intended to broaden its marketing appeal. The available discographies uniformly give the date of the concert as Wednesday, March 5, 1958, on account of Brubeck's unequivocal statement in the liner notes: "March 5th. The next day we went behind the Iron Curtain. That's how I can remember." According to the unanimous testimony of numerous archival documents, however, Brubeck misremembered, and the Copenhagen performances (there were two, at 7:00 and 9:30 p.m., in the Tivoli Concert Hall) actually took place on Tuesday, March 4. See, for instance, the field report from the American Embassy in Warsaw (Frank J. Lewand, "Report on Dave Brubeck Jazz Quartet Concerts in Poland," Foreign Service Dispatch #355 to Department of State, March 24, 1958; General Records of the Department of State, Record Group 59); a letter from the secretary of Brubeck's booking agent to Brubeck's manager (Frances Church to Mort Lewis, February 26, 1958 [Brubeck Collection]); and the travel journal of the Brubecks' ten-year-old son Darius https://scholarlycommons.pacific.edu/jdttj/ (accessed March 14, 2018).

58 Benjamin also substituted for Wright on the live album *Newport 1958* (Columbia CL 1249).

must be considered a predecessor to the more famous "Blue Rondo à la Turk." In the liner notes, Brubeck mentions that the rhythmic pattern of the theme was derived from the Turkish phrase *çok teşekkür ederim* (thank you very much), and that the title refers not to Desmond's saxophone but rather to the "narrow inlet of the Bosporus called the Golden Horn that divides Istanbul."

CHAPTER 3

WATERSHED

THE YEAR 1959 has been widely recognized as unusually significant for the development of jazz. To mark its fiftieth anniversary in 2009, the BBC produced a one-hour documentary with the provocative title *1959: The Year That Changed Jazz*. The promotional materials characterized it as a "seismic" and "pivotal" year, and the program was organized around four major jazz albums, "each a high-water mark and a powerful reflection of the times." These included *Time Out*, along with Miles Davis's *Kind of Blue*, Charles Mingus's *Mingus Ah Um*, and Ornette Coleman's *The Shape of Jazz to Come*.[1] Similarly, the journalist Fred Kaplan examined a variety of important cultural, political, and scientific

---

1 "BBC Four—1959: The Year That Changed Jazz," http://www.bbc.co.uk/programmes/boojf64y (accessed March 14, 2018).

events and trends in a book titled *1959: The Year Everything Changed.*[2] 1959 also turned out to be a watershed for the Dave Brubeck Quartet—although no one could have known it at the time, of course. Not only was it the year of Brubeck's most famous creative project, *Time Out,* but it also marked the midpoint of the "classic" Quartet with Paul Desmond, which was formed in the latter half of 1951 and disbanded sixteen years later, on December 26, 1967.

Specific factors involved in the production of *Time Out* include early concert performances of the repertoire, the recording sessions, and decisions concerning the album's title, cover art, and liner notes. One might expect that such an iconic project would loom large in Brubeck's voluminous correspondence. But, surprisingly, it is conspicuous in its absence. Several important matters that were uppermost in Brubeck's life and career even as he was creating his pièce de résistance fed through his letters instead. Chief among them were an enormous amount of domestic and international travel, a high-profile stand against racism and segregation in the South, an all-out effort to finish his musical and see it produced on Broadway, and a series of performances with the New York Philharmonic in Carnegie Hall.

THE EARLIEST LIVE PERFORMANCES OF THE TIME OUT REPERTOIRE

As 1958 came to a close, Dave Brubeck was planning to stay as close to home as possible in the coming year, with the exception of a tour in February. At the beginning of December, Brubeck's manager informed one of the booking agents, "We expect to work every possible day we are on the road in February, . . . and when we return home, Dave plans to remain here until the fall." He urged him, therefore, to "pull out all the stops and to get every open date filled and keep the price up!"[3] Around the same time, Brubeck himself stated plainly to the president of the agency, "I intend to spend the rest of the year 1959 here in California, . . . so that the February tour should be as lucrative as possible for both of us, as it is liable to be the only one for the year."[4] Things didn't turn out that way at all—and, in fact, Brubeck ended up traveling quite a bit in 1959. But somehow, in the midst of all his peripatetic activities, Brubeck found time to piece together the elements of his new album.

---

2   Fred Kaplan, *1959: The Year Everything Changed* (Hoboken, NJ: John Wiley & Sons, 2009).
3   Mort Lewis to Paul Bannister, December 1, 1958 (Brubeck Collection).
4   Dave Brubeck to Joe Glaser, December 3, 1958 (Brubeck Collection).

There is relatively little documentary evidence concerning the origins of the tunes on *Time Out*. The backstories on each of them generally do not provide more than an approximate chronological frame. For instance, the first cut, "Blue Rondo à la Turk," must have originated sometime after the end of March 1958, when the Quartet performed in Istanbul and Brubeck heard the street musicians who inspired his muse. On the other hand, the final cut, "Pick Up Sticks," already existed by the early days of the same month in its guise as "Watusi Drums," since it was performed in Copenhagen and was included on the live *In Europe* album, discussed in Chapter 2. In most cases, the handwritten sketches and charts—which are not very plentiful in the first place—provide no information by which they can be securely dated. A happy exception is found among the original materials for "Everybody's Jumpin'," which includes a page of sketches dated January 21, 1959 (see Chapter 7). This was just one day before Brubeck left California for a four-day tour in the East, followed some ten days later by a six-week stint on the road. In addition to supplying a rare bit of specific information concerning the chronology of his compositions, this manuscript source provides evidence that Brubeck was active in his compositional workshop until nearly the last moment before he had to leave town.

In an essay drawn from his master's thesis on four landmark recordings of 1959 (the Davis and Coleman albums, along with *Time Out* and John Coltrane's *Giant Steps*), Brubeck's son Darius characterized the intent of *Time Out* as experimental and "entirely dedicated to the working out of a particular musical idea." He mentioned that Columbia was reluctant to release such an unusual record, and that the label agreed to do so "only on condition that he also record an album of standards."[5] The project that served as a hedge against the company's fears of commercial failure was titled *Gone with the Wind* (Columbia CL 1347). This immediate predecessor of *Time Out* was recorded in Los Angeles on April 22 and 23, 1959. The repertoire was so familiar that it required only a minimum of commentary in the liner notes. The southern-themed tunes included two by Stephen Foster ("Swanee River" and "Camptown Races"), as well as "Ol' Man River" from Jerome Kern and Oscar Hammerstein's musical *Show Boat* (1927), and "Georgia on My Mind" (1930) by Hoagy Carmichael and Stuart Gorrell. The album achieved

---

5 Darius Brubeck, "1959: The Beginning of Beyond," in *The Cambridge Companion to Jazz*, ed. Mervyn Cooke and David Horn (Cambridge: Cambridge University Press, 2002), 198–199.

commercial and critical success, including a five-star review in *Down Beat*.[6]

Despite its conventional music, *Gone with the Wind* represented a milestone of sorts, for it was Teo Macero's first assignment as a producer at Columbia.[7] Macero subsequently served in this capacity for most if not all of Brubeck's numerous projects for that label. Regarding Brubeck's "interest in exploring unusual time signatures," George Avakian, the executive who had signed Brubeck in 1954, later recalled that he left Columbia to help start Warner Bros. Records in 1958 and that *Time Out* was "produced by Teo Macero, a Varèse student I had hired at Columbia after hearing his compositions played by the Charles Mingus Quartet."[8] In a letter to Macero one week after the 1959 recording sessions, Brubeck noted that the brevity and familiarity of the selections on *Gone with the Wind* were intended to ensure the album's popular appeal, particularly for disc jockey programming.[9]

The premiere of the pieces that were to be recorded on *Time Out* took place on Friday, June 12, 1959, in Oakland, California. Approximately two thousand listeners attended the performance at the Woodminster Amphitheater in Joaquin Miller Park. The concert was reviewed in the *Oakland Tribune* by the newspaper's regular music critic Russ Wilson, who had a surprisingly keen sense that Brubeck's "venture into rhythmic fields new to this branch of music" represented jazz history in the making.[10] It began with a series of tunes from the Quartet's "forthcoming Columbia album," *Gone with the Wind,* and several standards, including "St. Louis Blues" and "Take the A Train." The first two of Brubeck's new originals were "a waltz in 4/4 time" ("Kathy's Waltz") and "a selection in which two bars of 3/4 were followed by two of 4/4 throughout" ("Three to Get Ready"). Encouraged by the audience's enthusiastic response, Brubeck was emboldened to try out "a still untitled composition whose opening and closing sections have a pattern of three bars in 2/8 time

---

6 Gene Lees et al., "In Review," *Down Beat* 26, no. 29 (October 1, 1959): 27. On the very next page (28) is a five-star review of Miles Davis's *Kind of Blue.*

7 Teo Macero, speech to the Pacific Alumni Association, University of the Pacific, on the occasion of Dave Brubeck's "Distinguished Alumnus" award, April 16, 1966 (Macero Collection, box 7, folder 22).

8 George Avakian, typescript of tribute to Dave Brubeck for commemorative program, Kennedy Center Honors, November 28, 2009 (Avakian Papers, box 18, folder 18).

9 Dave Brubeck to Teo Macero, April 29, 1959 (Macero Collection, box 7, folder 15).

10 Russ Wilson, "Brubeck Makes Jazz History with New Rhythm Patterns," *Oakland Tribune,* June 13, 1959.

followed by one bar in 3/8" ("Blue Rondo à la Turk"). Wilson characterized it as the "most provocative" and noted presciently, "When this piece
is polished and gets into general circulation, it should create a sensation."
He also quoted Brubeck's own remarks to his hometown audience: "That
was the first public performance of these rather odd tunes. They're going
to be part of an album of numbers done in different tempos [i.e., meters]
than those that have been basic to jazz. I believe we have pushed harmonies in jazz just about as far as we can but that a lot of advances can be
made rhythmically. The next tune ["Blue Rondo"] is the farthest out we've
ever been. We're going to try it because I know we're among friends."

Wilson mentioned at the end of his review that the Quartet was about
to embark on "an extended eastern tour." Columbia's weekly promotional
publication later supplied some of the details: "Dave tried out many
of the new sounds of *Time Out* on 1959 festival audiences at Newport
[Rhode Island], French Lick [Indiana], Boston, Detroit, El Paso [Texas],
and *Playboy*'s blockbusting jazzorama at Chicago's Soldier's Field."[11] And
Time magazine reported on Brubeck's success at the Randall's Island
(New York) Jazz Festival: "To no one's surprise, the festival's standout
was the Dave Brubeck Quartet. . . . The quartet usually started with well-
known tunes . . . , then varied the tempo [i.e., meter] (from 4/4 to 5/4
and back to 3/4) as it injected its own sometimes loud, sometimes soft
designs."[12]

The new repertoire was also performed during Brubeck's summer residency at the Music Inn in Lenox, Massachusetts. In his reply to a student from the University of Vermont, Brubeck wrote, "Last summer you
heard one of the first performances of the music from *Time Out* when
you went to the Music Inn concert. I think that I can tell you that *Time
Out* is one of my favorite recordings and one that I am very proud of."[13]
A gesture of solidarity at that time on the part of an eminent African

11 "Time Out for *Time Out*," *Insight*, January 20, 1960, p. 4 (Macero Collection, box 7, folder
    5). The Newport date took place on July 5, 1959; Chicago during the weekend of August 7–9;
    and Boston on August 22.

12 "An Island of Jazz," *Time* 74, no. 10 (September 7, 1959): 56. The performance took place on
    August 21.

13 Dave Brubeck to Bill Mithoff, May 17, 1960 (Brubeck Collection). Mithoff's original query
    of March 10, 1960, is preserved as well. See also Milton R. Bass, "The Brubeck Septet,"
    Berkshire Eagle, July 25, 1959, which reports that the Brubeck family had "moved lock, stock
    and tape recorder to a studio apartment on the grounds of Music Inn in Lenox where Dave
    and his wife, Iola, are composing a musical for possible Broadway production" (*The Real
    Ambassadors*).

American music historian impressed Brubeck so deeply that he was still talking about it more than four decades later. In an interview with his son Darius, Brubeck recounted the public support he received from the chair of the music department and director of the Glee Club at Spelman College (Atlanta). In the context of a roundtable at the Music Inn, "there was some discussion of whether what I was doing was jazz. Doctor Willis James went to the podium and started singing, and when he finished he said, 'Can any of you tell me what time signature that was in?' No one responded and there were many great musicians sitting there. He said, 'That was an African work song; it was in five-four time, and the Dave Brubeck Quartet is on the right track.'" Even though the inspiration for "Take Five" and other compositions came from many different sources, Brubeck was especially pleased that his time experiments were being linked to the African roots of jazz: "That was such an important statement in my life to have somebody with his background telling these musicians that what I was doing was on the right track. . . . To be vindicated in what I was trying to do was wonderful."[14]

THE RECORDING SESSIONS

Even before the debut concert in Oakland, discussions were well along concerning the recording sessions for *Time Out*. A letter from Brubeck's manager to the producer supplies some significant details. Surprisingly, Plan A was apparently to record the album live rather than in the studio. Mort Lewis wrote, "After discussing all the pros and cons, we have decided to come into New York a day or so earlier and record in the studio rather than put you people to an unnecessary expense on a gamble recording at the Red Hill Inn [a jazz club in Pennsauken, New Jersey]."[15] Judging from the number of takes required even in the studio, this was

14 Darius Brubeck, "Jazz 1959: The Beginning of Beyond" (MA thesis, University of Nottingham, 2002), 143–144. The interview was conducted in San Remo (Italian Riviera) on July 25, 2001.

15 Mort Lewis to Teo Macero, June 5, 1959 (Macero Collection, box 7, folder 15). Stan Kenton and His Orchestra were there around the same time (June 9–14, 1959). An album was released many years later as *"Live" at the Red Hill Inn, Pennsauken,* Magic Records UK, DAWE43, 1990, compact disc. The liner notes claim that the music is from the Red Hill Inn on June 12, 1959. But the Kenton aficionado Ed Chaplin confirmed in an email to the author (August 23, 2014) that nothing on the album is from the Red Hill Inn. Rather, its twelve tracks were recorded in Balboa, CA, on March 8, 1958; Cincinnati on June 15, 1961; and Salt Lake City on August 24–25, 1962. In a subsequent message (August 24, 2014), Chaplin stated that "Wally Heider, the master engineer, was there during the Stan Kenton booking [June

FIGURE 3.1. *Time Out* recording session in summer 1959.
Photo: Don Hunstein © Sony Music Entertainment.

a wise call. Lewis requested a lengthy session on Thursday, June 25, 1959, "probably six hours total."

As unrealistic as it now seems, evidently everyone hoped that a single session would suffice. In fact, the producer had in mind to record three albums over the course of just two days. In a memo to the president of Columbia Records, Teo Macero stated that the purpose of an upcoming luncheon with Brubeck was "to discuss a few new recording plans." Specifically, Brubeck "has at present, three new albums ready to be recorded. One or two, which will be recorded June 25th and the remaining one will be recorded on the 26th."[16]

In the end, the recording sessions for *Time Out* took place on three days during summer 1959: Thursday, June 25; Wednesday, July 1; and Tuesday, August 18 (see Figure 3.1). There were, in fact, two sessions on the June date. The later one ran from 7:00 until 10:00 p.m.[17] The earlier

11–12, 1959] with his stereo equipment," and he provided a list of recordings that were issued on various LPs and CDs from that gig.

16 Teo Macero to Goddard Lieberson, June 18, 1959 (Macero Collection, box 7, folder 15). The Quartet ended up recording on the first day only.

17 Columbia Records, Artist Job Sheet, Job No. 50183 (Sony Music Archives Library).

one apparently began at 3:00 p.m., and presumably concluded by 5:30 or 6:00, to allow for a dinner break between sessions.[18] In July there was a single, longer session, from 2:30 until 7:00 p.m.[19] And the hours of the August session were 2:30 until 5:30 p.m.[20] The total recording time for *Time Out,* then, was thirteen or fourteen hours, compared with nine for Miles Davis's *Kind of Blue* earlier that year.

From the paper documents that were created at the time and that are held by the Sony Music Archives Library in New York, coupled with the recordings from the original sessions preserved at the Brubeck Collection in California (about three and a half hours total), it is possible to form an accurate account of what transpired at each session.

The first job sheet is missing. It was for the afternoon session on June 25, and it would have been numbered 50183 (like the later session that day). From the artist contact cards, however, it appears that the order of events was as follows:

CO 62555	Kathy's Waltz
CO 62556	Three to Get Ready
CO 62557	Strange Meadow Lark
CO 62558	Everybody's Jumpin'
CO 62559	Blue Rondo à la Turk
CO 62560	I'm in a Dancing Mood

The job sheets for the remaining three sessions provide the following information:

June 25, 1959, 7:00–10:00 p.m. (Job No. 50183)

CO 62561	Someday My Prince Will Come	5:29
CO 62562	Five-Fourth Time	
CO 62555	Kathy's Waltz	5:25
CO 62556	Three to Get Ready	
CO 62557	Strange Meadow Lark	

18 The job sheet for this session has not been preserved, but the starting time can be inferred from a handwritten annotation on the letter from Mort Lewis to Teo Macero cited above (June 5, 1959). Over the typed line in which Brubeck's manager requested "probably six hours" of studio time, "5:00 p.m. till finish," Macero wrote "3:00" in blue pen.

19 Columbia Records, Artist Job Sheet, Job No. 50192 (Sony Music Archives Library).

20 Columbia Records, Artist Job Sheet, Job No. 50258 (Sony Music Archives Library).

July 1, 1959, 2:30–7:00 p.m. (Job No. 50192)

CO 62575	I Get a Kick out of You	
CO 62576	Kathy's Waltz	
CO 62577	Take Five	2:50
CO 62578	Take Five	6:00
CO 62579	Everybody's Jumpin'	
CO 62580	Strange Meadow Lark	5:45
CO 62581	Three to Make [sic] Ready	

August 18, 1959, 2:30–5:30 p.m. (Job No. 50258)

CO 62752	Blue Rondo à la Turk	6:45/2:59
CO 62753	Pick Up Sticks	4:16
CO 62754	Everybody's Jumpin'	

There is a surprise in the documentation for these sessions. In addition to the seven originals that ultimately comprised the album, the Quartet also recorded some standards. The July session began with Cole Porter's "I Get a Kick out of You," from the 1934 Broadway musical *Anything Goes*. Brubeck's version is best known from another recording nearly seven years later (February 1966), which was released on *Anything Goes! The Dave Brubeck Quartet Plays Cole Porter* (Columbia CL 2602). It is difficult to see any meaningful connection between this straight-ahead arrangement of a show tune and the five originals that occupied the rest of the *Time Out* session. Similarly, the evening session the previous week began with "Someday My Prince Will Come" from Walt Disney's animated film *Snow White and the Seven Dwarfs* (1937). This choice initially seems curious as well, since Brubeck had already recorded it a couple of years earlier for *Dave Digs Disney* (Columbia CL 1059), and he was to return to it in December 1961 for *Countdown: Time in Outer Space* (Columbia CL 1775), the second sequel to *Time Out*. But his liner notes for the latter album explain the connection between this arrangement of a standard in 3/4 meter and his preoccupations on *Time Out*. Brubeck first quotes from Steve Race's review of the earlier version, which characterized it as "an exercise in time signatures" that "breaks entirely new ground in the field of jazz rhythms" by exploring "the possibilities of double, triple, and quadruple time in simultaneous performance." The reasons for a new rendition, according to Brubeck, were that the Quartet had "progressed polyrhythmically in the intervening six [sic] years" and the tune had been "the seed for many subsequent time experiments."

Even more interesting than "I Get a Kick out of You" and "Someday My Prince Will Come" is the short version of "I'm in a Dancing Mood" that concluded the first June session. Like the other two, it originated in the 1930s, albeit in a more obscure venue. The song by Al Goodhart, Al Hoffman, and Maurice Sigler was from a 1936 movie, the British comedy *This'll Make You Whistle*, starring Jack Buchanan. This was not the first time Brubeck's group had recorded the tune. They played it at the Newport Jazz Festival in July 1956, and it appeared later that year on *Dave Brubeck and Jay & Kai at Newport* (Columbia CL 932). In his spoken remarks on that live album, Brubeck introduced it as their "newest arrangement" and explained, somewhat sardonically, that they had concocted it because television shows always wanted them to play in several different styles, but within the time constraint of no more than three minutes: "So we've decided to fill our whole life with one tune— fast, slow, tempos mixed together, tempos changing—a real spectacular for TV!"

Brubeck's rendition of "I'm in a Dancing Mood" is ingenious, highly entertaining, and worth further investigation. But the following brief rundown will provide a preliminary indication of what is afoot.

Section 1: fast 4—32 measures, the last 4 (16 beats) of which are recast as 3+3+3+3+4

Section 2: fast 3 (waltz) in the same tempo—32 measures

Section 3: return to fast 4—16 measures, in which the last 4 introduce a Latin feel

Section 4: Latin beat continues for 32 measures (piano vamp, alto saxophone solo)

Section 5: fast 4 continues without Latin feel—24 measures (8 more of saxophone solo, then 16 of piano, with last 4 recast as 3+3+3+3+4, as before)

Section 6: fast 3—32 measures

Section 7: slower 4 superimposed on 2 groups of 3, in a 3:2 ratio—20 measures

Section 8: return to fast 4—20 measures (increasingly swung toward the end)

Although the inclusion of this arrangement would have disturbed the "all originals" ethos of *Time Out*, the metrical experimentation would have fit there quite comfortably.

Time Out is such a succinct and appropriate title for a jazz album devoted to experiments with meter and rhythm that even Brubeck himself came to believe that it had always been so. Many years later he recalled that, around the time of the concert premiere in Oakland (June 1959), "I already had in mind a good title—*Time Out*—the phrase commonly used in sports and familiar in everyday life. It could be interpreted in many different ways—time out to listen and relax, and 'time' outside the normal 4/4 meter."[21]

But the documentary sources tell a different story. The date of Brubeck's second five-year contract with Columbia Records coincided with the second *Time Out* recording day (July 1). Under "Nature of Services," the section of the contract concerning "Exception as to Exclusivity" makes mention of two forthcoming projects: "the record tentatively entitled *Gone with the Wind,* and the record tentatively entitled *Out of Our Time.*"[22] Just a few days after the final recording session, Dave's brother Howard used the same clunky title when he mentioned that his personal agenda included transcribing for publication the new "*Out of Our Time* album."[23] But the sleeker two-word formulation apparently originated shortly thereafter. Several weeks later Teo Macero referred to the album simply as *Time Out,* and he boasted with the pride of an expectant father, "This is truly an exciting album."[24]

The cover of *Time Out* is noteworthy for its departure from the usual depiction of the Quartet or its leader. Its abstract style (see Figure 3.2) is a significant example of the work of the eminent graphic designer S. Neil Fujita, head of the art department at Columbia Records. The *Time Out* painting is one of Fujita's most iconic works, but he also created provocative cover art for albums by other jazz musicians, including Art Blakey, Miles Davis, and Charles Mingus, as well as for bestselling novels such as Truman Capote's *In Cold Blood* (1966) and Mario Puzo's *The Godfather* (1969).

Fujita's piece was a fallback. Brubeck wanted a different painting for *Time Out,* one by the Spanish surrealist Joan Miró, but it wasn't possible

---

21 Dave Brubeck, "A Time to Remember" (unpublished autobiography, coauthored with Iola Brubeck).

22 Columbia Records to Dave Brubeck, July 1, 1959 (Macero Collection, box 7, folder 15).

23 Howard Brubeck to Dave and Iola Brubeck, August 26, 1959 (Brubeck Collection).

24 Teo Macero to Russ Wilson (*Oakland Tribune*), September 22, 1959 (Macero Collection, box 7, folder 4).

FIGURE 3.2. Cover of *Time Out*, with painting by S. Neil Fujita.
Courtesy of Sony Music Entertainment.

to obtain permission for its use in time for the album's release. The Miró
work appeared instead on the cover of the sequel, *Time Further Out* (1961).
The original, signed Fujita painting—which is apparently untitled—
hung for many years in Brubeck's home in Wilton, Connecticut.[25]

It's a good thing that Brubeck's producer thought *Time Out* was "exciting," because to hear Brubeck tell it—and he did so countless times
in the course of his long career—nearly everyone else at Columbia was
against it. The album's cardinal sins included the abstract art on its cover,
which the marketing moguls feared would be off putting to the general

25 It is singled out as the "most eye-catching of all the pictures in Brubeck's music room"—
    including the 1954 Boris Artzybasheff portrait mentioned in Chapter 1—in Michael Bourne,
    "Classic Time," *Down Beat* 70, no. 9 (September 2003): 46. During summer 2014, after the
    passing of both Dave (December 2012) and Iola (March 2014), their daughter, Catherine,
    confirmed via email that the painting was still there at that time.

public. Equally egregious was the fact that it ended up including seven originals, and no standards that everybody would already know and love. Moreover, those originals used mostly odd time signatures and rhythms that might not be suitable for dancing. All of this led to predictions of commercial failure.

Fortunately, Brubeck had at least one heavy hitter on his side. The president of Columbia Records, Goddard Lieberson, was himself a composer and a stalwart supporter of the *Time Out* project. In an interview on the fiftieth anniversary of the album's release, Brubeck recalled, "Goddard told me I was on the right track. I remember him saying, 'I am so tired of "Stardust" and "Body and Soul," and this is something fresh.'"[26] Although Brubeck's memories of such events occasionally morphed over time, this recollection remained stable and therefore seems quite reliable. Brubeck's contribution to a scrapbook that was compiled in 1964 in connection with the celebration of Lieberson's twenty-fifth anniversary with Columbia expressed gratitude for his encouraging words during the *Time Out* sessions: "How many versions of 'Body and Soul' and 'Stardust' do we need? Keep writing original experimental jazz." Brubeck told Lieberson that these remarks "were enough to convince *this* jazz man of your ability to lead Columbia in directions *he'd* like to go."[27]

Given the generally low level of corporate enthusiasm for the album, and anxiety about its potential to fail, it was especially important to recruit an articulate apologist to write the liner notes, and thereby to cement a triumvirate of support, along with Macero and Lieberson. The ideal candidate for this role was the British critic Steve Race.

In his later years, Race was best known as a radio and television personality, and as the composer of advertising jingles, most notably "Sweet as the moment when the pod went pop" for Birds Eye frozen peas. But he was also a frequent contributor to jazz periodicals, and his first interface with Brubeck was a lukewarm review of a group of Octet and Trio recordings. On the basis of this material, Race was "inclined to think the ballyhoo" about Brubeck had been "overdone." As of the early 1950s, he considered Brubeck's music to be "interesting but just a little over-publicised."[28] Three years later, however, Race began an article about two LPs with the unambiguous statement, "I'm sold on Dave

26 David Sprague, "Brubeck's Timeless 'Time Out,'" *Daily Variety* 302, no. 26 (February 6, 2009): A4.

27 Dave Brubeck to Goddard Lieberson, June 24, 1964 (Brubeck Collection).

28 Steve Race, "Analysing Brubeck: Bags of Ballyhoo—Little Technique," *Melody Maker* 28, no. 958 (January 26, 1952): 4.

Brubeck. . . . I think Brubeck is the musician we've been waiting for." He was impressed, above all, by Brubeck's ability to unite composition and performance in his improvisations: "Brubeck is neither our finest composer nor our finest performer. But as a fusion of the essential properties of both, working along paths hitherto untrodden in any realm of music, he's the most important man in new jazz."[29]

Race's encomium elicited a warm response from Brubeck. He had learned of the article from American critic Nat Hentoff, and he told Race that he felt "you have come closer to understanding my purpose in jazz than any of the critics who have written both favorable and unfavorable criticism." Race's support was especially welcome in the wake of the recent "barrage of unfavorable criticism" sparked by the *Time* magazine cover story. Brubeck appreciated that Race had tried to understand what he was attempting to accomplish, and that he judged his work accordingly.[30]

A couple of years later, in April 1957, the two finally met in person, when Race joined the Brubecks for dinner during a visit to San Francisco.[31] When the Quartet traveled to England the next year, at the beginning of their first international tour, Race was among the delegation that met them at the airport.[32] Moreover, he contributed a piece to the souvenir program, and Brubeck appeared on his radio program.[33] Not surprisingly, Race also wrote a rave review of a live performance at Royal Festival Hall in London, which was published alongside two less flattering portrayals by other critics.[34]

29 Steve Race, "Brubeck," *Melody Maker* 31, no. 1121 (March 12, 1955): 3–4.
30 Dave Brubeck to Steve Race, June 17, 1955 (Brubeck Collection).
31 Steve Race to Iola Brubeck, March 20, 1957 (Brubeck Collection): "I was delighted to receive your letter and am greatly looking forward to the pleasure of having dinner with you during my stay in San Francisco." A notation in Iola's handwriting indicates that Race was due to arrive on April 16. Race had just published a positive review of the new solo album *Brubeck Plays Brubeck* (Columbia CL 878). Steve Race, "Brubeck and the Future," *Melody Maker* 32, no. 1222 (April 6, 1957): 6.
32 Brubeck, "Time to Remember."
33 Steve Race to Dave Brubeck, November 11, 1957 (Brubeck Collection): "I am looked upon as the principal author of your following here. . . . I have just heard from the organisation promoting your tour in this country (The National Jazz Federation), and they have asked me to write about 3,000 words about you and the quartet for the printed programs." Mort Lewis to Harold Davison (British promoter), January 22, 1958 (Brubeck Collection): "In your letter you indicated that you have arranged for Dave to appear on Steve Race's radio program. Dave is delighted with the news."
34 Steve Race, Tony Brown, and Bob Dawbarn, "Brubeck in 3D," *Melody Maker* 33, no. 1267 (February 15, 1958): 10–11.

These and other communications and publications in the course of 1958 and 1959 formed the background for Brubeck's own suggestion that Race write the liner notes for *Time Out*.[35] Race apparently was approached by early September, not long after the third and final recording session.[36] He was compensated by Brubeck himself, a practice that seems to have been standard.[37]

More than two-thirds of the 864 words Race wrote for *Time Out* are devoted to thumbnail sketches of individual cuts. The first four paragraphs, along with the final one, portrayed Brubeck as a visionary and trailblazer. Despite the laudatory contributions of Coleman Hawkins, Charlie Parker, Dizzy Gillespie, Thelonious Monk, and Duke Ellington—all mentioned by name—to the realms of harmony, form, and orchestration, "jazz has not progressed" in the rhythmic sphere, according to Race. He asserted that Brubeck was "really the first to explore the uncharted seas of compound [sic] time." Although he acknowledged that Benny Carter, Max Roach, and others had experimented with 3/4 meter (jazz waltz), Race announced that "Dave has gone further, finding still more exotic time signatures, and even laying one rhythm in counterpoint over another." In his peroration, Race made the following bold claims, which were undoubtedly worth every penny Brubeck paid for them: "In short: *Time Out* is an experiment with time, which may well come to be regarded as more than an arrow pointing to the future. Something great has been attempted . . . and achieved. The very first arrow has found its mark."

THE LURE OF THE TOUR

Fifty years after the fact, Brubeck said that in 1959 he was "concentrating on doing the 'Time Out' album. That took up most of my time."[38] Although he may have remembered it that way, this project actually

---

35 Brubeck, "Time to Remember."

36 Russ Wilson (*Oakland Tribune*) to Teo Macero, September 8, 1959 (Macero Collection, box 7, folder 4): "Dave told me that the notes for the new album probably will be done by an English critic."

37 Mort Lewis to Howard Lucraft (British composer and music critic who lived in Hollywood), January 26, 1960 (Brubeck Collection): "Enclosed you will find a check for our mutual friend, Steve Race. Please keep it in a safe place until Steve calls for it, whenever that may be." Steve Race to Iola Brubeck, February 29, 1960 (Brubeck Collection): "The payment for the 'Time Out' liner has been received by Howard [Lucraft] in Hollywood." Race mentioned, too, that he hoped to visit America again in April 1960.

38 John Soeder, "Brubeck's Still Calling His Own Tune," *Cleveland Plain Dealer*, May 31, 2009.

played a surprisingly minor role within the complex story of his personal and professional commitments. Judging from the mass of correspondence and other relevant documentation that has been preserved, much of Brubeck's time and energy was devoted to domestic and international travel—despite his avowed intention to go out on the road as little as possible.

Brubeck had told his representatives in no uncertain terms that he wanted to make as much money as possible during the February tour, so he could spend the rest of the year in California. But several attractive opportunities conspired against this plan. First, the "February" circuit expanded on both ends to encompass a full three months. Brubeck initially traveled East on January 22, but only for a long weekend. After ten days back in California, he left again on February 3 for a more extended period.[39] The Quartet worked in and around New York for three weeks, including a weeklong stint at the Apollo Theater in Harlem.[40] In March they traveled south—with Iola and their son Chris, just short of his seventh birthday—for concerts in Jamaica, Trinidad, Aruba, and Venezuela.[41] More domestic dates—in Oklahoma, Texas, Arkansas, the Pacific Northwest, and Los Angeles—kept Brubeck on the move until April 22.[42]

Brubeck's summer in the East was filled with recording sessions in New York, jazz festivals in many different locales, and a residency in western Massachusetts.[43] Immediately after dates at Basin Street East in New York the weekend of September 12–13, the Quartet departed for their second European tour, which included performances in France and Italy as well as England, and concluded in early October.[44] After a brief respite, they set off again with several other groups—including Maynard

39 Mort Lewis to Art Thurston (promoter in Australia), January 12, 1959; Mort Lewis to Bob Willoughby (photographer in Los Angeles), January 19, 1959 (Brubeck Collection).

40 Mort Lewis to Leonard Feather, January 27, 1959; Mort Lewis to Art Thurston, January 29, 1959 (Brubeck Collection).

41 Mort Lewis to Frances Church (Associated Booking Corporation), November 30, 1958; "Dave Brubeck, Group Here for Concerts at Carib Tonight," *Daily Gleaner* (Kingston, Jamaica), March 10, 1959, p. 20; "'King' Brubeck on Stage Tonight," *Trinidad Guardian*, March 12, 1959; Larry Bennett to Iola Brubeck, March 17, 1959; Iola Brubeck to Mary Jeanne Sauerwein, March 28, 1959 (Brubeck Collection).

42 Mort Lewis to Dave Brubeck, March 14, 1959; Mort Lewis to Art Thurston, March 17, 1959 (Brubeck Collection).

43 Milton R. Bass, "The Brubeck Septet," *Berkshire Eagle*, July 25, 1959.

44 Mort Lewis to Art Thurston, May 19, 1959; Mort Lewis to Art Thurston, September 2, 1959; Mort Lewis to Iola Brubeck, September 16, 1959 (from Paris); Joe Glaser to Dave Brubeck, September 17, 1959 (letter sent to London) (Brubeck Collection).

Ferguson and his band, the Chico Hamilton Quintet, and Lambert, Hendricks & Ross—for the promoter Ed Sarkesian's "Jazz for Moderns" package tour, which occupied them through the end of November.[45] The Quartet ended the year with a two-week run in New York in December, featuring a week at Basin Street East and several concerts with the New York Philharmonic.[46]

An excursion to Australia and New Zealand took place the following year, yet most of the vast amount of planning and preparation occurred in 1959. The quantity of correspondence and other documentation that has been preserved concerning this trip greatly exceeds the evidence pertaining to the creation of *Time Out*; its origins are to be found in a letter from Art Thurston, a promoter in Sydney, to Dave Brubeck's manager, Mort Lewis, during summer 1957. Thurston thanked Lewis for a previous letter and reported that the Dave Brubeck Quartet was already famous in Australia.[47] These initial communications engendered a robust discussion, reflected in some eighty documents in the Brubeck Collection, about how and when the Quartet might travel Down Under. It didn't abate until the tour was over, and even then the talk was of "a return tour of Australia in 1961, as well as a tour of the Far East."[48] The lion's share of this material was penned (and typed) by Thurston and Lewis. But an extensive cast of characters entered the proceedings at various points, including promoters and public-relations men in Australia, New Zealand, and the United States, representatives from Coronet Records and Qantas Airlines, plus Dave and Iola Brubeck, of course. In the end, the tour ran a full month (March 11–April 11, 1960), and it involved performances in Honolulu on the way over, several major cities in Australia (Sydney, Melbourne, Adelaide, and Brisbane) and New Zealand (Auckland and Wellington), and a number of cities in Germany (Frankfurt, Essen, Hamburg, Munich, and Berlin) and the Netherlands (The Hague and Amsterdam) on the way back to San Francisco.[49] In several internal documents (letters to booking agents and an itinerary), Lewis referred to this project explicitly as the Quartet's "round the world

---

45 Mort Lewis to Iola Brubeck, September 16, 1959 (Brubeck Collection).
46 Mort Lewis to Howard S. Richmond, November 3 and December 16, 1959 (Brubeck Collection).
47 Art Thurston to Mort Lewis, June 10, [1957] (Brubeck Collection).
48 Kenn Brodziak (promoter in Melbourne) to Iola Brubeck, April 8, 1960 (Brubeck Collection).
49 The Brubeck Collection also holds a substantial number of contemporary reports (more than twenty) from the press in Australia and New Zealand.

tour."[50] As it represented Brubeck's natural next step on the world stage, following his three-month tour in 1958, all the discussion and activity leading up to the trip overshadowed *Time Out* considerably.

TROUBLE IN GEORGIA

In May 1959, a month before the first *Time Out* sessions, Charles Mingus entered the same space in New York (Columbia's 30th Street Studio), under the supervision of the same producer (Teo Macero), and recorded his masterpiece, the album *Mingus Ah Um* (Columbia CL 1370).[51] One of its most famous and significant cuts is "Fables of Faubus," a biting satire about Arkansas's governor, Orval Faubus, in protest of his racist actions in connection with the desegregation of Central High School in Little Rock. Although the music of *Time Out* is not explicitly political, Brubeck had recently taken a very public stance on a similar issue.

About halfway through his week at the Apollo Theater in Harlem (February 20–27), Brubeck received a phone call from Stuart Woods, a senior at the University of Georgia and president of the collegiate Jazz Society under whose auspices the Quartet was booked to perform the following week. According to a newspaper article that day, Brubeck "confirmed reports that a March 4 engagement at the University of Georgia has been canceled because his bass player, Eugene Wright, is a Negro." In response to the possibility of employing a white musician for the gig instead, Brubeck said, "If they paid me $1,000,000, they couldn't get me to drop Gene because he's a Negro. You can't buy self-respect. Their attitude seemed to be, all-white, OK, but mixed, it's no go." The piece went on to report that Woods "had realized only after some publicity pictures arrived yesterday that the concert would have to be canceled." He said, "I didn't realize Brubeck's group was mixed until I saw Wright's picture. The university has a rule against mixed functions and I knew we wouldn't be able to hold it. I think, personally, it would have been all right to have a mixed group but the school officials felt it was pretty touchy. We are a state school and I think they realized the type of reaction the politicians would have had. It's unfortunate when a man can't play on a stage with another man just because of his color."[52]

---

50 Mort Lewis to Bobby Phillips (Associated Booking Corp.), March 1, 1960; Mort Lewis to Paul Bannister (Associated Booking Corp.), March 12, 1960; "Round the World Tour (Thirty Day Plan)" (Brubeck Collection).

51 Another parallel between Mingus's album and *Time Out* is that its cover featured an abstract painting by S. Neil Fujita.

52 "Why Brubeck's Band Won't Play in Georgia," *New York Post*, February 24, 1959.

When the Associated Press picked up the story, they abbreviated and intensified it.[53] Two of the five sentences mention that officials at the university "decreed" that the group wasn't allowed to perform there, and that Brubeck called the decree "unconstitutional and ridiculous."[54] The students' own point of view isn't mentioned at all.

When Ralph Gleason got wind of it, he wrote a caustic column about the episode, which ridiculed the South and blamed the students, especially Woods:

> The president of the jazz club . . . said he didn't know Eugene Wright was a Negro until he saw the publicity photographs of the group. One wonders just what sort of a jazz club this is and where they have been. Who do they think plays jazz, Herman Talmadge [Georgia senator who opposed desegregation and civil rights legislation]? . . . I don't know who enfranchised that Georgia jazz club but I'd like to revoke their permit right now. There has been no news story that the club (125 members) resigned in a body or even that the president had the grace to resign. It's the least they could do, since apparently they haven't got the guts to go ahead and hold their concert somewhere else. Jazz music is the music of democracy and it just might be that it's too good for the students at Georgia—who called that club a jazz club, anyway? They might have had the grace to make some gesture on this event. . . . I would now like to see all jazz musicians refuse to play at the University of Georgia. The jazz club president was a "sociology senior," the news stories said. What a recommendation for the University of Georgia as a center for the study of social sciences![55]

Echoes of this showdown reached around the world. A March letter to Brubeck's manager reported that the news was "mentioned over the media in Sydney," and "as Gene Wright has many friends in Australia, all the folks felt Dave's attitude was very commendable."[56] The Brubeck

---

53 "Georgia Bans Negro Player in Jazz Band," n.p., n.d. (Brubeck Collection). The AP also introduced some minor factual errors. The date of the concert is given as March 3 instead of March 4; the Quartet is referred to as an "orchestra"; and Eugene Wright's surname is listed as "White."

54 The account in the *Post*, on the other hand, quoted Woods as saying that Brubeck "was very understanding about it."

55 Ralph J. Gleason, "Georgia Jazzists Aren't That at All," n.p., n.d. (March 1959) (Brubeck Collection).

56 Art Thurston to Mort Lewis, March 23, 1959 (Brubeck Collection).

Collection also holds magazine clippings about the incident in Swedish and German.[57]

Its resonances were also felt in the lives of its protagonists. In Brubeck's case, his high-profile unwillingness to submit to Jim Crow laws at the University of Georgia in 1959 (and at East Carolina College in 1958) surely fed his resolve a year later, when nearly his entire southern tour was canceled for similar reasons. The other principal—Stuart Woods, the twenty-one-year-old sociology major from Manchester, Georgia—eventually became a highly successful novelist, with about forty *New York Times* bestsellers to his credit.[58] Fifty-six years after the fact, Woods was eager to share his story, which was remarkably congruent with the initial report in the *New York Post* but also provided significant new details about the institutional power play in the late 1950s.[59]

When he was an undergraduate, Woods had decided to form the University of Georgia Jazz Society. Shortly thereafter, the university's Director of Student Activities informed him regarding the concerts they planned to produce, "You may have white bands or you may have black bands, but you may not have black-and-white bands." This directive originated with the Board of Regents, apparently influenced by one of its members, Roy Harris, who published the *Augusta Courier*, a racist tabloid, and who wanted to prevent biracial entertainment.[60] When Woods objected, he was told, "If you can't accept that, then you won't be producing these concerts, and you won't have an organization either." Accordingly, he sought bands that fit those criteria.

After signing Brubeck, then printing posters and tickets, Woods received publicity photographs in the mail, which showed an African American bassist, Eugene Wright, playing in the Quartet.[61] Although his first impulse was to go ahead with the concert anyway, his faculty advisors convinced him to speak with the Director of Student Activities and explain what had happened. Woods did so and was told in no uncertain terms to cancel the concert. When he and some other students

57 "Basist kostade Brubeck 17.000 dollars," *Estrad* (April 1959); "Selbstachtung nicht käuflich," *Schlagzeug* (May 1959).

58 http://www.stuartwoods.com (accessed March 14, 2018).

59 Stuart Woods, interview with the author, August 7, 2015.

60 Christopher A. Huff, "Roy V. Harris (1895–1985)," *New Georgia Encyclopedia* (January 10, 2014). http://www.georgiaencyclopedia.org/articles/history-archaeology/roy-v-harris-1895-1985 (accessed March 14, 2018).

61 According to the report in the *New York Post*, Woods opened this package on Monday, February 23, 1959.

decided to send Brubeck a telegram, apologizing for the cancellation and explaining the reason, Woods was called into the office of the university's Director of Public Relations and told that if they did so, there would "never be a jazz concert of any kind held on this university campus again."

That night, while he was visiting a friend at the campus radio station, a reporter from the Associated Press called and Woods told him the whole story. Within a few days Woods started getting hate mail because it had been reported by Herb Caen, a gossip columnist at the *San Francisco Chronicle*, and others that he was the one who objected to having a racially mixed band and had canceled the concert. When Brubeck played another gig in Atlanta, Woods went backstage, explained what had happened, and apologized. Brubeck said he understood that Woods was dealing with a bunch of racist idiots. After that "it kind of blew over," Woods graduated, and he moved away from Georgia.

The creative residue of this anxious historical moment is preserved in one of Paul Desmond's alto saxophone solos. In the bridge of "Georgia on My Mind"—recorded about two months later, on April 22, 1959, for the *Gone with the Wind* album—Desmond deployed his acerbic wit to offer an unspoken commentary on the situation, by quoting from Artie Shaw's theme song "Nightmare" (1938).[62]

HIGH HOPES FOR BROADWAY

In 1959, while Brubeck's manager was obsessively planning a tour to Australia and New Zealand, Dave and Iola Brubeck were intently focused on their dream of producing a musical on Broadway. This never came to pass, although music from *The Real Ambassadors* was recorded in 1961 and subsequently released as an album (Columbia OL 5850), and a concert version (with Iola as narrator) was performed at the Monterey Jazz Festival in September 1962.

Dave and Iola Brubeck conceived the idea in 1956 of writing a musical together.[63] During the first couple of years, they shared their plans with only a select group of close associates. For instance, toward the end of 1957 Dave sent to George Avakian (the executive who had signed him to Columbia a few years earlier) "the story outline, the first act of the book, lyrics, and a list of the tunes," and asked for his advice "about where we

---

62 Robert Rice, "The Cleanup Man," *New Yorker* 37, no. 16 (June 3, 1961): 47.

63 Iola Brubeck's handwritten response to a questionnaire from Milan Schijatschky (Swiss broadcaster), January 13, 1964 (Brubeck Collection).

go from here." At that time, the show's working title was *World Take a Holiday*. He told Avakian, "It is still in the beginning stages, and will be rewritten and revised probably many times before we get a version we think *ready* for production."[64]

During most of the next several months, the Quartet was on tour in Europe, Asia, and the Middle East. Shortly after their return, Dave mentioned to his brother Howard their plan to discuss it with the president of Columbia, Goddard Lieberson, and their hope "that he will show some interest in" their show. He also confessed his weariness from "this constant touring," and said he intended to concentrate on composition as his plan of escape from the itinerant lifestyle. The linchpin was the new musical: "If we can just see this first show in production, I will be encouraged to develop this field of writing."[65]

Central to the Brubecks' vision for their project was a starring role for Louis Armstrong. By their own testimony, they designed the show around him. One week before Thanksgiving in 1958, Dave told his booking agent, Joe Glaser, who represented Armstrong as well, that he and Iola "have been working night and day on [the show] and have rewritten it." He dreamed of "owning a night club jointly" with Armstrong, "while the play is running on Broadway, with me performing the early part of the evening at the club and Louis coming in for one set after the show."[66] After the Christmas holidays, Brubeck met with Armstrong in Chicago and evidently reported back to Glaser that Armstrong was interested in the show.[67] One week after New Year's, however, Brubeck requested Glaser's "frank appraisal" and said he wanted "Louis to do the show only if he *believes* in *it*." The idea was for it to be produced on Broadway during the 1959–1960 season. Brubeck's manager, Mort Lewis, was so optimistic about its prospects that he included an exit clause in the agreement for the November 1959 "Jazz for Moderns" tour, in the event that Brubeck "cannot possibly make the tour this year because of the Broadway show."[68]

As the year wore on, the Brubecks did their level best to get the show on Broadway. They reached out beyond their inner circle, initiated innumerable new contacts, and followed up every lead. In late March, their spirits were still high. Lewis told his colleague in Australia that the

---

64 Dave Brubeck to George Avakian, December 13, 1957 (Brubeck Collection).
65 Dave Brubeck to Howard Brubeck, May 29, 1958 (Brubeck Collection).
66 Dave Brubeck to Joe Glaser, November 20, 1958 (Brubeck Collection).
67 Joe Glaser to Dave Brubeck, January 5, 1959 (Brubeck Collection).
68 Mort Lewis to Ed Sarkesian (promoter in Detroit), January 13, 1959 (Brubeck Collection).

Brubecks' show was "at present being submitted to a few Broadway producers," and "from the looks of things, it will be produced sometime soon." He confided, moreover, that "this very success may . . . mean the end of the Quartet as we know it."[69] The same day, Iola informed her close friend, "This summer we will go to New York (all of us), and Dave and I will concentrate on trying to snag a producer to do our 'bang up' musical." With a light touch, she added, "We are proud of it, if we did write it ourselves."[70]

Three months later, Dave went so far as to approach Jerome Robbins, the famous choreographer, whose work with Arthur Laurents, Stephen Sondheim, and Leonard Bernstein on *West Side Story* was all the rage around that time. In the draft of this remarkable letter, written in Oakland on June 20, Brubeck makes reference to his own use of "odd rhythm patterns," just days before the first *Time Out* recording sessions in New York:

> To come directly to the point of this letter, I would like very much to talk to you and play for you some of the music I have written for a Broadway production starring Louis Armstrong and Carmen McRae. I have the assurance of Mr. Joe Glaser, Armstrong's manager, that Louis will be available to me for a Broadway production, as both he and Louis have heard and approved of the score. . . . I think you will be interested in the manner I have treated the chorus and the dance. For example, *I have superimposed rhythms in the crowd scenes to create a feeling of mass movement, and of tensions, of mass forces pulling against each other. In an "Around the World" ballet sequence I have employed odd rhythmic patterns based on the folk music of various countries of Europe, the Middle East, India and Africa. . . .* The time is now ripe for a jazz show on Broadway, and I think mine is ready. . . . I plan to make some positive moves toward production this summer.[71]

The second recording day for *Time Out* was July 1, less than two weeks after Brubeck penned this letter. In addition to the artist job sheet for that session (2:30–7:00 p.m.), there are two more pages with the same job number, for a three-hour session on July 2 (1:30–4:30 p.m.), marked "experimental takes."[72] Eleven of the sixteen tunes listed are from *The Real*

69 Mort Lewis to Art Thurston, March 28, 1959 (Brubeck Collection).
70 Iola Brubeck to Mary Jeanne Sauerwein, March 28, 1959 (Brubeck Collection).
71 Dave Brubeck to Jerome Robbins, June 20, 1959 (Brubeck Collection); emphasis added.
72 Columbia Records, Artist Job Sheet, Job No. 50192 (Sony Music Archives Library).

Ambassadors.[73] This evidence suggests that the show was actually more important to the Brubecks in 1959 than was *Time Out*. At all events, they were deeply involved with its creation and promotion at exactly the same time as Brubeck's most famous album was taking shape. Paradoxically, although it never really got off the ground, *The Real Ambassadors* was the endeavor that occupied first place in Brubeck's affections and to which he devoted the greatest amount of time and effort—instead of the project that ultimately became one of the best-selling albums in jazz history.

WITH BERNSTEIN AT CARNEGIE HALL

The official release date for *Time Out* was Monday, December 14, 1959, although the album seems not to have been generally available until after the holidays. During the preceding weekend, Brubeck was kept busy with a gig that ought to have raised any spirits sagging from the disappointing inertia surrounding his show. On a program that also included concertos by Bach, Mozart, and the Juilliard composition professor Robert Starer, the Quartet performed *Dialogues for Jazz Combo and Orchestra* by Dave's brother Howard Brubeck, at Carnegie Hall with the New York Philharmonic under the direction of Leonard Bernstein.[74]

Taking place on the eve of the release of *Time Out,* this was an event of considerable cultural complexity. Despite the fact that this particular piece of music is not everyone's cup of tea, the spectacle of the leading jazz combo performing with America's most famous orchestra under the baton of its flamboyant new conductor in one of the nation's premier concert venues was a high-water mark for all concerned. Although the liner notes for the Columbia recording claim that "Bernstein conducted the première of *Dialogues for Jazz Combo and Orchestra*" in December 1959, the work had actually been performed several times during the previous three years, and its origins stretch back even further.[75]

---

73 The specific titles are "World Take a Holiday," "Cultural Exchange," "Good Reviews," "King for a Day," "Swing Bells," "Since Love Had Its Way," "Easy as You Go," "The Real Ambassadors," "They Say I Look Like God," and "Lonesome," plus another Brubeck original with "title to be given later."

74 The liner notes for *Bernstein Plays Brubeck Plays Bernstein* (Columbia CL 1466) give the performance dates as December 10, 11, and 13—and this information has therefore been widely disseminated. According to the official printed program, the "6064th," "6065th," and "6066th" concerts of the Philharmonic's "One Hundred Eighteenth Season" (1959–1960) took place at 8:30 p.m. on Thursday, December 10, 2:15 p.m. on Friday the 11th, and 8:30 p.m. on Saturday the 12th.

75 Liner notes, *Bernstein Plays Brubeck Plays Bernstein.*

In the early 1950s, when the Dave Brubeck Quartet was just getting under way, Howard Brubeck was teaching composition, first at San Diego State College and then (from 1953) at Palomar College, just thirty-five miles up the road in San Marcos. On August 10, 1954—three months before his brother appeared on the cover of *Time* magazine—Howard had a triumph of his own, when the San Diego Symphony Orchestra played his *Overture to "The Devil's Disciple"* under the direction of Robert Shaw. The work had been commissioned by the Symphony Association, and this was its first performance.[76] The pathway from there to the *Dialogues* began with a detour, described many years later by Howard Brubeck himself: "The president of the San Diego Symphony. . . became obsessed in 1955 with the idea that Dave should be scheduled to play the *Rhapsody in Blue* [by George Gershwin] with the orchestra, then conducted by Robert Shaw. When I explained that Dave was essentially a jazz musician and confined himself to on-the-spot improvisations based on traditional popular tunes, she responded by saying that I should write some tunes on which he could improvise with the orchestra. . . . The opportunity appealed. Dave accepted the challenge and Bob [Shaw] kindly invited me to conduct the first performance in July, 1956."[77]

The première of Howard Brubeck's *Dialogues* on July 31 was itself reported in *Time*, which claimed this was "the first time that a jazz group improvised in a concert with a symphony orchestra."[78] The Cleveland Summer Orchestra performed a revised version in July 1958, and it was reworked a second time before the Oakland Symphony programmed it in December 1958.

Ralph Gleason devoted one of his "Rhythm Section" syndicated columns in November 1959 to the upcoming December performances of a fresh incarnation of the *Dialogues* with the New York Philharmonic. In language redolent of the 1956 *Time* report, Gleason credited Brubeck with another "first," noting that his "appearance there with Bernstein will mark the first time a working jazz group has played with the symphony at Carnegie Hall."[79]

76 "1954 Summer Symphony Season" program (Brubeck Collection).

77 Thomas P. Lewis, ed., *Something about the Music 2: Anthology of Critical Opinions* (White Plains, NY: Pro/Am Music Resources; London: Kahn & Averill, 1990), 126–127. A copy of Howard Brubeck's August 30, 1990 letter to Lewis is in the Brubeck Collection.

78 "Symphonic Jam Session," *Time* 68, no. 7 (August 13, 1956): 45. Duke Ellington appeared on the cover of the next issue.

79 Ralph J. Gleason, "Brubeck to Play with N. Y. Philharmonic," n.p., n.d. (Brubeck Collection). The same column appeared under a different title in the *Boston Daily Globe*. On the clipping in the Brubeck Collection is the handwritten date of November 1959.

The reception of these New York concerts was extremely enthusiastic. From Dave Brubeck's own point of view, of course, they were an unqualified success. In her eulogy many years later for her brother-in-law's memorial, Iola Brubeck characterized the experience of "sharing with Howard the angst and the joy of performing . . . in Carnegie Hall with Leonard Bernstein" as "one of the most glorious moments in Dave's career."[80] A review of the first concert indicates that the listeners that night were equally enthralled: "The standing-room-only audience at Carnegie Hall gave the Brubeck quartet a five-minute applauding tribute. Bravoes were shouted. The quartet was called back three times for bows. Howard Brubeck, Dave's brother, took two bows."[81]

There were two attendees who were equally unexpected, yet who differed from each other in nearly every respect, including their reactions to the event. The first was Edgard Varèse, the famous experimental composer from France, who lived in New York for many years beginning in 1915. He had recently achieved new heights of fame with his *Poème électronique,* which formed part of an installation at the 1958 World's Fair in Brussels, with a pavilion designed by Le Corbusier. Brubeck's producer at Columbia, Teo Macero, himself an avant-garde composer, had befriended Varèse in the 1950s. Macero later recalled, "I was there when he was doing the *Poème électronique* in Paris. He would show me all the pieces, all of the elements. . . . We used to see each other for lunch. We'd talk on Saturdays and Sundays on the phone and he'd come to all the concerts that I gave. He was like a second father, with a tremendous amount of knowledge."[82]

The Brubeck brothers benefited from Macero's friendship with Varèse. In a remarkable passage from a set of liner notes that ultimately didn't see the light of day, Macero told the story of Varèse's surprisingly warm response to the *Dialogues,* shortly before his seventy-sixth birthday:

> While listening to the performance with Edgard Varèse, I could see from the look on his face that he was really enjoying it as much as I was. Some of his comments after each movement were, "wonderful, magnificent," etc. Immediately after the performance at Carnegie

80 Iola Brubeck, "A Wonderful Man," read by Theodore Kilman, March 28, 1993 (Brubeck Collection). She also noted, as did several published accounts, that Howard Brubeck and Leonard Bernstein had been classmates at Tanglewood.

81 Doc Quigg, "Symphony, Plus Brubeck, Is Cool, Man," *Oakland Tribune,* December 11, 1959.

82 Iara Lee, interview with Teo Macero, September 1997, *Perfect Sound Forever* (online music magazine), www.furious.com/perfect/teomacero.html (accessed March 14, 2018).

Hall, Mr. Varèse and I met with Dave and Howard on the street, as it was impossible to get backstage to see them. Mr. Varèse proceeded to embrace both Dave and Howard Brubeck, telling them both that it was not only a great performance but an excellent composition as well. Since this performance, we have talked many times about the excellence of Howard's composition, and how it far surpasses most of the music being written today.[83]

The other unexpected visitor was the twenty-nine-year-old saxophonist and composer Ornette Coleman, who reacted quite differently. He had recorded his pathbreaking album *The Shape of Jazz to Come* in May, and had met Dave Brubeck at the Lenox School of Jazz in western Massachusetts during the summer.[84] He had also caught the attention of Leonard Bernstein during his New York debut at the Five Spot, beginning in mid-November. Unlike Miles Davis, who declared that Coleman was "all screwed up inside," Bernstein famously voiced his support and approval. Moreover, Bernstein invited Coleman to hear an upcoming performance of the *Dialogues for Jazz Combo and Orchestra*. It was reported that "Coleman was bored by the music, and was stunned by the scenes of homage in the Green Room where Bernstein receives visitors after the concert." Moreover, one of Coleman's biographers noted that "this was apparently the end of their association."[85]

In his 1963 essay on "Third Stream Problems," Martin Williams had tart words for the music of both Macero and the Brubecks: "Leonard Bernstein and the New York Philharmonic premiered a rather pretentious and aridly 'experimental' piece by Teo Macero for jazz group and orchestra. Under the same auspices, there was performed Howard Brubeck's *Dialogues for Jazz Combo and Orchestra*—an example of bad conservative classical writing, with sometimes genially *ersatz* jazz from Howard's brother Dave."[86] However the concert itself was received, a small but characteristically thoughtful gesture on Dave Brubeck's part

83 "Brubeck-Bernstein 'Dialogues for Jazz Combo & Orchestra,'" unpublished typescript (Macero Collection, box 6, folder 6).

84 See Jeremy Yudkin, *The Lenox School of Jazz: A Vital Chapter in the History of American Music and Race Relations* (South Egremont, MA: Farshaw Publishing, 2006), 78–99 (Chapter 10: "The 1959 Season: Apogee of the School, Arrival of 'Student' Ornette Coleman, Problems of Success").

85 David Lee, *The Battle of the Five Spot: Ornette Coleman and the New York Jazz Field* (Toronto: Mercury Press, 2006), 112–113 n. 152.

86 Martin Williams, *Jazz Heritage* (New York: Oxford University Press, 1985), 74.

following that weekend undoubtedly served as a catalyst in bringing together the worlds of jazz and classical music. At the very end of the year, Brubeck's manager mentioned to Macero that they had received a thank-you note from the New York Philharmonic for "the gift of Dave's *Time Out* album (one to each musician)," and Brubeck's manager, in turn, thanked Macero for his role in making this possible.[87]

87 Mort Lewis to Teo Macero, December 29, 1959 (Macero Collection, box 7, folder 15; also Brubeck Collection).

CHAPTER 4

CREATIVE PROCESS I
COMPOSITION AND
IMPROVISATION

THE SEVEN CUTS on *Time Out* were the product of an intensive creative ferment in 1959, some of which had its roots earlier that decade.

"BLUE RONDO À LA TURK"

A few weeks after Dave Brubeck's passing in 2012, the eminent jazz pianist Herbie Hancock—twenty years Brubeck's junior—penned a short but eloquent tribute for *Time* magazine. After characterizing him as "a legend" and "a master who was instrumental in the shaping of modern jazz," Hancock shone the spotlight on Brubeck's compositional abilities: "Let's not forget that he was also an amazing composer. He constructed his pieces not just as tunes but as real compositions: architectural arrangements that were reminiscent of classical works." In this connection, Hancock mentioned "Blue Rondo à la Turk" in particular.[1]

The autograph manuscripts reveal the structure of the piece quite clearly. The first page of the final copy of the bass part, which was penned in black ink, consists of a series of eight-bar segments numbered from one through seven (see Figure 4.1).[2] Each segment falls into two halves with the same rhythmic pattern: three bars of 9/8 with three quarter notes and a dotted quarter, followed by one bar of 9/8 with three dotted quarters. Expressed in groups of eighth notes, the resultant metrical pattern is 2+2+2+3 | 2+2+2+3 | 2+2+2+3 | 3+3+3. The seven segments alternate between two pitches: f is articulated in the odd-numbered ones and a in the others, with doubling at the lower octave in the second half of segment six (the system used here is Helmholtz pitch notation, in which middle C is notated as c′; the octaves above as c″, c‴, and c⁗; and the octaves below as c, C, and CC).

Segments eight and nine depart from the established eight-bar format, running to twelve bars (three four-bar phrases) and ten (two plus four plus four), respectively. Each phrase of segment eight—which begins at the bottom of the first page and continues on the top two staves of the second—includes a prominent descending chromatic scale. The first two (mm. 57–58 and 61–62) trace the same pitches, beginning on c♯′, but flow into different harmonic territory: A in m. 59, and F in m. 63. The third phrase of segment eight features a mostly chromatic descent starting on b (mm. 65–66), which resolves into F again, in m. 67. Segment nine begins with a two-bar scale that descends more than an octave, from e to AA, this time using mostly white notes (diatonic instead of chromatic). The balance of the segment remains fixed on the low A, but a new rhythm is introduced. Within each phrase (mm. 71–74, 75–78), there are three bars in which two sets of duplet eighth notes are followed by a regular set of three eighth notes. In the last bar of the first phrase, all nine eighth notes are articulated (3+3+3). In the second phrase, this pattern is extended to four sets of eighth notes (3+3+3+3). This pattern sets the stage for the shift to common-time blues at the beginning of the next segment.

1 Herbie Hancock, "Dave Brubeck," *Time* 180, no. 27 (December 31, 2012/January 7, 2013): 136.
2 This leaf is in a folder marked "Blue Rondo à la Turk—Bass Part" (Brubeck Collection). The folder also contains an incomplete pencil draft, which apparently preceded the one in pen and pencil, and which includes essentially the same material. In both manuscripts the title is shortened to simply "Blue Rondo." A fifteen-bar pencil manuscript with the heading "9/8 Alto" in a separate folder labeled "Blue Rondo Sketch" comprises the transposed (E♭) saxophone part of the eighth segment and the beginning of the ninth.

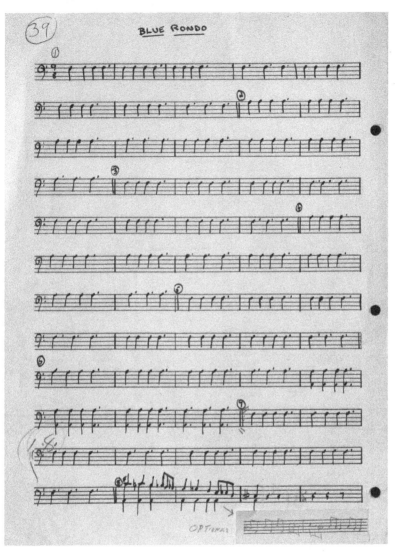

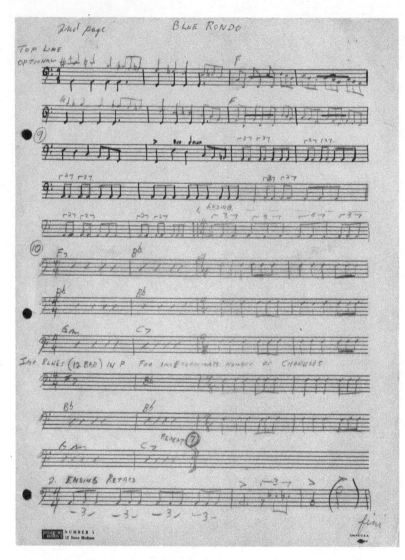

FIGURE 4.1A AND 4.1B.   Continued

Though segment ten has the form of the twelve-bar blues, it remains a metrical hybrid—alternating between two bars of 4/4 and two of 9/8 (2+2+2+3). Thereafter, the longest portion of the piece—from 2:13 to 5:34 in the recording on *Time Out*—is summarized simply as "IMP [i.e., improvised] BLUES (12 BAR) IN F FOR INDETERMINATE NUMBER OF CHORUSES." This portion is followed by a reprise of the "metrical hybrid" passage, which flows into a return of segments seven through nine, this time with an altered ending that grinds to a halt instead of transitioning to the blues.

In addition to its formal design and rhythmic profile, the architectural features of "Blue Rondo à la Turk" include its motivic content, its palette of chord types, its tonal blueprint, and the relations between these factors. The piece is noteworthy in its economy of motivic material. Consider, first of all, segment one (see Example 4.1). The initial gesture is a two-note descending third motive (a' and f') that is articulated three times in each of the first three measures. The other component is a three-note scalar figure—first ascending and encircling f' (m. 1), then descending and encircling a' (m. 2). M. 3 follows the pattern of m. 1, but the ascending figure is subsequently treated as the first leg of a sequence that continues through m. 4. Meanwhile, the left-hand part consists of the pedal tone f, over which a chromatic line oscillates between e' and c'. On *Time Out*, Brubeck plays this four-bar passage first as a piano solo and then repeats it (joined by the bass and seasoned with a few light cymbal strokes) to form segment one.

Nearly all of the foregoing description applies to segment two as well (see Example 4.2), except that it is transposed up a third, the saxophone plays the tune, and the cymbal work becomes increasingly prominent. Segment three matches segment one, and its melody reverts to the piano. Segment four is closely allied to segment two, yet the tune remains in the piano and it introduces some fresh permutations of earlier material (see Example 4.3). Instead of the static alternation between two pitches that has graced three-quarters of the measures so far, the motive is transformed into a sequence that ascends (mm. 25 and 27) and descends (m. 26). Moreover, the directionality of these melodic units is varied. This is apparent, for instance, if one compares m. 28—a descending scalar figure arranged as a descending sequence—with the ascending versions in mm. 4 (Example 4.1) and 12 (Example 4.2).

Segment five follows the pattern of segments one and three, but the saxophone harmonizes the tune at the upper third (see Example 4.4). The most prominent feature of segment six is the repeated a, which is hammered out incessantly in the left hand of the piano part (see Example 4.5).

The parallel motion of the second-inversion triads in the right hand, however, is a significant precursor to similar passages shortly thereafter. Segment seven mirrors segment five.

As segment eight stretches out to twelve bars (instead of eight) and incorporates several chromatic scales, the whirling descending sequence heard earlier in the treble migrates to the left hand in mm. 60, 64, 68, and their anacruses (see Example 4.6). Moreover, chords in the right hand—which move upward in parallel motion—punctuate the third note of each leg. The last set consists of root-position triads, but the two previous sets introduce the pungent sonorities of quartal harmony.

Segment nine, which accomplishes the transition to the blues section, begins with a set of chords that move in contrary motion until

EXAMPLE 4.3.   Dave Brubeck, "Blue Rondo à la Turk," first half of segment four (mm. 25–28).

EXAMPLE 4.4.   Dave Brubeck, "Blue Rondo à la Turk," first half of segment five (mm. 33–36).

EXAMPLE 4.5.   Dave Brubeck, "Blue Rondo à la Turk," first half of segment six (mm. 41–44).

EXAMPLE 4.6. Dave Brubeck, "Blue Rondo à la Turk," segment eight (mm. 57–68). Copyright © 1960 (Renewed) by Derry Music Company. Used by permission.

they reach their climax on an A-major triad (see Example 4.7). The underlying meter of the following eight bars—immediately preceding the first hint of the blues—is the regular compound version of 9/8 (3+3+3). But there are two wrinkles. In about half the passage, two duplet eighth notes substitute for three regular eighth notes (see Example 4.8).

76   *DAVE BRUBECK'S* TIME OUT

Moreover, the shift to the blues involves metric modulation. Another group of three eighth notes is added, forming a 12/8 bar, which then sets up swing 4/4.[3]

The subsequent course of "Blue Rondo à la Turk" described earlier bears repeating. Although the initial turn toward the blues occurs in m. 79 (immediately following the last measure of Example 4.8), the transition doesn't occur all at once. Mervyn Cooke's account aptly captures the magic of this hybrid passage: "In a delicious moment of unpredictability, the music sideslips effortlessly into a bluesy and swinging four-beat tempo. This attempt to establish a conventional jazz idiom is checked three times with brief interruptions by the edgy 2+2+2+3 rondo theme, before the music finally settles into a twelve-bar blues."[4] Paul Desmond and Brubeck each take four twelve-bar choruses, in that order.[5]

The piece is rounded out with a reprise of the hybrid segment and a greatly abbreviated version of the opening material.[6] The last two bars of the hybrid passage are elided with the recapitulation. Accordingly, mm. 197–198 serve simultaneously as the end of the twelve-bar blues and the beginning of the head. At the very end, the 12/8 measure that formerly slipped so "deliciously" into the blues is followed instead by a straightforward A-major chord (see Example 4.9). This focuses attention on the fact that the piece starts and ends in different keys. The opening tonality and the key of the longest section (eight choruses of blues) is F major. The concluding sonority, on the other hand, is A major, and indeed A is the secondary tonal center throughout the composition. With A and F firmly in mind, a glance back at the initial oscillating motive reveals that the melodic kernel (micro level) and the overall harmonic plan (macro level) both are derived from these same two pitches.

---

3 Darius Brubeck, "Jazz 1959: The Beginning of Beyond" (MA thesis, University of Nottingham, 2002), 141.

4 Mervyn Cooke, *The Chronicle of Jazz*, rev. ed. (New York: Oxford University Press, 2013), 147.

5 This is the usual pattern. According to Robert Rice, "Desmond's solo—by Desmond's choice—precedes Brubeck's in almost every number, causing Brubeck to refer to himself as 'the cleanup man.'" Robert Rice, "The Cleanup Man," *New Yorker* 37, no. 16 (June 3, 1961): 50.

6 The opening nine segments (mm. 1–78) are telescoped to just thirty bars:

mm. 197–200 = 1–4 (first half of segment six)

mm. 201–204 = 53–57 (latter half of segment seven)

mm. 205–216 = 57–68 (segment eight)

mm. 217–227 = 69–78 (segment nine), plus concluding A-major chord

"EVERYBODY'S JUMPIN'"

"Everybody's Jumpin'" also is an elegantly constructed composition. Its fundamental pattern consists of three four-bar units (4/4, 3/2, 4/4). This twelve-bar structure (see Example 4.10) underlies all six choruses—two on the saxophone, three on the piano, and one on the drums. In the head, it is extended by four additional measures of 3/4, marked throughout with the rhythm of a dotted eighth followed by a sixteenth note, and then four 2/4 measures subdivided into eighth-note triplets, a telescoped version of the preceding phrase (see Example 4.11).

The tune begins on a dominant seventh chord in F major. The following 3/2 passage in A♭ major is therefore to be understood as a tonicization of the flat three. The material that comes next, including the eight-bar extension, revolves around an F⁷ chord, which functions as the dominant seventh in B♭ major, the key of the second iteration of the head. What this progression means is that the full twenty-bar version of the head modulates from the tonic, down a fifth to the subdominant.

EXAMPLE 4.11. Dave Brubeck, "Everybody's Jumpin," head, part 2 (mm. 13–20). Copyright © 1960, 1962 (Copyrights Renewed) by Derry Music Company. Used by permission.

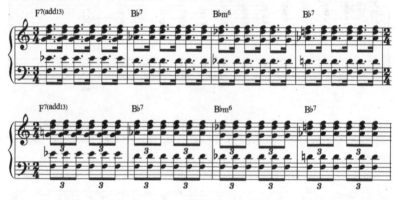

EXAMPLE 4.12. Dave Brubeck, "Everybody's Jumpin," beginning of second statement of head (mm. 21–24). Copyright © 1960, 1962 (Copyrights Renewed) by Derry Music Company. Used by permission.

The boundary between the end of the first statement of the head and the beginning of the second (at m. 21) is camouflaged ingeniously, by continuing the rapidly pulsating triplet eighth-note chords from the previous measures while simultaneously stating the tune in the new key (see Example 4.12). The same procedure is repeated in mm. 21–40, yielding a trajectory from B♭ major, through D♭ major, and on to E♭ major. The harmonic spiral downward through the circle of fifths is impeded by the subsequent omission of the extension and the use of just the first dozen bars of the head as the basis for Desmond's, Brubeck's, and Joe Morello's

solos. All of these passages move from E♭ major (tonic) to G♭ major (flat three) and back to the tonic.

The allocation of solos in "Everybody's Jumpin'" follows the usual sequence. Desmond improvises first, taking two choruses (1:23–2:07). Brubeck then enters and takes three (2:08–3:15). The only thing out of the ordinary here is that Brubeck's improvisation remains rather benign. He forgoes the intensification into block chords so often heard in his solos, opting instead for gentle single notes throughout. Indeed, the most surprising and engaging passage is the brief drum solo (3:16–3:37), in which Morello skillfully mimics not only the rhythms but also the pitches of the tune. This amelodic episode serves as a kind of musical "palate cleanser," which enables the final statement of the head to begin in F major again (after several minutes of E♭ major), without any awkwardness.

The first twelve measures of the head at the end match the version at the beginning. But the original eight-bar extension, with the modulation and the intensification from dotted rhythms to triplets, is replaced by a slightly longer passage. As before, it consists of repeated block chords. This time, however, the outer voices move in contrary motion toward resolution in F (see Example 4.13).

"THREE TO GET READY"

"Three to Get Ready" begins with a mock-classical theme that is purposely square. Brubeck's piano solo, accompanied by light percussion and bass, is in the 3/4 meter of a waltz or minuet (see Example 4.14).[7] Its

---

7 Steve Race's liner notes for *Time Out* invoke the music of Joseph Haydn (1732–1809), characterizing Brubeck's tune as "a simple Haydn-esque waltz theme in C major." If his nod to Haydn is apt at all, then it would have made more sense for Race to refer to a different social dance, the minuet rather than the waltz. Haydn composed many minuets in the course of his long career, but the waltz didn't become popular until later in the nineteenth century, and Haydn would have been familiar with it only at the end of his life.

EXAMPLE 4.14.   Dave Brubeck, "Three to Get Ready," theme (mm. 1–12).
Copyright © 1960, 1962 (Copyrights Renewed) by Derry Music Company. Used by permission.

four phrases, each of which is three measures long, sound cut and dried
and remain benignly close to the tonic C major. The first, second, and
fourth phrases begin identically. Moreover, the first two phrases essentially consist of a one-measure gesture that is repeated a step higher—
that is, a sequence. Only the last note of the two passages is different.
Instead of dropping back down to the starting pitch (m. 3), the second
phrase continues its ascent (m. 6). The latter half of the fourth phrase
is an inverted form of the last four notes of the second phrase. Rather
than moving upward by step to the leading tone b′ (m. 6), it proceeds
downward to the tonic c′ (m. 12). The third phrase provides the greatest
contrast with the other three, but it too consists of not much more than
a two-leg sequence of eighth notes.

When the saxophone enters for the second chorus, just twelve
seconds into the cut, the tune is altered in two ways, both of which are
plain to see in Brubeck's manuscript chart for Paul Desmond (Figure
4.2). Each phrase is extended from three bars to four, for a total of sixteen. Moreover, the meter and feel of the latter two bars of each unit
(4/4, foxtrot) are quite different from the first two. From this point forward, the next fourteen choruses—almost the rest of the cut—feature
regular alternation between two measures in 3/4 and two in 4/4. This
pattern is retained even in the sixteenth chorus (4:38–4:57), the first restatement of the head, which is followed by the original all-3/4 version,
rounded off with a chromatic and polytonal cadential extension (see
Example 4.15).

In addition to the compact and expanded versions of the theme, the
performing part for the saxophone includes Desmond's annotations
in pen, which designate the subsequent course of the piece. Above the
opening chorus in 3/4, Brubeck had written "Piano 1st Chorus Alone." In
the passage with Brubeck's heading "2nd Chorus," Desmond indicated
that the piano was to play fills in the 4/4 measures. The order of events in

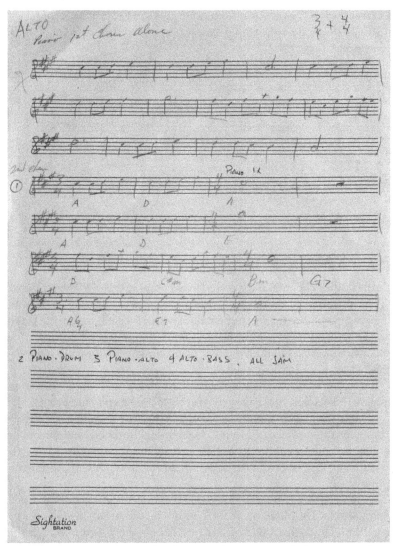

FIGURE 4.2. Dave Brubeck, "Three to Get Ready," manuscript alto saxophone part, pencil, autograph, with Paul Desmond's annotations in pen.

Brubeck Collection, Holt-Atherton Special Collections, University of the Pacific Library. © Dave Brubeck.

the next three choruses is expressed in telegraphic style: "Piano—Drum," "Piano—Alto," and "Alto—Bass." The middle one is similar to the second chorus, except that the instrumental roles are reversed, so that the piano plays the melody (3/4) and the saxophone supplies the fills (4/4). The other two choruses highlight either drums or bass, by providing opportunities for solos in the 4/4 measures.

Desmond's last annotation reads simply "All Jam." On the *Time Out* album, this section runs to ten choruses—three for saxophone and seven for piano. Desmond's minute in the sun (1:29–2:26) is smooth and highly competent, as usual. But his solo is so straightforward, and devoid of quotations, that a full transcription and analysis is unnecessary. A few features of Brubeck's improvisation (2:26–4:37) merit brief comment, however.

It appears that Brubeck's initial creative impetus came from the saxophone solo. Desmond signed off with a lick that outlines a C-major triad in second inversion (m. 124 in Example 4.16). Brubeck took the first five notes of that passage as the point of departure for his own solo (see Example 4.17). His second bar forms a sequence with the first (mm. 125–126). Similarly, there is a symmetrical relationship between the first four-bar segment (mm. 125–128) and the second (mm. 129–132). The introduction of the flat third scale degree (m. 137) signals Brubeck's turn toward blues inflection. This eventually leads to some biting dissonances in the fourth piano chorus (beginning around 3:27) and continuing into the fifth.

EXAMPLE 4.16. Dave Brubeck, "Three to Get Ready," alto saxophone (Paul Desmond), end of chorus 3 (mm. 121–124), transcription.

EXAMPLE 4.17. Dave Brubeck, "Three to Get Ready," piano (Brubeck), chorus 1 (mm. 125–140), transcription.

"KATHY'S WALTZ": ANALYSIS

"Three to Get Ready" and "Kathy's Waltz" belong together by virtue of their position side by side as the first two cuts on Side Two of *Time Out* and, more importantly, because they both involve metrical experimentation with groups of three and four beats. As Steve Race observed in the original liner notes, "Three to Get Ready" starts in three, "but before long it begins to vacillate between 3- and 4-time, and the pattern becomes clear: two bars of 3, followed by two bars of 4." "Kathy's Waltz," on the other hand, "starts in 4, only later breaking into quick waltz time. . . .[In his solo,] Dave starts in triple time, then urges his piano into a rocking slow 4. Theoretically it is as if [drummer Joe] Morello's three beats had ceased to be the basic pulse, and had become triplets in a slow 4-beat blues." In other words, triple and quadruple time are used successively in "Three to Get Ready" and concurrently in "Kathy's Waltz."

"Kathy's Waltz" begins provocatively, in decidedly unwaltzlike common time (see Example 4.18). But brisk 3/4 waltz time is introduced at the end of the head (around 1:06), and it prevails for the rest

of the cut. The rationale for Brubeck's unusual opening gambit becomes clear a couple of minutes later, in his second chorus (just before the 3:00 mark), when he switches back to common time, while the rhythm section continues in 3/4. The effect of this move is to produce a species of polymeter in which two bars of waltz time (six beats total) are juxtaposed against one bar of common time (four beats), in the ratio 3:2. This intentional metrical clash continues through to the end of Brubeck's solo, encompassing another full chorus.

When the head is brought back (around 4:00), after two intervening choruses for alto saxophone and three for piano (including the polymetrical passages described previously), it is presented in the normal garb of a waltz in 3/4. Accordingly, it follows rather closely the manuscript lead sheet reproduced in Figure 4.3. The more straightforward version notated there features a tightly wrought melody, thirty-six bars in length, which falls into five phrases. Phrase 1 (mm. 1–8) consists of four iterations of a distinctive three-note motive that moves downward and includes a leap to each downbeat, followed by an ascending scale in quarter notes. Phrase 2 (mm. 9–16) begins with two statements of a six-note variant of the motive from Phrase 1, followed by another ascending scale. Phrase 3 (mm. 17–24) adheres to the pattern of Phrase 1, except that it is transposed, and the direction of the chromatic motion of the half notes is reversed (downward in mm. 1–4, upward in mm. 17–20). Phrase 4 (mm. 25–32) could have completed the usual thirty-two-bar form, but it turns out to be identical to phrase 1, which is tonally open. As a result, Brubeck tacked on an additional four-bar phrase (mm. 33–36), comprising the fifth and final scalar ascent in quarter notes, which ends on the tonic B♭. The *Time Out* recording doesn't conclude there, however. It dissolves instead in a series of polytonal chords that adds three more bars (see Example 4.19). The first five sonorities consist of

FIGURE 4.3. Dave Brubeck, "Waltz for Cathy," manuscript lead sheet.
Brubeck Collection, Holt-Atherton Special Collections, University of the Pacific Library.
© Dave Brubeck.

two different major chords whose roots are a minor third apart: D♭ (right hand)/B♭ (left hand)–C/A–C♭/A♭–B♭/G–A/G♭.

THE STORY OF "KATHY'S WALTZ"

Dave Brubeck passed away on December 5, 2012, just one day before his ninety-second birthday. Five months later, on May 11, 2013, he was memorialized in a public celebration at the Cathedral Church of Saint John the Divine in New York City. This event included performances of thirteen Brubeck compositions by a number of eminent musicians, including Chick Corea (piano), Jon Faddis (trumpet), Roy Hargrove (trumpet), Branford Marsalis (saxophone), Deepak Ram (flute), John Salmon (piano), and Paul Winter (saxophone). The first number on the program was "Kathy's Waltz," performed by four of Dave and Iola Brubeck's sons—Darius (piano), Chris (bass), Dan (drums), and Matthew (cello)—and introduced by its namesake, their daughter, Catherine Brubeck Yaghsizian. Later that year, Catherine was kind enough to meet me in person and share the story of "Kathy's Waltz" in a memorable two-hour interview near her home in Connecticut.

Catherine told me that when she was little her mother, Iola, gave her a blue tutu as a Christmas or birthday gift.

> When my father would come home from the road, he'd be so tired . . . , but to relax he would . . . play with the boys. . . . At the time I think Mike was playing drums, Darius played trumpet, and my dad would be on the keyboard, and Chris, who was just a year and a half older than me, would sit at the piano . . . and try to follow the bass line. . . . [Dad] would say, "Hey, let's play," . . . and we'd all get together, and then I took that as my cue. So I go booking down the hall to put my tutu on. And when I went back in the room, I was trying to dance,

FIGURE 4.4. Dave Brubeck at home, with daughter Catherine and sons Darius (trumpet), Mike (drums), Chris (piano, to his father's left), and Dan (sax), January 1959. Bob Willoughby/mptvimages.com. Used by permission.

and there were all these crazy time rhythms going on. . . . I think I was crashing into coffee tables . . . , trying to twirl around, and everybody was laughing, as usual. But I got a song out of it, and it was "Kathy's Waltz."[8]

Catherine wasn't sure of the year her waltz was penned. But if it was early in 1959, as seems most likely, she would have been five years old.[9] A photo taken at the Brubecks' home by the renowned photographer Bob Willoughby (1927–2009) during the last week of January 1959 shows the scene of the family music making and dancing (see Figure 4.4).[10]

8 Catherine Brubeck Yaghsizian, interview with the author, November 12, 2013.
9 Catherine was born on November 5, 1953, according to Fred M. Hall, *It's about Time: The Dave Brubeck Story* (Fayetteville: University of Arkansas Press, 1996), 108.
10 A letter from Brubeck's manager, Mort Lewis, requests that Willoughby try to arrange his work "sometime between January 26th and February 2nd," during a hiatus in Brubeck's travels. Mort Lewis to Bob Willoughby, January 19, 1959 (Brubeck Collection). When I shared this image with Catherine, she replied, "Great photo! But where's the tutu?" (Obviously, this was an optional accessory.) She also confirmed the identities of her brothers, including three-year-old Dan on "baby sax," whom she had not previously mentioned. Catherine Brubeck Yaghsizian, email message to author, April 15, 2017.

Catherine remarked on the downward contour of the melody and its accentuation, speculating that these musical features may have represented her father's attempts to capture the kinesthetic aspects of her contribution to their domestic entertainment: "When I listen to the melody, I do think of somebody sort of twirling and falling, because the line of it is like [sings] 'da-da-DUM, da-da-DUM'. . . . I don't know if he meant it that way, but that's how I think of it. It's just twirl and plop, and twirl and plop." She also confirmed my hunch that the three-note motive might simultaneously constitute a wordless setting of the song's title. In support of this notion, she observed that her father "wrote a song for every child."[11]

Another significant aspect of the story of "Kathy's Waltz" is the fact that the name of its dedicatee was spelled incorrectly. The booklet for the fiftieth-anniversary rerelease of *Time Out* includes a photo of Catherine Brubeck as a child, with a caption that acknowledges this circumstance: " 'Kathy's Waltz' is dedicated to Dave's daughter Cathy (misspelled due to a typographic error by Columbia Records)."[12] This administrative blunder has accompanied Catherine throughout her life. In 2013, I asked her whether she was aware of the misspelling when the album was released, and whether she cared about it. She recalled, "I probably wasn't reading much, if I was six. So it must have been later, when I was a little older, [that I said], 'How come it's spelled like that?' " She said it didn't bother her, though she was glad when it got corrected. But she also acknowledged that she was always mixing her name up, because her middle name is Ivey: "For some reason I got it confused because, I guess, I had heard about that old piano player, Ivory Joe [Hunter] . . . and I thought my name was Catherine Ivory Joe Brubeck. I mean, I really did. Like, I would fight over it, you know . . . So they did humor me on that for quite a while."[13]

---

11 In addition to compositions for his children, such as "Michael, My Second Son" (1986) and "Charles Matthew Hallelujah" (recorded on *Time Further Out* in May 1961, a couple of weeks after the birth of his sixth and final child), Brubeck wrote pieces in honor of his grandchildren, including two of Catherine's daughters, "Elana Joy" (1986) and "Mariel" (2001). Sometimes the pronunciation of a name gave rise to a tune's rhythmic and motivic content—e.g., "Marian McPartland" (1997), which was inspired by his esteemed fellow jazz pianist and friend.

12 Dave Brubeck Quartet, *Time Out*, Columbia/Legacy 88697 39852 2, 2009, three compact discs.

13 Yaghsizian, interview, November 12, 2013. According to his obituary, Hunter wrote between 2,000 and 3,000 songs, and he had two million-selling records in the 1950s. See "Ivory Joe Hunter, Blues Pianist, 63: Song Writer Who Had Two Gold Records Is Dead," *New York Times*, November 10, 1974.

Confusion about the orthography of her name affected even members of the inner family circle. For instance, when Catherine was ten, her uncle Howard wrote the following query to Sally Slade, Dave's personal secretary: "Incidentally—how is that poor mispelled [sic] child's name supposed to be spelled? The spelling used by Columbia records is KATHY. Please help me. I will paste the answer on the wall of my study, never again to be confused." Slade replied, "Cathy is spelt with a 'C.' Columbia made a mistake when they first wrote out the album notes." Then she quipped, Cathy "sometimes feels like calling them Kolumbia."[14]

"STRANGE MEADOW LARK": ANALYSIS

"Strange Meadow Lark" is a gentle ballad that begins with a lyrical piano solo in tempo rubato. Even when the bass, drums, and alto saxophone enter (at around 2:10), the pace is fairly laid back, never exceeding 125 beats per minute. The piece includes complex harmony—and some polytonality at the very end—but nothing remotely discordant. It is, indeed, some of Brubeck's easiest listening.

"Strange Meadow Lark" is not only the most accessible but also the longest cut on *Time Out,* clocking in at about seven-and-a-half minutes. Perhaps the most important observation about "Strange Meadow Lark" in the present context is that it is *not* a time experiment. On an album devoted to breaking the hegemony of 4/4 meter in jazz, it stands out in bold relief as the only cut in straightforward common time. Brubeck himself said, "Rhythmically, there's nothing complex about it, but it seemed to belong on that album."[15]

But even though its meter is unadventurous, the piece's phrase structure is novel. At its core is a series of four-bar passages, which are frequently combined to form eight-bar phrases. Many of these symmetrical constructions are disrupted, however, by extensions of two or more bars. Take, for instance, the beginning (see Example 4.20). A clearly articulated antecedent (mm. 1–4) is answered by a consequent that initially traces the same contours a third lower (mm. 5–7), but is extended by

14   Howard Brubeck to Sally Slade, June 27, 1964; Sally Slade to Howard Brubeck, July 3, 1964 (both in Brubeck Collection). When I shared this archival tidbit with Catherine fifty years later, she told me she didn't remember saying it but found it to be quite humorous. She also mentioned that, even today, she is frequently asked about that mistake. Catherine Brubeck Yaghsizian, email message to author, July 10, 2014.

15   Michael Bourne, "Classic Time: Dave Brubeck's Tireless Journey as a Global Jazz Ambassador," *Down Beat* 70, no. 9 (September 2003): 46.

two bars of pitch repetition (mm. 9–10). Instead of 4+4, then, this initial phrase stretches to 4+6 (or 4+4+2), for a total of ten bars. The second phrase (mm. 11–20) is identical to the first, except that the repeated pitch at the end is b♮′ rather than b♭′, which signals modulation from the tonic E♭ major (three flats) to the major key a third above—namely, G major (one sharp).

The two phrases described in the previous paragraph (mm. 1–20) constitute the A section. The B section (mm. 21–36) remains in the new key. Its phrase structure is symmetrical and rather square (see Example 4.21). Apart from a few minor alterations of pitch or rhythm, the melody in the second phrase (mm. 29–36) is identical to the first (mm. 21–28). The second half of each phrase essentially repeats the first half a third lower, the same procedure as was noted in A. The overall result is (4+4)+(4+4). Despite all this repetition and symmetry, however, monotony is skillfully avoided by wholesale reharmonization of the second phrase (compare the chord symbols of mm. 21–28 and 29–36 in Example 4.21).

The third and final section is a shorter and varied version of A, creating the overall form A B A′. The first eight bars of A′ are virtually identical to A. The ninth is slightly reharmonized, simply adding a flat nine to the B♭13 chord, halfway through the measure. The remainder of the passage, however, diverges from A (see Example 4.22). The total length of A′ is sixteen measures, as opposed to twenty in A.

This fifty-two-bar tune in ternary form is played the first time through, mostly as a piano solo in a rhythmically free style. In the last two measures (the descending chromatic figure), however, the bass and drums join in and establish a medium-tempo groove (around 126 beats

EXAMPLE 4.21.   Dave Brubeck, "Strange Meadow Lark," B section (mm. 21–36).
Copyright © 1960, 1962, 1963 (Copyrights Renewed) by Derry Music Company. Used by
permission.

EXAMPLE 4.22.   Dave Brubeck, "Strange Meadow Lark," end of A′ section (mm.
44–52).
Copyright © 1960, 1962, 1963 (Copyrights Renewed) by Derry Music Company. Used by
permission.

per minute). Thereafter follows a nearly full-length chorus on the alto
saxophone. Paul Desmond's solo hews closely to the A and B sections of
the tune, spanning twenty and sixteen bars, respectively. But the varied
reprise (A′), which had already been shortened by four measures with
respect to A, is here curtailed by an additional two bars. The saxophone
chorus, in other words, is slightly shorter than the opening piano solo.

The details of Desmond's workmanly solo need not detain us—except
for one remarkable spot. The end of the saxophone chorus (mm. 88–103a)
is transcribed in Example 4.23. At mm. 91–92 (the third and fourth bars of
A′, around 3:21–3:24), he suddenly and unexpectedly breaks into a brief
quotation from the Christmas song "Santa Claus Is Comin' to Town."

This is a superb instance of one of the defining features of Desmond's
style. Doug Ramsey summed up the consensus when he stated, "No

EXAMPLE 4.23. Dave Brubeck, "Strange Meadow Lark," alto saxophone (Paul Desmond), end of chorus (mm. 88–103a), transcription.

one in jazz quotes more naturally or slyly than Desmond."[16] The "Santa Claus" reference is sly indeed, and it passes in a fleeting moment. Yet it bears the unmistakable imprint of Desmond's wit. The words most commonly associated with this fragment are, "You better watch out / You better not cry," at the beginning of the chorus (see Example 4.24). Whether Desmond was addressing his nonverbal admonition to a specific person (presumably one or more members of the Quartet, or perhaps someone on the production team), or he was commenting on a particular situation, is anyone's guess. The quotation's precise meaning—if it went beyond general leg pulling—is lost to the sands of time.[17]

16 Doug Ramsey, review of The Dave Brubeck Quartet, *The Last Time We Saw Paris*, Columbia CS 9672, 1967 (typescript, 1968, Macero Collection, box 6, folder 3).

17 The words "He's making a list and checking it twice" are sung to the same musical phrase and could possibly have been on Desmond's mind instead. If so, their application is similarly obscure. "Santa Claus is Comin' to Town" was written in 1934 by Haven Gillespie (words) and J. Fred Coots (music). The Dave Brubeck Quartet recorded it for *Jingle Bell Jazz* (Columbia CL 1893), a sampler that was released before Christmas in 1962. On the front of his copy of the sheet music, Brubeck wrote in pencil, "OK for kids" and "Recorded for Teo's Xmas album 1961 [sic]" (Brubeck Collection). The session date is given as October 25, 1962, in Klaus-Gotthard Fischer, "Discography," in Ilse Storb and Klaus-Gotthard Fischer, *Dave Brubeck, Improvisations and Compositions: The Idea of Cultural Exchange*, trans. Bert Thompson (New York: Peter Lang, 1994), 246.

EXAMPLE 4.24. Beginning of "Santa Claus Is Comin' to Town" aligned with mm. 91–92 of alto saxophone chorus.

You   bet - ter watch out,   you   bet - ter   not   cry

As is typical, Brubeck's improvisation comes next.[18] His first chorus (3:44–5:19) follows the contours of Desmond's solo—that is, it spans fifty bars:

mm. 103–122 = A (10+10)

mm. 123–138 = B (8+8)

mm. 139–152 = A′ (8+6)

Brubeck's second chorus falls into two parts. The first segment continues in the groove and encompasses thirty-six bars, corresponding to A and B (5:20–6:28 = mm. 153–188). With the return of the tonic E♭ after the bridge comes a shift back to the texture (piano solo) and free rhythm of the beginning. This final *tempo primo* section is similar to the latter part of the opening piano solo, but it is expanded by a few bars (mm. 189–207 ≈ 37–52). The polytonality of the ending—especially the superimposition of C-major triads over E♭ major—is simultaneously piquant and deeply satisfying (see Example 4.25).[19]

"STRANGE MEADOW LARK": ORIGINS

Nearly five years after recording it on *Time Out*, Brubeck mentioned in a letter that " 'Strange Meadowlark' is still one of my favorite ballads."[20]

18 Howard Brubeck's transcription is available in *Time Out, The Dave Brubeck Quartet, 50th Anniversary Edition, Piano Solos* (Van Nuys, CA: Alfred Music Publishing Co., 2009), 27–32.

19 Mark McFarland briefly considers the "intricate mixture of polychords and high tertian sonorities" in the first twenty measures of "Strange Meadow Lark," but he doesn't mention the ending. See Mark McFarland, "Dave Brubeck and Polytonal Jazz," *Jazz Perspectives* 3 (2009): 164–166.

20 Dave Brubeck to Allan Ferguson (Victoria, Australia), January 23, 1964 (Brubeck Collection). Although the title is given here as two words, it appears as three ("Strange

EXAMPLE 4.25. Dave Brubeck, "Strange Meadow Lark," ending (mm. 203–207).
Copyright © 1960, 1962, 1963 (Copyrights Renewed) by Derry Music Company. Used by permission.

The creative spark for the tune is reflected in its title. A couple of months after the album was released, in response to a query ("How did you get your ideas for composition themes?"), Brubeck wrote, "Ideas are everywhere. . . . One piece I wrote was based on the call of the meadowlark."[21] About a dozen years later, he pinpointed its origins even more precisely: "Strange Meadow Lark" "has always been one of my favorite tunes. I can recall writing it down, on a train, coming back to San Francisco from Denver. I used to love that Feather River Canyon line, where you could look out the window and see the swift stream and deer, and yes, even a meadowlark. Anyone raised in the hills of California, as I was, knows the call of the meadowlark."[22]

Meadow Lark" rather than "Strange Meadowlark") on *Time Out* and in the earliest manuscript and printed sources.

21 Dave Brubeck to Ron V. Brown (Los Angeles), February 25, 1960 (Brubeck Collection).

22 Dave Brubeck to Hayden Richards (San Francisco), November 3, 1972 (Brubeck Collection). Hayden T. Richards and his twin brother Donald L. Richards were born in Massachusetts on October 28, 1934. Both were members of the Class of 1955 at Harvard, and Hayden served as vice president of the Harvard Dramatic Club. Brubeck had come into his own (with the *Time* magazine cover story, for instance) during the Richards brothers' senior year in college (1954–1955), and they were twenty-five years old when *Time Out* was released. Don Richards died in Santa Clara, California, on March 4, 1972. In August of that year, his brother sent a letter to Brubeck in care of Shawnee Press, and the press forwarded it to Brubeck's home. In addition to his own cover letter, Hayden included a letter from his brother and a set of lyrics that Don had penned for "Strange Meadow Lark." The lyrics are dated December 18, 1971. Presumably, Hayden either found these materials among Don's effects and took it upon himself to pass them along to Brubeck, or he was perhaps fulfilling his brother's dying wish. Don's letter says that he considered "Strange Meadow Lark" to be "a masterpiece which seemed unduly overshadowed by the popularity of 'Take Five' and 'Blue Rondo,'" and that he regarded Dave as "one whose position in the top rank of jazz greats is forever assured." In his reply to Hayden, Brubeck expressed sympathy for Don's passing and noted that Don's lyrics were "very similar to the words my wife wrote for the

It is impossible to adequately describe in words the song of the western meadowlark. Fortunately, the Cornell Lab of Ornithology maintains a website that includes field recordings. The one that is closest to the opening motive of Brubeck's tune was recorded by Robert C. Stein in Oregon in June 1961, about two years after the studio sessions for *Time Out*.[23] The most striking similarity is the long-short-short-long pattern of the birdsong, which Brubeck renders in common time as a quarter note and two eighths, followed by a quarter note with a fermata (the rhythm of the first three beats of m. 1, without the anacrusis). The contours of the pitches are also similar, though more difficult to specify.

In most cases, the written origins of the compositions on *Time Out* have been preserved only fragmentarily, if at all. For "Strange Meadow Lark," however, there exist four pages of pencil sketches (see Figure 4.5) that provide a more substantial glimpse into this aspect of Brubeck's creative process. The sketches pertain to all three sections: A (mm. 1–20), B—that is, the bridge—(mm. 21–36), and A' (mm. 37–52). Three of the pages include lyrics; significantly, they are in Dave's handwriting, because the words have been attributed to—and almost certainly originated with—his wife, Iola.

The sketches for the A section reveal that the ballad's principal melody didn't occur to Brubeck immediately in its final form. Rather, he worked it out in stages. The first six notes (g'–$a\flat'$–$b\flat'$–d''–$b\flat'$–f''), which incorporate the long-short-short-long rhythm of the birdsong for the latter four notes, remain constant from one version to the next. Brubeck's initial conception of the second measure continued in the same vein, with a quarter note, two eighths, and two more quarters (see Example 4.26a). In a subsequent draft, however, he subdivided the quarter notes into eighths (top of Example 4.26b). Moreover, the starting point of the second subphrase (note 7) is different in the two

song." Don's letter and lyrics are preserved in the Brubeck Collection. The biographical information on the Richards brothers (Hayden died in Santa Clara, California, on February 14, 1976) was compiled from a number of sources, including the following:

http://www.thecrimson.com/article/1954/2/19/college-news-in-brief-pbjubilee-committee/
http://www.thecrimson.com/article/1954/1/5/phantom-public-pto-the-editors-of/
(accessed March 15, 2018).

23 "Western Meadowlark—Media Search—eBird and Macaulay Library," Macaulay Library ML12729, https://search.macaulaylibrary.org/catalog?taxonCode=wesmea&yr=YCU STOM&mediaType=a&sort=rating_rank_desc&ey=1961&by=1961&q=Western%20 Meadowlark (accessed March 15, 2018).

A

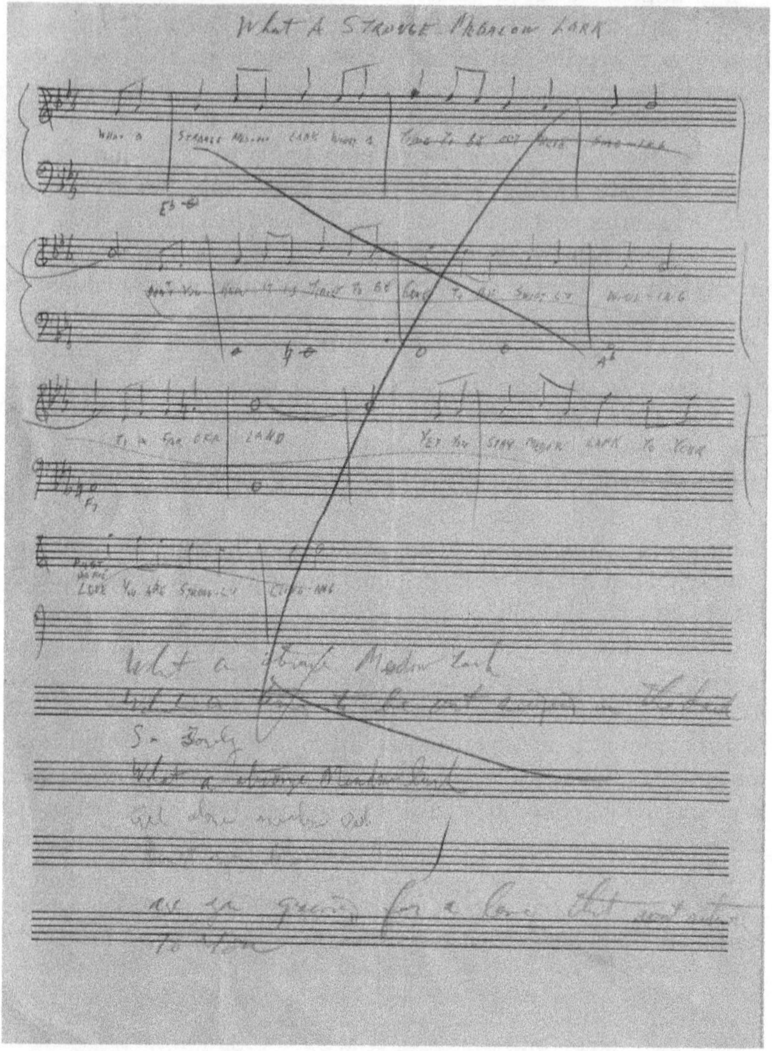

FIGURE 4.5A, 4.5B, 4.5C, AND 4.5D. Dave Brubeck, "Strange Meadow Lark," pencil sketches, autograph.

Brubeck Collection, Holt-Atherton Special Collections, University of the Pacific Library. © Dave Brubeck.

B

FIGURE 4.5A, 4.5B, 4.5C, AND 4.5D.   (Continued)

C

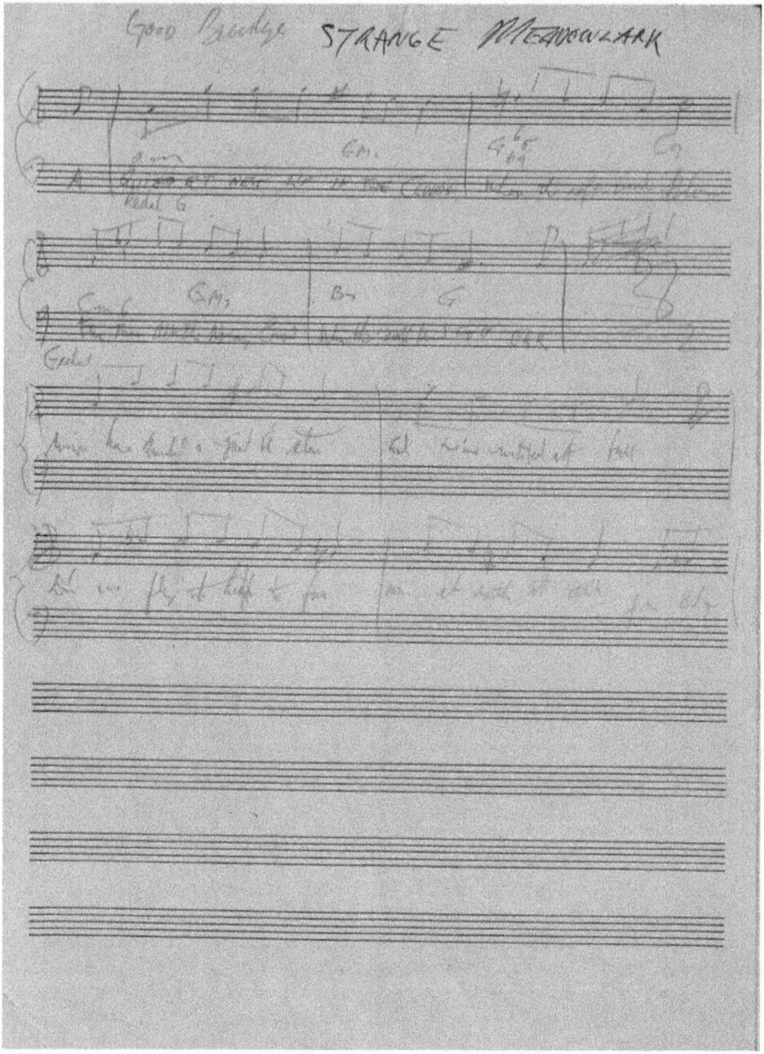

FIGURE 4.5A, 4.5B, 4.5C, AND 4.5D.   (Continued)

D

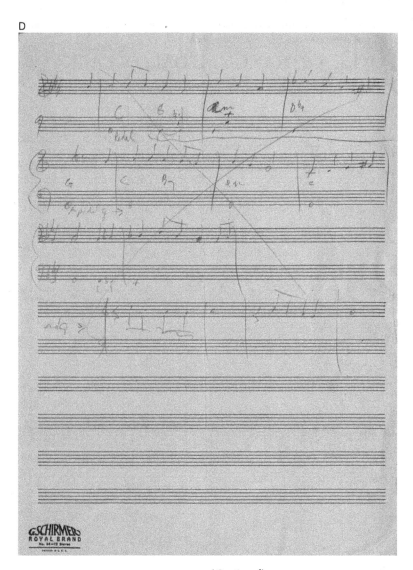

FIGURE 4.5A, 4.5B, 4.5C, AND 4.5D. (Continued)

EXAMPLE 4.26A, 4.26B, 4.26C, AND 4.26D. Dave Brubeck, "Strange Meadow Lark," transcription of pencil sketches, autograph.

What A STRANGE MEDALOW LARK

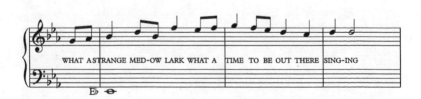

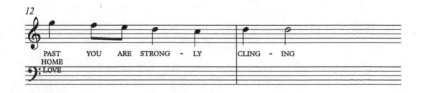

GOOD Bridge STRANGE MEADOWLARK

A QUI-ET NEST UP IN THE CLOUDS where the soft wind Blow

Am   GM.   G(b5)   C9

Pedal G

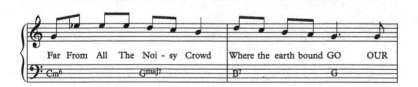

Far From All The Noi - sy Crowd   Where the earth bound GO   OUR

Cm6   Gmaj7   B7   G

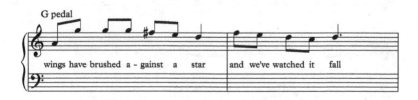

G pedal

wings have brushed a - gainst a   star   and we've watched it   fall

Did we fly to high to far   was it worth it   all

Fm   Bb7

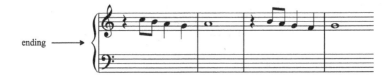

versions. Brubeck replaced the stepwise ascent to g″ in the first version with a similar ascent to b♭′ in the second. Unfortunately, this replication of the opening three-note motive was a retrogressive move that served to neutralize the dynamism of the eighth-note activity. The final version (Example 4.20) satisfyingly incorporates both the forward motion of the eighth notes and the original shape of the melody, except that it comes to rest on c″ in m. 3 rather than d″.

Nearly the same can be said of the second phrase, beginning with the anacrusis to m. 5. Thereafter, in both sketches as well as in the final version, the cadential pitch in the ninth and tenth measures is b♭′. But the run-up to it in m. 8 differs between the two sketches—both of which have a straightforward scalar ascent—and the final version, which descends by step, then ascends by leap.

Brubeck's sketch of the B section, which he labeled "Good Bridge" (Example 4.26c), is nearly identical to the final version (Example 4.21), except that the note values are halved (predominantly eighths and quarters, rather than quarter and half notes). At some point, however, he also sketched an alternative version of the second half of the bridge (mm. 29–36) (see Example 4.26d). Although its rhythmic pace matches the final version, it differs in numerous details, especially the arpeggiation of chords in mm. 30, 31, and 34.

The sketches for A′ show that, on the one hand, the content of the first part (mm. 37–47) was settled by the time Brubeck notated it here. At all events, that passage (bottom of Example 4.26b) is substantially the same as the final version. On the other hand, the end of the tune was still in flux. Brubeck crossed out his first attempt, a seven-bar passage following m. 47. In the second draft (last stave of Example 4.26b), he hit upon the rhythm of the final version (dotted quarter followed by two eighth notes). And a brief notation marked "ending" (bottom of Example 4.26d) comprises Brubeck's work on the scalar segment that eventually became mm. 46–47.

"TAKE FIVE": ANALYSIS

"Take Five" is the best-known cut on *Time Out* and the most famous composition associated with the Dave Brubeck Quartet. Even listeners with little affinity for jazz have heard it—whether they are aware of it or not—on the playlists for background music in restaurants and other public places, or elsewhere in popular culture. One writer, the New Jersey poet Joel Lewis, referred to it as "a cultural and musical landmark" and

EXAMPLE 4.27. Paul Desmond, "Take Five," piano vamp.

Copyright © 1960 (Renewed) Desmond Music Company (United States) and Derry Music Company (World excluding United States). Used by permission.

"a part of musical Americana."[24] Surprisingly, it was the first record that Billy Joel purchased as an adolescent, and the famous pop musician later said that "Take Five" was as important to him as the Beatles' *Sergeant Pepper* was to rock and roll aficionados in the 1960s.[25] For decades it served as the closer for live performances by the Quartet, and "Take Five" was inducted into the Grammy Hall of Fame in 1996.[26] The creation of "Take Five" was credited not to Brubeck, however, but to his saxophonist Paul Desmond.

The harmonic palette of "Take Five" is quite limited. Oscillation between the tonic (E♭ minor) and dominant (B♭ minor) has a nearly exclusive monopoly in this piece (see Example 4.27). The only passage that includes a broader range of changes than these two chords is the eight-bar bridge that is heard just twice, in the head at the beginning (mm. 21–28) and end (mm. 159–166):

C♭ – A♭m⁶ / B♭m⁷ – E♭m⁷ / A♭m⁷ – D♭⁷ /

G♭maj⁷ / C♭ – A♭m⁶ / B♭m⁷ – E♭m⁷ /

A♭m⁷ – D♭⁷ / Fm⁷ – B♭⁷ /

The harmonic ostinato in "Take Five" has melodic implications as well. Even though *Time Out* is different from *Kind of Blue* in nearly all

24 Joel Lewis, liner notes, *The Essential Dave Brubeck*, Columbia/Legacy C2K 86993, 2003, compact disc.

25 Hank Bordowitz, *Billy Joel: The Life and Times of an Angry Young Man*, rev. ed. (Milwaukee, WI: Backbeat Books, 2011), 10; Ted Gioia, *West Coast Jazz: Modern Jazz in California, 1945–1960* (Berkeley: University of California Press, 1998), 68.

26 "GRAMMY Hall of Fame | GRAMMY.com," https://www.grammy.com/grammys/awards/hall-of-fame (accessed March 15, 2018).

EXAMPLE 4.28. B♭ Aeolian.

other respects, "Take Five" partakes of the modal jazz approach made famous in Miles Davis's album. Paul Desmond's saxophone solo in particular, about forty-five seconds in length, is in B♭ Aeolian, employing the pitches listed in Example 4.28.

"Take Five" entails much repetition of the five-beat tonic-dominant pattern (Example 4.27), but at the macro level the basic unit is four bars in length. For instance, the introduction spans twelve measures, and it falls into three units. First, the drummer Joe Morello establishes a distinctive groove, with ride cymbal and snare drum at the forefront (mm. 1–4). Next, Brubeck joins in with the piano vamp (mm. 5–8). Then Eugene Wright begins accentuating beats 1, 4, and 5 with the bass notes E♭—B♭—BB♭ (mm. 9–12).

At this point, Desmond plays the head, which is in ternary form: A (mm. 13–20), B (mm. 21–28), A′ (mm. 29–36). Each of these phrases is subdivided, however, so that the tune actually consists of six four-bar segments (see Example 4.29).

Desmond's improvisation follows immediately thereafter. It is about as long as the head, with the same kind of thematic parallelism (see Example 4.30). But this modal rhapsody unfolds over consistent alternation between the tonic and dominant chords. It ends with a pair of "extra" measures (mm. 61–62). This brief cadential extension before the onset of Morello's drum solo is the only departure from the strict four-bar mold in the entire cut.

It is a challenge to write meaningfully and intelligibly about a drum solo. And indeed nearly half of "Take Five"—about two and one-half minutes—is exactly that. Morello begins his improvisation as soon as Desmond's ends (at 1:51). Strictly speaking, however, it is not a "solo," because Brubeck and Wright continue the vamp all the way through. Morello's chorus extends to no fewer than twenty-two four-bar segments—nearly four times the length of Desmond's. Since it includes eighty-eight iterations of the two-chord vamp in unrelieved succession, it is not difficult to understand why Ira Gitler characterized it (using hyperbolic and ethnically insensitive language) as being "like a Chinese water torture."[27]

27 Ira Gitler, review of *Time Out*, *Down Beat* 27, no. 9 (April 28, 1960): 37.

The beginning of the solo (segments 1–4, 1:51–2:18) is dominated by the snare drum and ride cymbal, and there is a conspicuous increase in the volume level toward the end of the third segment (around 2:09). The bass drum comes to the fore in segment 5 (2:18–2:25), even leading the

EXAMPLE 4.30. Paul Desmond, "Take Five," alto saxophone (Desmond), chorus (mm. 37–62), transcription.

articulation of a triplet figure that is echoed by the cymbal. In the next segment (2:25–2:31), however, the cymbal drops out for the remainder of the solo and is replaced by the tom-tom drum. The snare and bass drums are featured in segments 7 and 8 (2:31–2:45), and the tom-tom sneaks back in at the end of segment 9 (around 2:51). For the next minute

EXAMPLE 4.31. Paul Desmond, "Take Five," comparison of melodic contour of head at beginning and end.

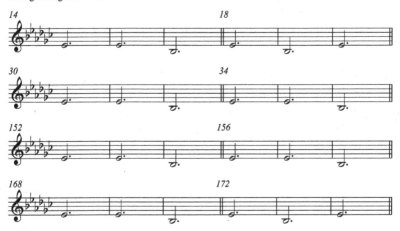

or so (segments 10–19, 2:52–4:01), Morello employs the snare, tom-tom, and bass drums on an equal basis, in a kaleidoscopic sequence of complex rhythmic patterns. Segments 12 and 13 (3:06–3:20) include a second, even more pronounced, crescendo than was heard in segment 3. The end of the solo (segments 20–22, 4:01–4:21) favors the tom-toms, paving the way for the return of the head.

Desmond's performance of the head during the last minute of the cut (4:21–5:24) requires relatively little commentary. Its most notable difference from the beginning is the addition of a nine-measure tag (5:04–5:24). But its melodic contour is also slightly different. This can be readily perceived if one compares the dotted half notes at the beginning with the analogous pitches at the end (see Example 4.31). The dominant pitch (b♭) in m. 36, of course, leaves the section tonally open, in preparation for Desmond's chorus. The tonic pitch (e♭') in m. 174, on the other hand, provides closure—as does the tag.

"TAKE FIVE": ORIGINS

Among the business papers of Teo Macero, who served as producer for the *Time Out* album, is a paragraph about "Take Five," typed and signed by Paul Desmond.[28] The little blurb, presumably drafted as liner

28 This page is reproduced on p. 20 of the booklet for the 50th Anniversary edition of *Time Out*, cited previously in note 12.

notes or for a similar purpose, reveals more about Desmond's personality and wit than it does about the origins of the tune. Desmond writes that it was "intended mainly as an entrance and exit for a pentagonistic drum solo by my favorite drummer." Joe Morello was hardly his "favorite drummer." The two worked together for eleven years (1956–1967) and eventually became close friends, but the first few years were rough. As was mentioned in Chapter 2, at one point, Desmond threatened to leave the Quartet, telling Brubeck, "Morello goes or I go."[29] A glimmer of the tension between them can be detected in Desmond's characterization of the drum solo as "pentagonistic," a clever neologism that combines "pentagon" (referring to the five beats of the tune's time signature) with "antagonistic."

Desmond's claim that the melody "was assembled rapidly in the studio, and consists of fragments which occurred to me here and there" is similar to the canonical description of the tune's origin, which Brubeck repeated for the rest of his career, and which will occupy us presently. But Desmond's tale about receiving inspiration from "a slot machine in Reno which produced an ominous but regular series of 5 clicks as the coins vanished" is apocryphal. His biographer noted that Desmond "amused himself by concocting stories about the piece's origins," and he quoted Brubeck's reaction to this particular yarn as, "Come on, Paul, no."[30] Yet this bit of mischief has persisted. It even turned up in Desmond's *New York Times* obituary, which reported the musician's account straight-facedly: "The rhythm of the machine suggested [the tune] to me, and I really only wrote it to get back some of the money I'd lost in the machine. That has now been accomplished."[31] And it was still rattling around in jazz periodicals nearly two decades after Desmond's passing.[32]

The true story of the composition of "Take Five" is more workaday. The version Dave and Iola Brubeck told their son Darius in an interview during summer 2001 includes the essential elements. In response to Darius's query about the contributions of each member of the Quartet to the making of *Time Out,* Dave took credit for the idea of

---

29 Doug Ramsey, *Take Five: The Public and Private Lives of Paul Desmond* (Seattle: Parkside Publications, 2005), 187. The vicissitudes of the fraught relationship between Desmond and Morello are narrated on 185–188.

30 Ramsey, *Take Five,* 207.

31 John S. Wilson, "Paul Desmond, Alto Saxophonist with Dave Brubeck Quartet, Dies," *New York Times,* May 31, 1977.

32 See, for instance, Dave McElfresh, "Paul Desmond: Still Waters Run Deep," *Coda* 264 (November 1995): 10.

EXAMPLE 4.32. Johnny Burke and Jimmy Van Heusen, "Sunday, Monday, or Always," mm. 1–4, transcription.

doing "an album using different time signatures." Dave recalled hearing Morello play a rhythmic pattern in 5/4 when he was warming up backstage, over which Desmond would improvise. Dave asked Desmond to compose a tune along those lines, saying, "Just write down something [in which] Joe has a five-four drum solo and bring it to rehearsal when we rehearse [for] the *Time Out* album." According to Dave, Desmond "came with two melodic ideas, but he didn't have a tune." So Dave helped to shape those inchoate ideas into an intelligible tune that could be included on the album. Though "Take Five" was essentially written by Desmond, clearly Morello and Brubeck both had a hand in its genesis as well.[33]

Two additional facets of the origins of "Take Five" deserve attention. Doug Ramsey has stated unequivocally that the second of the two themes that Desmond brought to the rehearsal—the bridge—is "a chromatic reduction of the opening theme of the Johnny Burke–Jimmy Van Heusen popular song 'Sunday, Monday, or Always,' a 1943 hit for Bing Crosby, a piece that Desmond frequently quoted in solos."[34] Comparison of the first two bars of this tune (see Example 4.32) with mm. 21–22 of Example 4.29 reveals that the two passages do indeed follow a similar trajectory. It is certainly possible that this song supplied the generative idea for the bridge of "Take Five." On the other hand, the theme is not especially distinctive—entailing only the arpeggiation of a sequence of two seventh chords (plus a third leg of the sequence in "Take Five")—so there remains some lingering doubt about this.

There is greater clarity, however, concerning the evolution of the tune's catchy title—no small part of the secret of its success. Ramsey mentions that "the piece had no name when Desmond brought in the

---

33 Brubeck, "Jazz 1959," 129, 237–238.
34 Ramsey, *Take Five*, 208.

CREATIVE PROCESS I

113

EXAMPLE 4.33.   Dave Brubeck, "Pick Up Sticks," bass ostinato.

two themes."[35] Brubeck recalled that there was "great discussion" about what to call it. Desmond toyed with "Penthouse" and "other titles that referred obliquely to the five beats to a measure, but no one was enthusiastic about any of the ideas."[36] According to Iola Brubeck, "The title 'Take Five' was Dave's idea." In an email to her son Darius, she revealed that Desmond "didn't like the title. He said nobody would know what it meant. But Dave insisted that everybody in the world knew what it meant except Paul."[37]

"PICK UP STICKS"

The final cut on *Time Out* brings us full circle. The first number, "Blue Rondo à la Turk," was inspired by Brubeck's exposure to sounds from a different part of the globe—namely, Turkish folk music. Similarly, the origins of "Pick Up Sticks" are connected with a recording of African drumming. The fundamental feature that distinguishes "Pick Up Sticks" is the use of an ostinato. "Take Five" is based on a harmonic and rhythmic pattern that is repeated throughout. Another famous example, recorded just a few months earlier (March 2, 1959), is the vamp on "So What" from Miles Davis's *Kind of Blue* (Columbia CL 1355). In both of those cases, it is not a melody that recurs but rather a characteristic rhythm and set of chords. The ostinato in "Pick Up Sticks," on the other hand, is a six-note figure in the bass (see Example 4.33), similar to a ground bass or *basso ostinato* in Baroque music (the lament "When I am laid in earth" from Henry Purcell's opera *Dido and Aeneas* in the late seventeenth century is a famous example). The pattern begins with a leap from the tonic B♭ to the third D, which strongly reinforces the tonality of B♭ major (or, more accurately, the modality of B♭ Mixolydian). When repeated, however, it

35 Ramsey, *Take Five*, 208.
36 Dave Brubeck, "A Time to Remember" (unpublished autobiography, coauthored with Iola Brubeck).
37 Iola Brubeck to Darius Brubeck, January 18, 2002, cited in Brubeck, "Jazz 1959," 125. Dave was correct. In jazz circles in 1959, anyway, the term "Take Five" was so familiar that John Tynan published a regular column under that heading in *Down Beat* magazine.

EXAMPLE 4.34. Dave Brubeck, "Pick Up Sticks," mm. 1–4.

can be seen to consist of two chromatic passages: notes 2–5 (ascending) and notes 6 and 1 (descending).

In "Pick Up Sticks" the ostinato is played by the bass and it is heard no fewer than ninety-nine times in a row. It is therefore incumbent on Brubeck and Desmond to vary their solo work as much as possible— and this cut is perhaps not their most successful effort in that regard. The order of events is fairly straightforward. Brubeck first presents what amounts to the head (0:00–1:04), then Desmond and he each play his improvisation in turn (1:04–2:02 and 2:02–3:24), followed by a varied version of the head (3:24–4:16). Each of the four segments lasts only about one minute, so there is little opportunity for deep-seated ennui to set in. Especially in view of the light texture that was observed in "Everybody's Jumpin'," the cut that immediately precedes it, it is note-worthy that Brubeck plays in block chords throughout the entire first section, beginning straightaway. The chords are heavy and syncopated, and they make liberal use of the flat seven pitch (A♭), in addition to the usual B♭ and E♭ in the key of B♭ major (see Example 4.34).

The large-scale organization of "Pick Up Sticks" can best be under-stood in terms of a series of four-bar groups, rather than as an undif-ferentiated stream of individual measures. The first segment is given in Example 4.34, and Brubeck subsequently plays five more (mm. 5–24), for a total of six four-bar passages in block chords. This initial section stands in for the head, although it lacks the usual thematic content associated with that term.

Desmond's solo noodles around in B♭ Mixolydian. As mentioned before, though undeniably competent, it is not one of his more inspired improvisations. This realization leads one to wonder whether Desmond perhaps felt a bit hemmed in by the ostinato and the use of a mode rather than chord progressions. Oddly, his solo also peters out halfway through the expected final four-bar segment. In other words, whereas Brubeck had just played a full twenty-four bars in the head (4+4+4+4+4+4), Desmond stops short after twenty-two (4+4+4+4+4+2).

Following Desmond's five-and-a-half segments, Brubeck stretches out to eight sets of four bars in his solo. The first twelve bars (three sets of four) are spun out of single notes in the treble, up to two octaves above middle C, as opposed to chords. The accidental E♮ receives special emphasis, but the improvisation is otherwise rather aimless and marred by a couple of missed notes (around 2:16 through 2:20). Brubeck gathers steam as he moves into the fourth set of four measures, by introducing a repeated short-long rhythm (sixteenth and dotted eighth notes). It starts with single notes (2:33–2:43), but quickly changes to chords for the remaining sixteen bars of Brubeck's solo (2:43–3:24). At this point (3:24), the sonorities from the beginning return—albeit in a slightly different, but still syncopated, rhythm—marking the beginning of the head. The parallel with the beginning lasts only eight bars, however. In fact, toward the end of the eighth bar (around 3:44), Brubeck begins an oscillation between A♭ major and B♭ major chords in first inversion, which continues to the end and cuts across the prevailing 6/4 meter. This creates a kind of built-in "repeat and fade" effect, which is reinforced by the sound engineer's electronic fade-out, and whose open-endedness seems especially appropriate for the concluding number on this album.

CHAPTER 5

CREATIVE PROCESS II
RECORDING SESSIONS

"TAKE FIVE"

It is always interesting, and frequently instructive, to hear recordings of the original sessions. In the case of "Take Five," however, the original recordings are nothing short of revelatory. Among Dave Brubeck's personal audio recordings, preserved in the University of the Pacific Library, are about two dozen takes. These include the full-length version on *Time Out* and the shorter single release version, both of which were recorded on July 1, 1959. The previous week (during the evening session on June 25), however, the Quartet spent more than forty minutes, attempting unsuccessfully to get "Take Five" off the ground.

The paperwork for the session that ran from 2:30 until 7:00 p.m. on July 1 includes two entries for "Take Five."[1] The latter, with its time listed as six minutes, includes the instruction "use this for album releases." The raw audio for this take (CO 62578) is identical in all respects to the version released on *Time Out* (which was examined in Chapter 4), except that Morello can be heard counting off at the very beginning.

The previous entry (CO 62577/ZSP 48255) is listed as being just 2:50 in length, and its rubric specifies its use "for all single releases." The raw audio includes an announcement by the producer, Teo Macero, that it was a second attempt, implying that another recording preceded it. That version has not been preserved among these materials. But the one we have begins with a distinctive cymbal pattern, given in Example 5.1.

The introduction is layered, beginning with drums alone (four bars), adding piano (four), then bass (four), for a total of twelve bars—the same as in the full-length album version. The twenty-four-bar head is nearly identical to the longer version as well. The only significant difference is rather subtle. The sustained pitches in all of the four-bar segments on either side of the bridge are identical (e♭' e♭' b♭), whereas the album version has e♭' b♭ e♭' (i.e., a cadence on the tonic) in mm. 18–20 (see Example 4.31). Given that the single release version is only about one-half the length of the performance on *Time Out*, it is surprising that Desmond's solo here is two bars longer. On the other hand, Morello's drum solo—accompanied by the piano/bass vamp as on *Time Out*—breezes by in a mere twenty seconds. This is followed by a truncated version of the head (only the last third), and a coda similar to the one on the album.[2]

Six days earlier, after recording "Someday My Prince Will Come" (from Walt Disney's 1937 animated film *Snow White and the Seven Dwarfs*), the Quartet turned their attention to a new original, which Macero announced as "Five-Four Time."[3] Their efforts are preserved in

---

1 Columbia Records, Artist Job Sheet, Job No. 50192 (Sony Music Archives Library).
2 The sustained notes at the end of the head are e♭' e♭' b♭ again, which undermines the expected tonic closure and shifts this responsibility to the coda.
3 Columbia Records, Artist Job Sheet, Job No. 50183 (Sony Music Archives Library). It is listed in this document as "Five-Fourth Time," under the matrix number CO 62562. Apparently, the tune received its more familiar title in the course of the following week.

EXAMPLE 5.2. Paul Desmond, "Take Five," opening cymbal pattern, original version, June 25, 1959, evening recording session.

a remarkable set of tapes that include dialogue involving the musicians and audio engineers, as well as more than twenty attempts to record "Take Five."[4]

In 1966, about a year before Brubeck's "classic" Quartet dissolved, he told an interviewer in London that by then his combo could "play a new thing in five-four without any trouble." But he recalled vividly how difficult it was at first: "Believe me, when we first recorded 'Take Five' my toes were really counting in my shoes."[5] Brubeck's recollection is borne out in dramatic fashion by these session recordings. There was no single weak link. All four of these fine musicians made mistakes that produced ragged results and frequently led to musical "train wrecks." At the same time, however, one can detect a clear trajectory of progress that enabled the group's successful recordings a few days later.

A fundamental issue that ran like a thread through this early session concerned the opening gambit. Instead of the more filled-in drum pattern, etched so deeply into our collective consciousness through repeated listening, Morello initially opted for a minimalist approach. He played a sparse pattern four times in a row (Example 5.2). Brubeck added his piano vamp in the next four bars, and Eugene Wright was supposed to supply bass support in the last segment of the introduction. At first, Wright played only two pitches, the dominant (B♭) and tonic (E♭), and he placed them incorrectly on beats 4 and 5 of each measure. After several attempts, Morello suggested adding another quarter note one octave higher, which he called a "grace note." This produced the pattern shown in Example 5.3, which Wright was able to lock in consistently.

A related issue was the tempo, which was set by either Brubeck or Morello. More often than not, when Brubeck counted off, Morello would err sooner or later. Apparently sensing his drummer's unease, Brubeck ceded control several times and asked Morello to count off instead.

4 The producer, Teo Macero, first announces takes 1 through 12, and then inexplicably shifts his nomenclature to a subsequent series encompassing takes 1A through 9A. Only a few are full-length recordings, and many are quite short.
5 Bob Houston, "Dave Brubeck: Such a Long Time over This Matter of Time," *Melody Maker* (November 5, 1966): 8.

EXAMPLE 5.3. Paul Desmond, "Take Five," excerpt from bass part.

Regardless of who was giving the signal, the tempo throughout this session was considerably brisker than the pace enshrined in the *Time Out* recording. After the eighteenth take (6A), in fact, Desmond even stated his concern that "it's getting a little faster." At this point, the tempo had reached 220 beats per minute, about fifty beats higher than the versions that were eventually released. The rapid pulse was surely a byproduct of the energy and excitement associated with recording this tune. But it also engendered many opportunities for missteps, and it made the session feel as if the group were walking a musical tightrope.

When all was said and done, the Quartet emerged that night with only two full-length takes, which were quite similar to each other in their overall shape but somewhat different from the version on *Time Out* (see Table 5.1). All three recordings begin with the additive introduction (drums–drums/piano–drums/piano/bass) and head (saxophone). And in all three cases these sections are followed by a saxophone solo, though it varies in length. Next on the *Time Out* version is Morello's drum solo,

TABLE 5.1. Paul Desmond, "Take Five," comparison of takes 8 and 11 from June 25, 1959 recording session and July 1 version on *Time Out*

Take 8	Take 11	Time Out
Introduction (12 bars)	Introduction (12)	Introduction (12)
Head (24)	Head (24)	Head (24)
Saxophone solo (44)	Saxophone solo (24)	Saxophone solo (26)
Piano solo, with drums and bass (13)	Piano solo, with drums and bass (24)	
Drum solo (2:43)	Drum solo (2:40)	Drum solo, with piano and bass (2:30)
Reprise of introduction (8)	Reprise of introduction (8)	
Head (24)	Head (24)	Head (24)
Coda (8, with fade out)	Coda (10, with fade out)	Coda (9)

120   *DAVE BRUBECK'S TIME OUT*

which was famously (or infamously) accompanied by the piano/bass vamp. By contrast, in both recordings from the previous week, Brubeck plays a relatively brief piano solo (accompanied by drums and bass) at this point. These piano solos generally maintain the rhythm of the vamp but include some inventive and piquant chord substitution. The drum solos that follow are for drums alone—that is, the piano/bass vamp goes on hiatus. At the end of his solos, Morello reintroduces the sparse cymbal pattern that he played at the beginning. Brubeck and Wright then re-enter in sequence, for a reprise of the introduction, a segment that is absent on *Time Out*. All three versions conclude with a full restatement of the head, and a coda. The earlier version of the coda, however, has a more active rhythm than the familiar ending (see take 11, Example 5.4), and it fades out because the musicians play more softly and sparingly.

The remaining takes from the evening of June 25 are fragmentary. In a couple of cases (takes 2 and 3A), the Quartet got no further than the introduction. A number of other times, they played the introduction and all or part of the head, before running into trouble (takes 1, 4, 5, 12, 1A, 5A, 6A, 8A). And a few include only false starts (takes 3, 4A, 7A), an index of the difficulty of what they were attempting. This leaves six takes that include the introduction, head, and some improvisatory material before breaking down. Not surprisingly, the problems generally involve miscounting. In take 6, for instance, after Brubeck and Morello improvise together for forty-eight bars, Brubeck drops out, and Morello subsequently loses the pulse only a few bars into his solo. Something similar happens in takes 10 and 9A, except that Morello's downfall is provoked (inadvertently) by Brubeck. In both cases, Brubeck accidentally adds a beat midway through his solo, playing a measure of 6/4 instead of 5/4.

EXAMPLE 5.4. Paul Desmond, "Take Five," coda, take 11, June 25, 1959, evening recording session, transcription.

The unfortunate result is that the piano part is consistently one count behind the drums. Astonishingly, they play out of phase for eight bars in the first instance and sixteen in the second. Both times, though, Morello loses his way not long after beginning his solo.

As mentioned, Wright was the first Quartet member to have trouble playing his part. But once he got the bass groove squared away, his problems were few and far between. The other three had their challenging moments, though. Take 7 starts in a promising manner, with successful solos by Desmond and Brubeck, after the usual introduction and head. When it comes to the drum solo, though, Morello immediately plays a measure of 6/4 instead of 5/4, then halts in his tracks and mutters, "I blew it again." Brubeck's impassioned (and rather humorous) response is, "N-n-n-n-n-n-no!" Morello has some difficulty in take 9, too. His false starts are punctuated with comments like "Oh, man!" and "I forget my beat now." But after they finally get it off the ground with an acceptable introduction and head, Desmond improvises for only eight bars before he stops short and says, "Ah, forget it!" Then he declines to solo in the next take: "I'd better just split after the melody [i.e., the head], 'cause I always get hung there."

Even Brubeck himself encounters some obstacles. Take 2A begins with Morello grousing about how "ridiculous" it is that he "can't get the count." Then later, at the end of his thirty-two-bar solo, Desmond says, "Forget it" (as he had done in take 9). Despite the sagging morale of his sidemen, however, Brubeck is apparently feeling adventuresome. At all events, he launches into his signature two-against-three polyrhythm, playing duplets against the group of three quarter notes at the beginning of the 5/4 measure. Because the remainder of the bar contains only two quarter notes, the proportions do not work out evenly. By the time Brubeck plays a series of four chords up and four chords down, and repeats this pattern three times, the performance grinds to a halt. Brubeck asks, "Was I on that, or did I get off a beat?" Morello replies diplomatically, "I wasn't sure." And Brubeck sums up the situation: "Yeah, it's crazy."

Brubeck's skills as leader of his combo are prominently on display in these tapes. When Wright was having trouble playing his bass notes on the correct beats (take 1), Brubeck's compassionate response was, "Yeah, it's very hard. Now, we've got all day." Shortly thereafter, when Desmond stopped playing midway through the head (take 4), Brubeck wondered aloud, "Did I blow it?" When Desmond replied, "No, I did," Brubeck kept the tone positive: "OK, try it again. That's great!" He then declared (and later repeated several times), "This is all rehearsal!"

Brubeck's comment made Desmond laugh and provoked the following rejoinder: "You're goddamn right it is! And I'm not getting paid for it either!" Nearly every time the Quartet got hung up, Brubeck demonstrated his willingness to take responsibility for the glitch and his disinclination to single anyone out for blame. He said, for instance, "That's a bad spot. I did two bad chords" (take 5), and "I made a mistake. We all did, everybody but Joe [Morello]" (take 9). And after numerous unsuccessful attempts, when his colleagues were probably becoming rather discouraged, Brubeck had nothing but good things to say: "This is such a ball! I really dig this!" (take 10). It ultimately fell to Macero to suggest, after more than twenty attempts, "Why don't we come back to this?" Brubeck agreed and called "Waltz for Cathy" (i.e., "Kathy's Waltz"). Six days later, the Quartet returned to "Take Five" and made one of the most successful jazz recordings of all time.

"KATHY'S WALTZ"

Although the artist job sheet for the first *Time Out* recording session on the afternoon of June 25, 1959, has not been preserved, the order of events can be reconstructed from the matrix numbers announced by Macero on Brubeck's personal copies of these recordings. "Kathy's Waltz" (CO 62555) was the first tune to be recorded, followed by "Three to Get Ready" (CO 62556), "Strange Meadow Lark" (CO 62557), "Everybody's Jumpin' " (CO 62558), "Blue Rondo à la Turk" (CO 62559), and "I'm in a Dancing Mood" (CO 62560). The evening session, for which written documentation is available, began with "Someday My Prince Will Come" (CO 62561) and "Take Five" (CO 62562). The Quartet then recorded remakes of "Kathy's Waltz," "Three to Get Ready," and "Strange Meadow Lark," before calling it a night.

It is fortunate that two takes of "Kathy's Waltz" from the afternoon session have come down to us, as well as two more from the evening session. Macero announced these four versions as follows:

1. "CO 62555, Kathy's Waltz, take 1"
2. "Take 2, Kathy's Waltz"
3. "Take 1, remake, Waltz for Cathy"
4. "Take 2, remake"

Immediately after Macero's fourth announcement, Brubeck instructed the other members of his combo to "Play that waltz, no matter what I do."

Unlike the Quartet's frequently abortive attempts to record "Take Five," the takes of "Kathy's Waltz" proceeded fairly smoothly. Only once, before the first remake, did the proceedings grind to a halt, to peals of laughter. The group tried out various tempos. In the first two takes, the head (which Brubeck consistently counted in fast 4/4) moves at around 136 beats per minute. When the 3/4 meter kicks in, the tempo is about sixty-six beats per minute, with the dotted quarter note receiving the beat. The first remake is a shade faster, and the second is considerably slower (123 beats per minute in the head, and sixty-three beats per minute thereafter). Brubeck varied other aspects of the tune as well, especially its rhythms but also the specific pitches employed. In the second half of the melody (beginning at m. 17), where the last pitch of each three-note motive forms an ascending chromatic scale beginning on f, Brubeck sometimes alternates between the upper and lower octaves (as in the *Time Out* version) and at other times he favors the upper octave (take 2) or the lower (second remake). In all four cases, the choruses are played by the saxophone and piano, in that order, but the lengths of the solos vary from one recording to the next:

Take 1 = saxophone (2 choruses), piano (2 choruses)

Take 2 = saxophone (2), piano (3)

Remake, take 1 = saxophone (3), piano (2)

Remake, take 2 = saxophone (2), piano (4)

In take 1, Brubeck begins hinting at the superimposition of quadruple and triple meter (4/4 vs. 2 × 3/4) fairly early on, but he doesn't move definitively in that direction until the end of his first chorus. In the other three takes, the polymeter begins almost immediately. After the piano choruses, the return of the head generally is masked by the continuation of improvisation until m. 17. Finally, each take concludes with a coda that gradually slows to the end. But its length and specific chords are different each time.

Surely the most surprising result of the examination of the original sessions concerns the recordings of "Kathy's Waltz" from July 1, 1959. The artist job sheet for that day indicates that the session began at 2:30 p.m. with Cole Porter's "I Get a Kick Out of You" (CO 62575), followed by a fresh recording of "Kathy's Waltz" under the new matrix number CO 62576.[6] Among Brubeck's personal copies of the tapes are three tracks

6 Columbia Records, Artist Job Sheet, Job No. 50192 (Sony Music Archives Library).

that apparently document this portion of the session, before the Quartet moved on to "Take Five" (CO 62577 and 62578). In the first track, Macero announces the succeeding recording as a new version of "Kathy's Waltz." His specific words are "Waltz for Kathy, CO 62576, take 1, remake." Thereafter, the Quartet plays the familiar version of "Kathy's Waltz" from *Time Out*, with one exception. If my inferences are correct, this means that the version of "Kathy's Waltz" on *Time Out* was recorded on July 1 rather than June 25. This recording conflicts with the official information promulgated by Columbia (and its successor, Sony), which was evidently based on the July 1 job sheet, where CO 62576 is marked "N.G." (no good) and annotated with a note to "see 6/25/59 session for good take—CO 62555." There is absolutely no doubt, however, that the version that ultimately was released matches the CO 62576 remake rather than any of the four CO 62555 versions discussed before.

The other unexpected discovery is that the last sixteen seconds (eight bars) of the *Time Out* version were spliced from a supplemental take. The July 1 remake exactly matches the album up through the downbeat of m. 248 (around 4:31). The continuation of this passage originally remained more or less in tempo, included a conspicuous mistake (several incorrect chords), and it was a few bars longer. The spliced material came from a track lasting about thirty seconds, which Macero announced as "Take 3." It began with the polytonal chord in m. 239, formed by an F-sharp major triad in the right hand and a C major triad in the left (the analogous measure begins at 4:22 on *Time Out*). Only the latter half of "take 3" was spliced, beginning with the second beat of m. 248. The edit was accomplished so artfully that it is virtually inaudible.[7]

"STRANGE MEADOW LARK"

The recordings in the Brubeck Collection from the original studio sessions in 1959 testify that even "Strange Meadow Lark," a relatively straightforward ballad, required several takes. In addition, they reveal the surprising fact that the final version on *Time Out* was spliced from two recordings that were initially made separately.

The Quartet's first attempts occurred during the afternoon session on June 25. Macero announced the master number ("CO 62557") and asked, "Is there a title, Dave?" After answering his question ("Strange Meadow

---

7 Immediately after the conclusion of the "take 3" supplementary material, Brubeck requested another take and Macero announced "take 4." No additional music has been preserved, however.

Lark"), Brubeck said, "Here we go." He played the first three measures, then stopped abruptly and said, "Cut it. I forgot the 3/4." This comment is puzzling, because the tune is in common time, not 3/4. But apparently the rubato style of the opening piano solo—accompanied in this take by the bass, playing arco—skewed Brubeck's perception of its meter. His next attempt lasted only four beats, before he broke it off and said, "Wait a minute." He then counted under his breath—"One, two-and," then "One, two, three-and," the latter implying 3/4 meter (two quarters and two eighths). After announcing, "That's the way I'll count it," Brubeck immediately spoke and sang the tune in two different rhythms: "One, two, three-and," then "One, two-and, three." Apparently sensing the contradiction, he told his sidemen, "As long as we get in on the first one, I'm not too concerned."

Once Brubeck had gotten it off the ground, this first take paralleled the familiar version on *Time Out*, with one exception. The first three sections are similar. Brubeck plays the entire tune (mm. 1–52) as a piano solo in free rhythm, with light accompaniment by the bass (arco in A and A′, pizzicato in the second half of B). Then follow two choruses (in tempo) by the saxophone and piano, which are shortened slightly, to fifty bars each. The divergence occurs at this point. Instead of another statement of the entire tune (A B A′), the A and B sections (thirty-six measures total) are omitted. Moreover, the first part of A′ remains in tempo, rather than reverting to free rhythm, as in the version that was released on *Time Out*.

The next take also began haltingly. Brubeck played just the first measure before Macero announced, "Take two," whereupon Brubeck attempted it again and said, "I didn't even like the beginning." Despite his own urging ("Here we go—keep going"), Brubeck got through only seven bars on his next try, before stopping and saying, "I'll take another one." After Macero intoned, "Take three," Brubeck finally laid down another complete version, whose form matches the previous one—that is, it has an abbreviated reprise, following the saxophone and piano choruses.

For the most part, the alternative versions of Brubeck's and Desmond's solos—which are exceedingly familiar in their final incarnations—plow no unfamiliar territory and sound rather similar to material that can easily be heard elsewhere. One moment worth singling out, however, occurs midway through Desmond's chorus on the latter take. Just before he begins improvising on the changes for the bridge, he hits upon a three-note motive consisting of an ascending perfect fifth followed by an ascending half step (b-f#′-g′ in mm. 71–72 of Example 5.5). These are pitches used in the well-known popular song "Bewitched, Bothered and Bewildered," from the musical *Pal Joey* (1940) by Richard Rodgers and

Lorenz Hart. The pitches occur at the beginning of the song's refrain, to the words "[I'm] wild again." Desmond's solo in the first half of the bridge (mm. 73–76) is essentially a paraphrase of the Rodgers and Hart melody associated with the words, "I'm wild again / Beguiled again / A simpering, whimpering child again." Desmond could count on wide recognition of this tune and its lyrics. It had been recorded numerous times, including most recently by Ella Fitzgerald (1956), Anita O'Day (1957), and Frank Sinatra (1957) for the film version of the musical. Desmond's wry appropriation of this quotation is similar to his use of the melody associated with the words "You better watch out / You better not cry" from "Santa Claus Is Comin' to Town."

The attempted remakes in the evening session on June 25 (7:00–10:00 p.m.) were an exercise in futility. After Desmond played a brief solo, then petered out, Brubeck said, "Too bad it wasn't taped. That sounded good." When Macero replied, "We're taping it," Brubeck cried out in shocked disbelief, "Were you? Gee, I wish I'd known that." Macero then announced the first take of the remake. After Brubeck played his entire opening piano solo, Desmond began his chorus and uncharacteristically went off in the wrong direction about thirty seconds into it. Several more false starts ensued, before the Quartet finally got through the

EXAMPLE 5.6.   Dave Brubeck, "Strange Meadow Lark," mm. 36–39.

second take of the remake. Unlike the somewhat abbreviated renditions from the afternoon session, the return of the head after Desmond's and Brubeck's solos was a bit more expansive, because it included the first thirty-six bars (10+10+8+8) as well—like the final version—rather than just the end. Unfortunately, however, this second take was incomplete, since Brubeck started his opening piano solo with the pickups to m. 37, rather than at the beginning.

Six days later, on July 1 (2:30–7:00 p.m.), the Quartet was back in the studio, and this time they nailed it—almost. The biggest surprise of the original studio recordings is the revelation that the familiar version of "Strange Meadow Lark," as released on *Time Out*, was spliced from two separate takes. The lion's share of this track (5:45 out of 7:20 total) is from a recording that matches the form of the last remake of the previous session, described earlier. That is, Brubeck's solo at the beginning spans only sixteen bars, rather than a full fifty-two. Other than that, its content is identical to the released version. At the conclusion of this recording, Brubeck can be heard to say, "Let's do another one." But Macero ignored this request and announced instead, "Stand by, please. Insert 1, take 1. Beginning of 'Strange Meadow Lark.'" After one false start, Brubeck then played the entire opening piano solo, through the downbeat of m. 53. This shorter insert was subsequently spliced to the previous longer take. The splice is at 1:39 of the final version, after Brubeck reaches the top of the arpeggio in m. 37 (see Example 5.6).[8]

---

8 The first few beats of the longer take were evidently papered over in the editing process. A telltale clue is that the pickup notes had originally been eighth notes, but they were augmented to quarters in the inserted (and final) version.

Although it is startling to realize that the familiar version of "Strange Meadow Lark" was cobbled together from two separate recordings, editing of this kind was neither new nor rare by 1959. Barry Kernfeld mentions that cutting and splicing of recordings was made possible "from the late 1940s, when magnetic tape became the principal recording medium." He cites a 1956 recording of "Brilliant Corners" by Thelonious Monk, in which the issued track was formed in a similar manner to "Strange Meadow Lark." It is "a composite, in which the final statement of the theme is part of a different take from the remainder of the performance."[9]

A clear indication of the extent to which Brubeck's recordings were edited, from the very beginning of his tenure with Columbia Records, is provided in correspondence from the producer who signed him to the label. George Avakian discusses in detail several selections that appeared on *Dave Brubeck at Storyville: 1954* (Columbia CL 590). Four numbers were recorded live at George Wein's nightclub in Boston. In order to fill out the album, however, Avakian asked Brubeck to "go to the studio with Lowell Frank [in Los Angeles] and cut anything you want." Avakian would then "add room noise and applause to match the other tapes." For a recording of "Jeepers Creepers," which ultimately was not included on the album, Avakian specified no fewer than six cuts that reduced the playing time by nearly two minutes. In the end, he decided against "the version with the cuts," because he "found it impossible to completely disguise the splices."[10]

"THREE TO GET READY"

The process of recording "Three to Get Ready" appears to have been relatively unproblematic. Unlike "Take Five," which required numerous attempts and took shape in fits and starts, the Quartet recorded "Three to Get Ready" only five times, and the first take was ultimately selected for the album. Though the evidence is patchy, it indicates that the tune was recorded twice in each of the two sessions on June 25, 1959. In a ten-second snippet from one of Brubeck's personal copies of the session tapes, Macero can be heard to say, "Here we go; take two."

9 Barry Kernfeld, "II. History of Jazz Recording, 7. The Effects of Technological Change," in Gordon Mumma, et al., "Recording," *Grove Music Online*, accessed March 15, 2018, http://www.oxfordmusiconline.com/grovemusic/view/10.1093/gmo/9781561592630.001.0001/omo-9781561592630-e-2000371600

10 George Avakian to Dave Brubeck, July 12, 1954, and July 30, 1954 (Brubeck Collection).

Thereupon, Brubeck counts to three, plays the first two bars, breaks off, says "Here we go again," and counts to three a second time. The second take is about thirty seconds shorter than the version that was released on *Time Out* because Brubeck plays only five piano choruses instead of seven.

The most surprising aspect of the second take is a tiny detail whose sonic impact seems out of proportion to its modesty, and that underscores how deeply ingrained in our aural consciousness the final version has become. When Brubeck plays the first chorus, he holds the final notes of the first two phrases for a full three beats instead of clipping them after one beat (see Example 4.14, mm. 3 and 6). This is the way Brubeck had notated the melody in the alto saxophone chart for Desmond (see Figure 4.2), and it engenders a gentler and more laid-back feel in that chorus and the next one. Hearing the version with these elongated pitches calls attention to the melody's articulation and reveals the important role of the staccato notes in creating the tune's jaunty affect. This is reinforced at the end of the second take, after the solos for saxophone (choruses 6–8) and piano (choruses 9–13), when the version of the tune with long notes (chorus 14) is juxtaposed with the version with short notes (chorus 15).

"EVERYBODY'S JUMPIN' "

The recording history of "Everybody's Jumpin'" begins with the un-expected fact that a portion of the tune originated nearly nine years before the *Time Out* sessions, when the Quartet had not yet been consti-tuted. In October 1950, six months before the swimming accident that led to the formation of the Quartet, Brubeck recorded with Ron Crotty on bass and Cal Tjader on vibraphone (as the Dave Brubeck Trio) the 1940 standard "How High the Moon" by Nancy Hamilton (lyrics) and Morgan Lewis (music).[11] About halfway through his first chorus (around 1:17), Brubeck plays a pattern that bears more than passing re-semblance to the flat three passage (mm. 5–8) in "Everybody's Jumpin'" (see Example 5.7). Not only are the harmonic content and pitches iden-tical (albeit a step higher, in G major rather than F major), but the meter of mm. 13–15 would be more accurately represented as two bars of 3/2 rather than three bars of 4/4.[12]

---

11   The Dave Brubeck Trio, *Distinctive Rhythm Instrumentals,* Fantasy 3-4, 1952.
12   It is impossible to know whether Brubeck was aware of this motive's prehistory when he composed "Everybody's Jumpin'" in January 1959. I am grateful to his longtime manager for pointing it out. Russell Gloyd, email message to author, August 8, 2013.

EXAMPLE 5.7. "How High the Moon," excerpt from piano chorus (Dave Brubeck) in 1950 recording, with motive that later appears in "Everybody's Jumpin'," transcription.

"Everybody's Jumpin'" is the only tune on *Time Out* that the Quartet recorded on all three days in the studio. Their first attempt took place during the earlier of the two sessions on June 25, 1959. Macero announced it as "CO 62558, take one, Everybody's Jumpin'," and Brubeck warned his colleagues repeatedly to be prepared for an especially energetic performance: "Listen, I'm gonna play a lot louder on this one. It's gonna be a lot louder. Yeah, the first part's gonna be soft, but watch out in the middle!" After he started counting it off, Brubeck also reminded them to pay special attention to what he called "the leapfrog jump," although he didn't specify which part of the melody he was referring to. The first take is the recording that ultimately was selected for the album.

On July 1, after achieving the final version of "Take Five," the Quartet took another stab at "Everybody's Jumpin'." Only one recording of CO 62579 has been preserved among Brubeck's personal audio tapes, and Macero announced it as "take eight," implying that a great deal of effort had been expended beforehand on this tune. The remake was marked as "no good" on the artist job sheet.[13] It is remarkably similar to the familiar version on *Time Out*, although Paul Desmond's performance is uncharacteristically lackluster. Otherwise, it is simply shorter (3:10 rather than 4:25), because Desmond and Brubeck take just one chorus each, before Morello's drum solo and the return of the head. The artist job sheet for the session on August 18 indicates that the Quartet tried one more time (CO 62754). Unfortunately, this recording has not been preserved, but it is similarly marked "N.G." (no good).[14]

13 Columbia Records, Artist Job Sheet, Job No. 50192, July 1, 1959, 2:30–7:00 p.m. (Sony Music Archives Library).

14 Columbia Records, Artist Job Sheet, Job No. 50258, August 18, 1959, 2:30–5:30 p.m. (Sony Music Archives Library).

According to the artist job sheet, the final version of "Blue Rondo à la Turk" was recorded on August 18, 1959. But the Quartet first attempted it in the earlier of the two sessions on June 25, from which two takes have come down to us among Brubeck's personal recordings.[15]

By August, the full title was typed on the job sheet. But in the June session, Macero announced the piece simply as "Turkish." The first take vividly illustrates its technical difficulty. Following Macero's announcement of "CO 62559, Turkish, take one" is forty-five seconds of music, which disintegrates when Brubeck's fingers get crossed up in m. 27 (toward the beginning of C, the second episode) and he initially shouts "Paul!" before admitting "*I* missed it!"[16]

The second take is much more successful, although Brubeck plays a surprising number of wrong notes in the left hand during the first two minutes—that is, before the blues kicks in. The blues section here is more spacious than in the final version, chiefly because Brubeck stretches out to a full ten choruses. Even though Desmond's solo is shorter—just three choruses—he introduces some ideas that are subsequently picked up by Brubeck: a touch of polytonality in chorus 1 and the incorporation of motivic material from the rondo portion of the piece in chorus 3.

Brubeck's choruses 8 and 9 are arguably the closest of the ten to the spirit of the blues (see Example 5.8). After three phrases in which the lowered third (A♭) is emphasized (mm. 211–212, 213–214, 215–216), the natural third (A♮) is reintroduced in m. 217. This shift coincides with quotation of a truncated version of the rondo refrain (mm. 217–219 ≈ 1–3), whose implicit 3/4 meter cuts across the grain of the prevailing common time. Chorus 9—like Brubeck's fourth and final chorus in the album version (Example 6.3b)—is marked by emphasis on a sustained b″ (mm. 223 and 227), the raised fourth scale degree. The balance of the passage is constructed predominantly from pitches associated with the A♭ major triad (A♭-C-E♭), which are superimposed on the F-major blues progression in a gentle whisper of polytonality.

---

15 Columbia Records, Artist Job Sheet, Job No. 50258, August 18, 1959, 2:30–5:30 p.m. (Sony Music Archives Library). The job sheet for the first session has not been preserved, but the recordings are in the Brubeck Collection.

16 Even the version that was ultimately released on *Time Out* has some blemishes, most notably a missed note by Brubeck at 0:24 and a squeak by Desmond at 0:49.

EXAMPLE 5.8. Dave Brubeck, "Blue Rondo à la Turk," choruses 8 and 9 (mm. 211–234), piano (Brubeck), June 25, 1959, afternoon recording session, transcription.

"PICK UP STICKS"

"Pick Up Sticks" was recorded on August 18, 1959, but the session tapes for that day are not held by the Brubeck Collection.[17] There are two

17 The tune is listed under the matrix number CO 62753 on Columbia Records, Artist Job Sheet, Job No. 50258, August 18, 1959, 2:30–5:30 p.m. (Sony Music Archives Library).

EXAMPLE 5.9. Bass ostinato from jam, June 25, 1959, evening recording session.

tracks from the evening session on June 25, however, that are relevant. The first is just over one minute in length. During the last ten seconds, Macero announces, "CO 62561, Someday My Prince Will Come, take one." According to the artist job sheet, this was the first order of business that night, before the string of unsuccessful attempts with "Five Fourth Time" (i.e., "Take Five), which were described at the beginning of this chapter. Immediately beforehand, though—presumably right after their dinner break—Wright, Morello, and Brubeck can be heard jamming. The glue of this brief improvisation is a bass ostinato. As is evident from Example 5.9, this pattern shares some essential features of the ostinato from "Pick Up Sticks." It is in 6/4 meter, and it traces a similar melodic trajectory. On the other hand, its tonic pitch is F rather than B♭, and the sixth note leaps down an octave to the dominant (C) rather than to the flattened supertonic (G♭). Against Wright's ostinato, Morello plays a swinging pattern in common time, starting on the hi-hat. This pattern yields complex polymeter and polyrhythms that eventually expand to encompass other drums in the kit. Meanwhile, Brubeck superimposes some dissonant tone clusters and then improvises with both hands playing in unison a predominantly pentatonic pattern that includes two blue notes, the lowered third (A♭) and the lowered seventh (E♭).

The other track is much more substantial, lasting about five-and-a-half minutes. It is unclear where it fits within the recording session, because it includes no announcement by the producer, nor is it listed on the artist job sheet. But it obviously is related to the impromptu moment discussed above, which took place at the beginning of the evening session on June 25. Moreover, on Brubeck's personal tape the longer track is sandwiched between multiple takes of "Take Five" (though presumably out of order), which originated in that same session. The heart of this recording is a drum solo, but Morello plays entirely alone for only about two minutes. This outing begins with a few seconds of light solo percussion, alternating quickly between cymbals and drums. The bass then joins in, playing a six-note ostinato similar to Example 5.9, but an octave lower. Because it is near the bottom of the bass's range (this instrument's lowest note, under normal circumstances, is EE′), Wright had to substitute a repetition of the tonic pitch for the downward octave leap, yielding the melody given in Example 5.10. The bass plays this pattern

DAVE BRUBECK'S TIME OUT

EXAMPLE 5.10. Bass ostinato from complete take, June 25, 1959, evening recording session.

EXAMPLE 5.11. Piano ("Watusi Drums" theme) and bass ostinato from complete take, June 25, 1959, evening recording session, transcription.

seven times, along with the drums, before the piano enters. Brubeck plays a series of blues-tinged riffs, culminating after more than thirty bars with an important and distinctive theme, to which we will return in Chapter 6 (Example 6.5). Thereafter, the drum solo begins, but it is accompanied for the first forty seconds by the bass, playing an additional sixteen repetitions of the ostinato. When the bass reenters after a couple of minutes of nothing but drums, the pace of the ostinato is considerably brisker and Wright consistently raises the last note by a half step (i.e., it matches the pattern of "Pick Up Sticks," albeit in F rather than B♭). When Brubeck joins in after four measures, he plays the same theme as before the drum solo. This is the tune known as "Watusi Drums" (Example 5.11). The cut ends with the drums playing alone again, except for a single piano chord as the final stroke.

CHAPTER 6

CROSS-GENRE SYNTHESIS

THE STORY OF *Time Out* involves the surprising juxtaposition of seemingly disparate elements and an artistic vision that encompasses musical cultures from around the world. Dave Brubeck's liberal attitude toward many different kinds of music and his desire to invite their influence into his work as a composer and an improviser come through on many occasions, as does his skill in bringing together aspects of classical and world music with jazz, to produce a coherent artistic statement.

THE THREE STRANDS OF "BLUE RONDO À LA TURK"

Among the papers of Teo Macero, the producer of *Time Out,* are two copies of a typed statement that evidently was prepared in anticipation of the single release of "Blue Rondo à la Turk" and "Take Five." The blurb asserts that "Blue Rondo à la Turk" "brings to jazz a unique combination of elements from three different musical cultures." The anonymous author (presumably Macero himself) notes, first of all, Brubeck's addition of his "own theme and harmonic pattern to an ancient Turkish rhythm." These materials were shaped into the second element, the rondo, "an early European classical form." Finally, this merges into "the very American form of expression, the blues."[1]

The melding of these three traditions was foundational to this composition. The blues is closest to home, since it is a quintessentially American brand of art with African roots, and a significant branch of jazz, Brubeck's native musical language. Rondo form represents the practices of European art music ("classical"), and is a bit farther removed, both geographically and culturally. The Turkish component is the most remote, and it is associated with so-called world music, with its overtones of Orientalism and the exotic Other.

TURKISH JAZZ?

In the twenty-first century, the connections between the country of Turkey and the musical idiom of jazz are no longer as tenuous as they were in the late 1950s. Although the jazz scene in Istanbul, for instance, is relatively modest, it is robust enough to support regular activity in several clubs and other venues, and a major festival every summer.[2] Moreover, a full-length documentary on *Jazz in Turkey* (2014) traced this music's storied history during the past century.[3] Nonetheless, "Turkish" and "jazz" are words that many people still find surprising when paired together.

When the Dave Brubeck Quartet first visited Turkey, for a week in late March 1958, their style of music wasn't completely unknown. In fact, Brubeck reported that in Ankara they invited three Turkish musicians (bass, drums, French horn) to join them on stage, and together they jammed fifteen choruses of the Jerome Kern standard "All the Things You Are"

---

1 Macero Collection, box 7, folder 4. The carbon copy includes Macero's editorial emendations, which shift the statement into the first person ("I added my own theme and harmonic pattern" instead of "Dave added his own . . .") and characterize the blues as a "very American form of expression" (added in pen).

2 Susanne Fowler, "Young Jazz Musicians Find a Niche in Istanbul," *International Herald Tribune*, February 17, 2011.

3 Alissa Simon, "Film Review: 'Jazz in Turkey,'" *Variety*, May 12, 2014. http://variety.com/2014/film/reviews/film-review-jazz-in-turkey-1201178822/ (accessed March 14, 2018).
   The film may be viewed at https://www.youtube.com/watch?v=ohJ38Es2P-c (accessed March 14, 2018).

(1939).[4] But for many, the Quartet's performances were *terra incognita*. Brubeck was especially proud that Turkey's Director General of Fine Arts, Cevad Memduh Altar (1902–1995), attended one of the performances in Ankara. Altar was a friend of the German modernist composer Paul Hindemith, and he had published studies on the music of Mozart, Beethoven, Chopin, and Bizet, yet this was reportedly the first time the diplomatic staff had been able to persuade him to attend a US function of any kind.[5]

The Quartet's week in Turkey seems to have been an especially successful example of cultural exchange. According to a report from the American Embassy in Ankara, the group "met with unqualified success in all of their appearances, whether professional or social." A scene at the airport upon Brubeck's departure from the city vividly illustrates the deep personal connections that were forged during the visit: "The morning that they left Ankara, two boys who had gone to the airport stood shaking their fists at the plane, and the young French horn player, with tears running down his cheeks, cried, 'It's terrible, terrible! We are like children without a father now that he (Brubeck) is gone!'"[6]

The impact of Turkey and its musical culture on Brubeck was equally profound. The diplomatic report mentions that, while he was in Ankara, Brubeck "asked a member of the USIS [United States Information Service] cultural staff to prepare a tape which would include representative music of Turkey." Accordingly, "a tape was made with excerpts of such early phases as the drums of Mehter (more commonly known as

---

4 Dave Brubeck, "The Beat Heard 'Round the World," *New York Times Magazine* (June 15, 1958): 32.

5 Brubeck, "Beat Heard." See also http://cevadmemduhaltar.com (accessed March 14, 2018).

6 C. Edward Wells (Country Public Affairs Officer, American Embassy, Ankara), "Cultural Presentation: President's Program—Dave Brubeck in Turkey," Foreign Service Dispatch #363 to Department of State, December 12, 1958; General Records of the Department of State, Record Group 59. This official account is corroborated by a personal one, the ten-year-old Darius Brubeck's travel diary ("Dari's Book 1958"). Brubeck's son recalled that, on the plane from Ankara to Istanbul (March 26, 1958), "my thoughts traveled back to just a few hours ago at the airport. When we left Ankara for Istanbul, our musician-friends had come to the airport to say goodbye. They were very sad that we had to leave so soon. . . . One, with tears in his eyes, turned to Miss [Patricia] Randles of the USIS [United States Information Service] and said, 'There goes my father,' meaning Dad. . . . It felt kind of strange to have your own father looked up to as a great musician in so many countries. To the man in Ankara, Dad was his musical father, yet to me Dad is just plain Dad." Audio recording, read aloud by Iola Brubeck (Brubeck Collection). https://scholarlycommons.pacific.edu/jdttj/ (accessed March 14, 2018).

Janissary music) up through today's better known Turkish composers' works."

This recording, a reel-to-reel tape, has been preserved in the Brubeck Collection. Written in pen on the back of the box are the words "Turkish music, with explanation in English," and on the side "M. Brubeck." Inside is a message in handsome calligraphic script, signed by Ahmet (surname undecipherable). It reads in part, "Dear Mr. Brubeck, I hope this tape will be of some use to you. . . . Have a nice trip. Hope to see you again."

The content of the recording is a half-hour program that explores "Turkish history and heritage through music." It had originally been presented several months earlier, "on the thirty-fourth anniversary of the founding of the Turkish republic"—that is, on October 29, 1957. Its nationalistic bent is evident from the very first words, which describe Turkey as a country that "blends a rich and colorful history with a vigorous present, a country which looks to the future with determination and hope."

The first musical example is the "Rondo alla turca" from Mozart's Piano Sonata in A major, K. 331 (300i). The remainder of the program weaves together a variety of selections drawn from the repertoires of classical, folk, and popular music. At one point, the narrator states that "there are many young Turkish jazz and dance music composers who blend Turkish motifs with Western techniques." In other words, those musicians were creating compositions with ambitions similar to those of "Blue Rondo à la Turk." By the same token, the specific type of folk music that gave rise to Brubeck's piece is never mentioned at all.

The tape concludes with a short personal greeting that was appended to the radio broadcast. It encapsulates the warmth and goodwill that permeated Brubeck's visit to Turkey: "Hello, Mr. and Mrs. Brubeck, Mr. Morello, Mr. Wright, and Mr. Desmond. This is your Turkish friend Ahmet from Ankara wishing you a very nice trip and much success. I hope you will like this tape, which will give you some briefing on the development of Turkish music. Goodbye now. Don't forget us. Have a nice trip. We were very glad to have you here in Turkey, and please don't forget us and write to us whenever you feel like. Goodbye."

The event that served as a catalyst for the creation of "Blue Rondo à la Turk" occurred in Istanbul, within a few days after the Quartet arrived there from Ankara. According to one version of this twice-told tale, Dave said,

I had walked to the Turkish radio station where there was a big band of Turkish musicians that I was going to do something with. And while walking through the streets, I heard street musicians playing in this 9/8 rhythm: 1-2-1-2-1-2-1-2-3. I was fascinated. I stopped for a while and heard this thing just keep going. When I got to the studio I asked a Turkish musician that spoke English very well, "What is this rhythm? It's so fascinating." And he said, "Well, what rhythm?" And I said, "1-2-1-2-1-2-1-2-3! 1-2-1-2-1-2-1-2-3," and he just turned to the band and they all started playing it. With no talking or anything, they all just fell into it, so I could see, boy, this is a rhythm that really works. . . . So I put a melody to the rhythm and called it "Blue Rondo à la Turk."[7]

The rhythmic pattern that intrigued and inspired Brubeck is known as *aksak,* a word that means "limping" and refers to a number of asymmetrical temporal designs in Anatolian folk music.[8] The article on Turkey in *Grove Music Online* notes that *aksak* meters appear "principally in dance-songs and instrumental dance melodies."[9] This is an especially sweet irony, given that the businessmen at Columbia Records were worried that Brubeck's tune would be "undanceable."

A JAZZ RONDO?

The place and time one is most likely to encounter rondos is, of course, Europe in the eighteenth and early nineteenth centuries. It is probably impossible to accurately quantify this enormous body of music, and the result would depend in large measure upon a multitude of gradations and distinctions. What is certain, however, is that the rondo is exceedingly common in classical music and relatively rare in jazz.

The defining characteristic of rondo form is the repeated return of an opening section of music (generally denoted by the letter A), which alternates with contrasting material. There are many different rondo designs, but it is customary to summarize them as ABAC . . . A.

The structure of "Blue Rondo à la Turk" in eight-bar segments can be considered in relation to the conventions of the classical rondo. If one

---

7 Dave Brubeck, "A Long Partnership in Life and Music," an oral history conducted in 1999 and 2001 by Caroline C. Crawford, Regional Oral History Office, The Bancroft Library, University of California, Berkeley, 2006. February 17, 1999 interview, p. 55.

8 See Eliot Bates, *Music in Turkey: Experiencing Music, Expressing Culture* (New York: Oxford University Press, 2011), 54–58. Substantial new contributions to the literature on *aksak,* as well as extensive bibliographies, may be found in *Empirical Musicology Review* 10, no. 4 (2015), a special issue on "Musical Rhythm across Cultures," guest edited by Justin London.

9 Kurt Reinhard, et al., "Turkey," *Grove Music Online/Oxford Music Online,* Oxford University Press, accessed March 14, 2018, https://doi.org/10.1093/gmo/9781561592630.article.44912

sets aside minor enhancements, such as doubling of the melody at the upper third or the addition of light percussion, the form of its first seven segments may be represented as follows:

mm. 1–8	A
mm. 9–16	B
mm. 17–24	A
mm. 25–32	C
mm. 33–40	A
mm. 41–48	D
mm. 49–56	A

The tonal center of the refrain is the pitch F, whereas the tonal center of each of the three episodes is A.[10]

Strictly speaking, then, the components of the first part of this composition are arranged in a type of rondo form. In point of fact, however, this piece differs from its European classical predecessors by virtue of the brevity of its constituent elements. So far as I know, there is no centralized source of information concerning the typical length of rondo refrains and episodes. But it is surely safe to say that classical rondos normally unfold over somewhat longer spans of time—and one would have to search high and low to find an example as compact as the quick eight-bar segments in "Blue Rondo à la Turk," each of which lasts only eleven seconds. Furthermore, the course of events that ensues departs from the regular rondo-like alternation of segments (ABACADA), and this orderly pattern never returns in its fully fleshed-out format.

The title "Blue Rondo à la Turk" is an odd macaronic construction, incorporating Italian ("rondo"), French ("à la"), and English ("blue" and "Turk") in an imaginative but linguistically inconsistent manner. The piece's relationship to Mozart's "Rondo alla turca"—the first item on the tape recording of Turkish music that was discussed earlier—is complex.

10 Since Brubeck's music has not yet received much searching analysis, it is worth mentioning here the treatment of "Blue Rondo à la Turk" in Henry Martin, *Enjoying Jazz* (New York: Schirmer Books, 1986), 64–67. Martin's account of its form matches the one given here, and it is hard to disagree with his judicious appraisal of the piece as "an admirable mixture of the experimental and the conventional, both of which are carefully planned and impeccably performed" (p. 67). Unfortunately, however, he confuses matters by incorrectly connecting its 2+2+2+3 meter with the European (Modernist) "fine-art aspects of the performance," rather than with the Turkish *aksak*.

On the one hand, Brubeck freely acknowledged that his title referred to the Mozart composition. But he also felt that there was no meaningful connection between the music of his piece and its classical predecessor. As a result, he thought he should have called it simply "Blue Rondo" instead, because "the title confused people"—that is, it led them to expect a closer kinship with the famous Mozart piece than actually existed.[11]

One can certainly understand Brubeck's scruples. Yet the very existence of the Turkish music tape strongly supports the continued use of the longer title. It was, after all, this specific "Turkish" rondo by Mozart that Brubeck heard first—before any indigenous music—when he listened to the recording of this radio program. Moreover, Mozart's "Rondo alla turca" was surely a standard in his mother's piano studio, and Brubeck must have heard it frequently at home in California when he was growing up. It was, in short, the spark that impelled Brubeck to create his own "Turkish rondo" in the jazz idiom, following his visit to the Middle East. To eliminate the words "à la Turk" might indeed lessen some confusion, but it would have come at the risk of obscuring his piece's connection to Mozart's eighteenth-century take on this exotic music as well as to the actual Turkish folk music Brubeck heard in the streets of Istanbul nearly two centuries later.

There is reason to think that Brubeck's decision to write "Blue Rondo à la Turk" was informed as well by his earlier compositional studies—and perhaps even by the desire to improve upon a failed experiment. One of the first items he produced as a graduate student at Mills College under the tutelage of Darius Milhaud was a short piece with the straightforward title "Rondo." It originated in 1946, shortly after Brubeck was discharged from the Army and resumed his studies, with the financial backing of the GI Bill.

"Rondo" is scored for trumpet, trombone, clarinet, alto and tenor saxophones, piano, bass, and drums. It was recorded in the same year it was composed, but it wasn't released until many years later (1954), on the album *Old Sounds from San Francisco* by the Dave Brubeck Octet (Fantasy 3-16). Ted Gioia has aptly characterized the piece as follows: "The 'Rondo' has all the marks of a student work. It lasts only ninety seconds,

---

11 Brubeck, "Long Partnership," p. 55; Dave Brubeck, raw interview audio with Russell Gloyd concerning the album *Time Out*, September 12, 2003 (Brubeck Collection). Portions of the latter are commercially available as "Dave Brubeck on *Time Out*," interview by Russell Gloyd, filmed on location in Wilton, Connecticut, September 12, 2003, directed by Chris Lenz, Sony Music Entertainment, 2009; included with 50th Anniversary edition of *Time Out*, Columbia/Legacy 88697 39852 2, DVD.

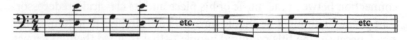

and though its dense harmonies would have been daring in a jazz context, the piece studiously avoids any reference to the jazz idiom, instead sounding like a classroom exercise written for Milhaud's benefit."[12]

Brubeck's "Rondo" sounds like a "classroom exercise," in part because it is so strongly derivative. Its apparent model was the opening movement of Stravinsky's *L'Histoire du soldat* (The Soldier's Tale) (1918). The "Marche du soldat" (Soldier's March) calls for an ensemble of seven instruments rather than eight. There are violin and bassoon instead of saxophones and piano. But the other five instruments (cornet, trombone, clarinet, bass, percussion) are virtually the same as in the Brubeck piece. Moreover, the duration of the Stravinsky movement is nearly identical to Brubeck's rondo—about ninety seconds. Finally, both pieces feature similar ostinato patterns in the bass, with the same starting pitch (see Example 6.1).

A contemporary review of the Octet recording enumerated some of the same shortcomings later mentioned by Gioia, plus a few more: "Musically, there's nothing here that has a wholly integrated worth of its own. . . . The next five numbers [including "Rondo"] are stiffly derivative of naively assimilated Milhaud, Hindemith, and exercise books. . . .The whole production is messy. The cover is unimpressively coy; the recording, even allowing for the date of recordings and the fact that some were audition sides, is quite bad." The reviewer expressed surprise that Brubeck allowed this album to be released, and he speculated that this was done "for historical purposes—to fill in further Brubeck's audiobiography."[13]

I think this is essentially correct, and that Brubeck released it in an effort to set the record straight. Specifically, he wanted the world to know that his Octet was active several years before Miles Davis's Nonet laid down the tracks in 1949 and 1950 that were eventually released as *Birth of the Cool* (Capitol T-762). By 1954, those recordings were widely available

---

12 Ted Gioia, *West Coast Jazz: Modern Jazz in California, 1945–1960* (Berkeley: University of California Press, 1998), 79.

13 Nat Hentoff, "Jazz Reviews," *Down Beat* 21, no. 21 (October 20, 1954): 14.

and critically acclaimed, and Brubeck was evidently disappointed that his own earlier achievements had been overlooked. Although Brubeck's liner notes for the Fantasy LP didn't name names, it isn't difficult to discern his intent: "In the spring of 1946 we were an organized band ready to work or record, but remained unnoticed until our first public concert in San Francisco in 1948. . . . An enthusiastic appreciation for jazz has grown to the point where we feel justified in releasing an LP of inferior technical quality on the premise that this Octet did much to shape the *new sounds* with the OLD SOUNDS from San Francisco."

For a 1956 reissue (Fantasy 3-239), Brubeck penned a new set of notes that were even more pointed but still didn't mention Davis. He had noticed "more and more of the Octet innovations being used and accepted in the 'mainstream' of jazz," and he complained that the Octet's work had been unacknowledged during the past decade, "except by flattery of imitation." His group hadn't received the credit it deserved, primarily because it was ahead of its time: "Much of what was considered so controversial when presented by us, is now being heralded as innovations in modern jazz." Brubeck concluded with the bold claim that "the Octet is a major contributor to jazz."

When the album was reissued as a compact disc in 1991 (Fantasy OJCCD-101-2), the veil was finally lifted. In addition to reprinting the 1956 liner notes, a blurb on the back declared that the group had "never been given its proper due," even though "some of these pieces were recorded in 1946, three years before the Miles Davis Nonet."

Notwithstanding all these protestations, the fact remains that knowledgeable writers both then and now have judged Brubeck's early "Rondo" to be weak and unoriginal. The composition of "Blue Rondo à la Turk," one of his most successful pieces, thirteen years later can therefore be viewed as a remedy for that earlier lapse. And this notion is supported by the fact that the form of his "Rondo" (ABACADA) matches the first section of "Blue Rondo à la Turk."[14]

---

14 If one counts the "Rondo" in bars of 2/4 meter at just under $\quarternote$ = 108, its structure can be summarized as follows:

mm. 1–8	Introduction
mm. 9–16	A
mm. 17–32	B (clarinet predominates)
mm. 33–40	A

The fraught question, to what extent it is possible for a middle-class or affluent white musician to play the blues authentically, bears on our examination of "Blue Rondo à la Turk" and situates this discussion in a larger conversation that extends well back into the twentieth century.[15]

About half of "Blue Rondo à la Turk" consists of eight choruses of straightforward twelve-bar blues: four by Paul Desmond on the alto saxophone (2:13–3:51) and four by Brubeck on the piano (3:51–5:34). Quite obviously, it was possible for these two white men to improvise in the style of the blues. The question then becomes, when they did so, what did it sound like? Examples 6.2a and 6.2b provide transcriptions of Desmond's first and fourth choruses. They are fluent, competent, and well constructed—words that probably apply equally well to nearly any of Desmond's solos. In addition to standard blues licks, each chorus has a moment of unusual harmonic interest. In chorus 1, it is the whiff of quartal harmony created by a series of leaps in perfect fourths (m. 97). In chorus 4, the arpeggiation of an augmented triad (F-A-C♯)

mm. 41–48	C (tenor saxophone)
mm. 49–56	A
mm. 57–64	D (trumpet)
mm. 65–76	A (with four-bar extension and ritard)

This clear structure is obscured in Frank Tirro, *"The Birth of the Cool" of Miles Davis and His Associates* (Hillsdale, NY: Pendragon, 2009), 37. Tirro labels the "introductory flourish" as A, the alternation of refrain and episodes as BCBDBEB, and the cadential extension as F.

15 A selection of representative texts includes Amiri Baraka, *Blues People: Negro Music in White America* (New York: Morrow, 1963); Ralph J. Gleason, "Can the White Man Sing the Blues?" *Jazz & Pop* 7, no. 8 (August 1968): 28–29; Joel Rudinow, "Race, Ethnicity, Expressive Authenticity: Can White People Sing the Blues?" *Journal of Aesthetics and Art Criticism* 52 (1994): 127–137; David Carr, "Can White Men Play the Blues? Music, Learning Theory, and Performance Knowledge," *Philosophy of Music Education Review* 9 (2001): 23–31; Patrice D. Madura, "A Response to David Carr," *Philosophy of Music Education Review* 9 (2001): 60–62; Mike Daley, "'Why Do Whites Sing Black?': The Blues, Whiteness, and Early Histories of Rock," *Popular Music and Society* 26 (2003): 161–167; Ulrich Adelt, *Blues Music in the Sixties: A Story in Black and White* (New Brunswick, NJ: Rutgers University Press, 2010); Michael Neumann, "Distributive History: Did Whites Rip-Off the Blues?" in *Blues— Philosophy for Everyone: Thinking Deep about Feeling Low,* eds. Jesse R. Steinberg and Abrol Fairweather (Chichester, UK: Wiley-Blackwell, 2012), 176–190; Steven P. Garabedian, "The Blues Image in the White Mind: Blues Historiography and White Romantic Racialism," *Popular Music and Society* 37 (2014): 476–494.

EXAMPLE 6.2A. Dave Brubeck, "Blue Rondo à la Turk," alto saxophone (Paul Desmond), chorus 1 (mm. 91–102), transcription.

EXAMPLE 6.2B. Dave Brubeck, "Blue Rondo à la Turk," alto saxophone (Paul Desmond), chorus 4 (mm. 127–139), transcription.

at m. 130 first catches the ear. This arpeggio is immediately followed by two measures, in which the second is a subtle transformation of the first.[16]

16 Moreover, the mutation of the descending three-note cell extends into the next measure as well: f′ d′ a (m. 131), f′ d′ g (m. 132), f′ d′ a♭ (m. 133).

EXAMPLE 6.3A. Dave Brubeck, "Blue Rondo à la Turk," piano (Brubeck), chorus 1 (mm. 139–150), transcription.

EXAMPLE 6.3B. Dave Brubeck, "Blue Rondo à la Turk," piano (Brubeck), chorus 4 (mm. 175–186), transcription.

This is sophisticated and intelligent music making, to be sure. But most listeners would probably not describe it as particularly soulful—which is certainly a limitation, if not a fatal flaw, for performance of the blues. Similar things can be said about Brubeck's choruses (Examples 6.3a and 6.3b). The most engaging passage is the roulade in chorus 1, which unfolds over the course of mm. 147–150 and traces a downward arc that spans more than two octaves. This passage is set up by four bars (mm. 139–142) that harp rather incessantly on a″ and f″, notes that were identified earlier as providing the composition's motivic and harmonic backbone. Chorus 4 is similarly fixated on b″—the raised-fourth scale degree, a tritone from the tonic F—which is rearticulated and sustained in mm. 175, 179, and 183. Brubeck's choruses 2 and 3, the only ones included in Howard Brubeck's published transcription, are dominated by his signature block chords in the right hand.[17] The thicker texture of these inner choruses forms a stark contrast to the spare single notes of the outer ones, especially the relatively static chorus 4.

This three-and-a-half minute stretch is the only instance of the blues on *Time Out*. This sparseness is a bit surprising, given the centrality of the blues within Brubeck's *oeuvre*—especially in the subsequent "time" albums. The blues were important throughout Brubeck's career. For instance, he recorded W. C. Handy's "St. Louis Blues" (1914) more than a dozen times in the three decades from *Jazz Goes to Junior College* (Columbia CL 1034; May 2, 1957 at Long Beach Junior College in California) to *Moscow Night* (Concord Jazz CJ-353; March 1987 at the Rossiya Concert Hall in Moscow).

Handy's famous tune had always been a favorite of Brubeck's. But it took on new significance at nearly the exact moment when "Blue Rondo à la Turk" was conceived, and it seems to have played a role in the genesis of Brubeck's composition. In an interview with Ralph Gleason four years after the 1958 tour, Brubeck mentioned that "St. Louis Blues" was "one of the things that they understood in almost every country. W. C. Handy had just passed away, and of course the jazz world was well aware of his passing and well aware of the wonderful blues he had written for jazz. So we played that throughout.... They knew about Handy in every country we were in."[18]

Handy died on March 28, 1958. That was also the day of Brubeck's last concerts in Istanbul, before he left Turkey for India. It would therefore have been very near to the time when Brubeck heard the street musicians in Istanbul playing in the *aksak* meter, after which a Turkish colleague is said to have commented, "It is equivalent to your playing the blues."[19] On some level, then—whether consciously or unconsciously—the news of the demise of the "Father of the Blues" must have combined with the cross-cultural analogy between *aksak* and blues to galvanize Brubeck's creative work on "Blue Rondo à la Turk."

---

17 *Time Out, The Dave Brubeck Quartet, 50th Anniversary Edition, Piano Solos* (Van Nuys, CA: Alfred Music Publishing Co., 2009), 20–21. Unfortunately, Howard Brubeck's fine work is not acknowledged in this reprint. The 1962 edition, however, distributed by Hansen, announces on the title page that it was "transcribed from the Columbia recordings, and edited by Howard Brubeck."

18 Dave Brubeck, interview with Ralph Gleason (KQED-TV, San Francisco), January 14, 1962 (Brubeck Collection).

19 Dave Brubeck, "A Time to Remember" (unpublished autobiography, coauthored with Iola Brubeck).

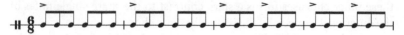

"WATUSI DRUMS" BECOMES "PICK UP STICKS"

Morello, Wright, and Brubeck were likely still experimenting with "Watusi Drums" in F on the evening of June 25, and "Pick Up Sticks" wasn't recorded until August 18. As a result, we simply don't know exactly when and how "Watusi Drums" morphed into "Pick Up Sticks." Even though "Pick Up Sticks" is more familiar, by virtue of its inclusion on the famous *Time Out* album, much more is known about the origins and recording history of "Watusi Drums."

A long rendition of "Watusi Drums" (more than eight minutes) appeared on the Quartet's *In Europe* album (Columbia CL 1168), which was recorded in Copenhagen on March 4, 1958.[20] This live performance begins with solo drums, about thirty seconds of continuous eighth notes, predominantly in groups of three (and sometimes two) and ending with the accentuation pattern shown in Example 6.4. Thereupon, the bass plays the ostinato four times in a row—but in Bb, like "Pick Up Sticks," rather than in F—while Morello articulates a pattern on the cymbals that produces a three-against-two rhythm. The next four iterations of the ostinato are punctuated by a saxophone wail consisting of three notes (d″ bb′ ab′) that are heard three times. When Brubeck finally enters, he plays with both hands in unison a tune very similar to the one in F major from the *Time Out* session more than a year later, on June 25, 1959 (Example 5.9). The earlier version from the live album (Example 6.5) is simpler, lacking the upward leap on the downbeat of m. 9, and repeating in mm. 23–28 the motive from m. 5 rather than forging a new one. After more than five minutes of stupendous solo drum work, Morello signals the end of his improvisation by repeating the same "square" rhythmic pattern as was heard at the beginning (Example 6.4). The next two segments are familiar as well, although Desmond sits out, and therefore the brief passage with the saxophone is missing this time. After Wright plays the ostinato four times with Morello, Brubeck joins them, playing exactly the same passage as before (Example 6.5).

20 See Chapter 2, note 57.

Although this cut might well have ended there, Morello gets the last word, with another thirty seconds of solo drumming.

When all is said and done, Desmond plays a total of only nine notes in this performance, and Wright and Brubeck only forty-five and thirty-five seconds at the beginning and end, respectively, while Morello is continuously active throughout the entire track. This emphasis on percussion is reflected in the tune's title, which underwent its own evolution, as Brubeck explained in the album's liner notes:

> Just before we left on tour [January 1958] I had written a number for Joe Morello, based on rhythmic ideas I had heard ten years before on an African recording. We originally called it "Drums Along the Thames," because it was first performed in London at the Royal Festival Hall which is on the Thames. When we went to Poland [March 1958] it became "Drums Along the Oder" or the "Vistula" or whatever river happened to be running near the town. Later, in Iraq [May 1958] I heard the same recordings from Africa I had heard years before, and discovered the source—the Watusi tribe. So we changed titles to give credit where credit is due.[21]

A couple of passages from Brubeck's autobiography fill in some additional details about the recordings of African music that inspired "Watusi Drums." Brubeck mentions that the tune's original title became a running joke, and that it was a reference to the 1939 film *Drums along the Mohawk,* set during the American Revolutionary War and starring Henry Fonda. According to Jean Jawdat, whose recollections Brubeck quotes at length, her brother-in-law Nizar (who died in Washington, DC, in 2017, at the age of ninety-six) and his wife Ellen hosted Brubeck for lunch at their home after his performances in Baghdad in May 1958. During this visit, "Nizar played for Dave a rare recording of Watusi tribe drums that . . . Roosevelt had made . . . Dave jumped to his feet and explained that he had heard this recording somewhere but didn't know what it was and that he had written a piece based on the rhythms." Elsewhere, Brubeck describes it more specifically as "a Denis-Roosevelt field recording."[22]

The project originated in the mid-1930s, when the Belgian documentary filmmaker Armand Denis (1896–1971) and his wife Leila Roosevelt

---

21 Liner notes, The Dave Brubeck Quartet, *In Europe,* Columbia CL 1168, 1958, 33⅓ rpm.
22 Brubeck, "Time to Remember."

(1906–1976)—daughter of André Roosevelt (1879–1962), a distant cousin of US President Theodore Roosevelt—traveled to the Belgian Congo (now the Democratic Republic of the Congo) in Central Africa for what was known as the Denis-Roosevelt Expedition. Their primary purpose was to shoot footage for films such as *Wheels across Africa* (1936) and *Dark Rapture* (1938). But soundtracks of the music of the Mangbetu, Tutsi (Watusi), and other peoples were also released as commercial recordings.[23] The track that most closely matches Morello's drum patterns in "Watusi Drums" is a three-minute selection titled "Royal Watusi Drums III."

This level of specificity about "Watusi Drums" is in stark contrast to the relative obscurity concerning the origins of "Pick Up Sticks." When Russell Gloyd interviewed Brubeck many years later, in September 2003, and asked him to say the first thing that came to his mind, Brubeck initially made the obvious connection between the tune's title and Joe Morello's drum sticks. But he then went on to situate it in relation to an ongoing dispute within the group: "I don't know why I called it that. Might be an inside joke, because Paul [Desmond] did not want Joe to play with sticks, because he wanted Joe to play softly, with brushes. And that argument was going on at that time, when I wrote 'Pick Up Sticks.'"[24]

Time Out was the end of the road for "Pick Up Sticks." Never again did the Quartet record it, despite outsized critical acclaim that it was "probably the most striking piece of music of its kind ever written" and it "transcends even the vague boundaries of modern jazz."[25] "Watusi Drums," on the other hand, not only was recorded more than a year

---

23 See Alan P. Merriam's review of the LP reissue of *The Belgian Congo Records: Primitive African Music, Stirring Rhythms and Unusual Melodic Tunes as Played and Sung by the People of the Great Equatorial Forest*, Denis-Roosevelt Expedition 1935–1936, in *Ethnomusicology* 7 (1963): 57–58. Also Martin A. Totusek, "Dave Brubeck: Interview [Seattle, May 21, 1993]," *Cadence* 20, no. 12 (December 1994): 15. Brubeck said, "I used to rent that recording from the record store. I was too poor to be able to buy it, so I'd save whatever I could and rent it as often as I could. This was back in '46, when I started the Octet. Right then I knew that jazz didn't reflect Africa hardly at all, that we were only using a little of it. This music was so complicated rhythmically by comparison. I used to tell jazz players that they needed to think about what came from Africa, instead of just thinking about what came from mostly western Europe."

24 "Dave Brubeck on *Time Out*."

25 "Dave Brubeck Pointer to New Jazz Form," *The Age* [Melbourne, Australia], March 11–17, 1960.

before "Pick Up Sticks," but it also appeared on two additional Brubeck albums during the 1960s and made it into print before "Pick Up Sticks."

"Watusi Drums" (in B♭) is the last of seven tunes that were edited by Howard Brubeck and published in 1960. The other six are associated with countries in Europe and Asia—Afghanistan, Germany, Turkey, Poland, England, and India—and their "themes were used as the basis for improvisation" on *Jazz Impressions of Eurasia* (Columbia CL 1251, 1958).[26] The geographical location assigned to "Watusi Drums" was the continent of Africa, rather than a specific country.[27] Beneath the heading "Africa" at the bottom of the page is the verbatim text of Brubeck's liner notes, quoted earlier, and the copyright date is listed as 1958. The tempo marking at the beginning indicates that it is to be played "like a work song"—a matter to be borne in mind when we examine the tune's brief appearance toward the end of *The Real Ambassadors*. In a moment of flippancy, the score also includes the following direction: "For improvisation, repeat 1st twelve bars until happy." Howard's prefatory comments at the beginning of the volume mention his own arrangement of "Brandenburg Gate" (the tune inspired by Germany) for "full orchestra and jazz combo," which was recorded and appeared on *Brandenburg Gate: Revisited* (Columbia CL 1963, 1963). He also refers to an arrangement of "Watusi Drums," "set for chorus," which may not have seen the light of day.[28]

It is possible, however, that Howard was speaking instead about a one-minute interlude in *The Real Ambassadors*, which was recorded in New York on September 12, 1961. The musical's finale begins with "Swing Bells," in which Lambert, Hendricks & Ross give voice to its utopian vision of universal civil rights:

Swing bells, ring bells!
The great day may now begin.
Ring out the new.
The world can laugh again.

26 Dave Brubeck, *Themes from Eurasia*, edited by Howard Brubeck (Delaware Water Gap, PA: Shawnee Press, 1960).

27 This seems strange for a volume titled *Themes from Eurasia*. But apparently it was included because "Watusi Drums" had appeared on the *In Europe* album (Columbia CL 1168), which was recorded in Denmark.

28 According to Nancy Wade, Brubeck's goddaughter and the person most knowledgeable about his choral music, it "was never arranged for chorus. It was probably one of those things that was 'a good thought,' but never happened." Nancy Wade, email message to author, August 15, 2014.

This day we're free.
We're equal in ev'ry way.
Ring bells, swing bells!
Declare a holiday.

After Louis Armstrong expresses his misgivings about the success of this project, the vocal trio encourages him with upbeat music. Among other things, they sing, "What are you waiting for? Blow, Satchmo! Make that trumpet roar!" After a passage dripping with Biblical imagery, including the story of Joshua bringing down the walls of Jericho with trumpet blasts, they finally ask, "Can it really be that you'll set all people free?" At this point (around 3:40), the music slows down and shifts to compound meter for a three-stanza interlude, in which the following religiously tinged words are sung to the "Watusi Drums" theme (in F):

Been waitin' so long, Lord!
How long will it be?
Been waitin' so long, Lord!
An eternity.
Been waitin' so long, Lord!
Will we ever see
The day that we long for,
The day we'll be free!
The day we'll be free!
The day we'll be free!
The day we'll be free!

So heavy the load, Lord!
Oh, help us to pray!
So heavy the load, Lord!
Oh, don't let us stray!
So heavy the load, Lord!
The sky's lookin' grey
Oh, lift up the load, Lord,
And show us the way,
And show us the way,
And show us the way,
And show us the way.

We're goin' to heaven,
We're goin' to fly.
We're goin' to heaven,

Way up in the sky.
We're goin' to heaven.
Oh, sweet by and by.
And we will be free, Lord,
The day that we die,
The day that we die,
The day that we die,
The day that we die.

This portion of the finale is also punctuated with repeated exclamations of the imperative "Work!"—which recalls the indication "like a work song" in the sheet music. Immediately thereafter, there is a return to the "Blow Satchmo" music, but this time Armstrong plays his trumpet, as the embodiment of this eschatological scenario.[29]

"TAKE FIVE" IN THE USSR

A live rendition of "Take Five" was recorded in Moscow in March 1987, nearly thirty years after *Time Out*.[30] As the Cold War was coming to a close, Brubeck was finally able to achieve his long-held goal of performing in the Soviet Union, with thirteen concerts in Moscow, Tallinn, and Leningrad over a two-week period.[31] The personnel on this recording were different (other than Brubeck, of course), as were two of the instruments. The drummer was Randy Jones, a British musician who joined the Quartet in 1979 and remained with the group until Brubeck's death in 2012.[32] Dave's thirty-five-year-old son Chris played the electric bass—which lent a distinctive (and funkier) timbre to this outing,

29 Although not nearly as complicated, the "Pick Up Sticks"—"Watusi Drums"—"Swing Bells" conglomeration illustrates the same facet of Brubeck's compositional process—the tendency to reuse material in multiple contexts—as his later "Jazzanians," whose five versions from 1987 through 2003 have recently been traced in painstaking detail. See Vasil Cvetkov, "Dave Brubeck's Definitive 'Jazzanians,'" *Journal of Jazz Studies* 9 (2013): 53–93.

30 Dave Brubeck, *Moscow Night,* Concord Jazz CCD-4353, 1988, compact disc.

31 A detailed account of Brubeck's performances in the Soviet Union in 1987 and 1988, and the events leading up to them, is provided in Stephen A. Crist, "Jazz as Democracy? Dave Brubeck and Cold War Politics," *Journal of Musicology* 26 (2009): 162–173.

32 Several sources, including Randy Jones's own obituary, published in the *New York Times* on June 26, 2016, report that he joined the Dave Brubeck Quartet in 1978. But, according to Russell Gloyd, who served as Dave's manager for many years and was part of the Brubeck organization for nearly forty years (1976–2015), Jones "was first with Dave in April of 1979." Russell Gloyd, email message to author, June 27, 2016.

as compared with the upright bass. Instead of a saxophonist, Brubeck brought along Bill Smith to play the clarinet.

The order of events in this version is generally unexceptional. Instead of the usual beginning with the drums, Brubeck leads off with the piano vamp (four bars), to which the bass and drums are added (four bars). The head is played by the clarinet instead of a saxophone, but it is otherwise intact (8+8+8). The core of the performance is comprised of a three-minute clarinet solo and a two-minute piano solo. Thereafter, a four-bar vamp (with all three instruments of the rhythm section) is followed by another complete statement of the head. It is extended by the regular nine-bar coda—which is spiced up, however, by an exuberant, over-the-top cadenza in which all four musicians improvise at once. The clarinet's high notes at the very end are especially wild.

Smith's intelligent and well-wrought solo is quite amazing. He spins out countless fresh ideas over the course of just a few minutes, all the while remaining firmly anchored in the same modal soundscape that Desmond had first used back in 1959. The real surprise, however, comes with the beginning of Brubeck's piano solo, which takes a sudden turn toward the parallel major and quotes the lyrical second theme from the first movement of Shostakovich's Fifth Symphony. Brubeck was just as surprised about this as anyone: "I had never played it before. I can't explain why. It just came out of that moment."[33] In an interview a few years later, he marveled at that solo: "You respond to your surroundings, and your mind will float at things you can't believe. It's the wonderful mystery of music and especially jazz and improvisation. You don't know what's going to happen from one bar to the next."[34] An experience that may have primed the pump was the Quartet's visit to the Union of Composers in Moscow. As Brubeck later recalled, "The Union was so filled with nostalgia for us; we felt a deep sense of reverence. I remember the room in which we had tea had pictures on the wall of Shostakovich, Khachaturian, and Prokofiev."[35]

Brubeck's quotation is astonishingly close to the original, especially for a spontaneous inspiration (see Examples 6.6a and 6.6b). A few of the pitches are different, but it is in the same key, and the outlines are sharp enough to be clearly recognizable.

It is worth considering, then, how this allusion by an American jazz musician to a well-known theme from a veritable staple of the Soviet

33 Brubeck, "Time to Remember."
34 Michael Bourne, "Dave Brubeck at 70," Down Beat 58, no. 3 (March 1991): 21.
35 Burt Korall, "Dave Brubeck: Ambassador of Jazz," BMI MusicWorld (Winter 1989): 17–18.

EXAMPLE 6.6A. Paul Desmond, "Take Five," excerpt from piano chorus (Dave Brubeck) at live concert in Moscow in March 1987, with allusion to Shostakovich theme, transcription.

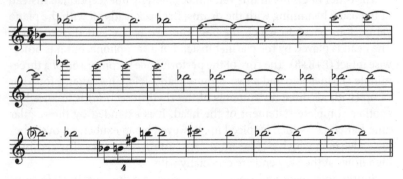

EXAMPLE 6.6B. Second theme from first movement of Shostakovich's Fifth Symphony.

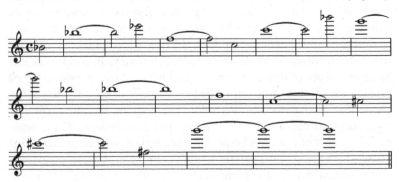

orchestral repertoire might have been understood by the audience in Moscow in 1987. Brubeck's manager, Russell Gloyd, viewed it as a political statement, uttered in the waning days of the Cold War: "Everything at that time in the Soviet Union was innuendo, with double meanings everywhere. Shostakovich's Fifth Symphony was his answer to Stalin, who had criticized Shostakovich's *Lady Macbeth [of the Mtsensk District]* opera. Shostakovich's answer was that artists must have their freedom. The Soviet audience knows this, and here's Dave playing this statement about needing freedom."[36]

36 John Soeder, "Brubeck's Still Calling His Own Tune," *Cleveland Plain Dealer*, May 31, 2009.

It is not out of the question that Brubeck intended his Shostakovich quotation as a subversive commentary on Soviet politics and a clarion call for basic human rights. That would certainly have been in line with his personal beliefs and commitments. But it seems unlikely that Brubeck spontaneously made that connection—or, frankly, that he was even aware of the Fifth Symphony's historic role as a response to Stalin's criticisms in the 1930s.[37] There is, moreover, reason to wonder whether the audience members in Moscow would have perceived the Shostakovich melody that way. Peter Schmelz provides a thoughtful alternative:

It's certainly possible that [Brubeck] had something like that in mind in playing [the Shostakovich quotation], especially given the political climate. To my mind, the lyrical second theme of the first movement [of the Fifth Symphony] is less politically loaded than the first theme (or a theme from the second or fourth movements). In any case, I bet the Russians just heard the reference as a sign of respect to Shostakovich and to them—an acknowledgement of a shared cultural touchstone. From what I can tell, the Russians were more fixated on the "musical" elements of foreign performances, rather than any political agenda of the performers or their sponsors. This was the case during Bernstein's 1959 visit to the USSR with the New York Philharmonic, for example.[38]

Either way, this moment in 1987 unexpectedly brought together two very different musical worlds to effect a powerful synthesis of jazz and symphonic music.

37 Though Brubeck's auditory memory and artistic creativity were prodigious, on numerous occasions when I pressed him for details about specific pieces, I discovered that he didn't know their titles or the circumstances of their composition. My first experience along those lines was a personal interview at Brubeck's home in Wilton, Connecticut, in April 1998—some of which was incorporated into my essay on "The Role and Meaning of the Bach Chorale in the Music of Dave Brubeck," in *Bach in America*, Bach Perspectives 5, ed. Stephen A. Crist (Urbana and Chicago: University of Illinois Press, 2003), 179–215.
38 Peter Schmelz, email message to author, February 23, 2015. On the 1959 New York Philharmonic tour to the USSR—which, coincidentally, began in Moscow on August 22, just four days after the last *Time Out* recording session—see Peter J. Schmelz, "'Shostakovich' Fights the Cold War: Reflections from Great to Small," *Journal of Musicological Research* 34 (2015): 110–117, 126–138.

CHAPTER 7

MUSIC AND LYRICS

TIME OUT IS a purely instrumental album. But several of its cuts either originated as songs or were later supplied with words. In fact, two singers—Claude Nougaro in the 1960s and Al Jarreau in the 1970s and 1980s—rose to fame largely on the basis of their vocal renditions of tunes from *Time Out*.

THE INTERDEPENDENCE OF "EVERYBODY'S JUMPIN'" AND "EVERYBODY'S COMIN'"

Among the manuscript source materials in the Brubeck Collection, the titles "Everybody's Jumpin'" and "Everybody's Comin'" are used more or less interchangeably. This exchange reflects the parallel genesis of the instrumental version for the *Time Out* album and the song for *The Real Ambassadors*.

At the top of the earliest sketch leaf, which includes the initial ideas for both main components of the theme, Brubeck wrote "EVRY Body's Comin" (see Figure 7.1). Although his manuscripts usually do not include

FIGURE 7.1.   Dave Brubeck, "Everybody's Comin," pencil sketches, autograph.
Brubeck Collection, Holt-Atherton Special Collections, University of the Pacific Library.
© Dave Brubeck.

chronological information, this page bears the date of January 21, 1959—a Wednesday, just before Brubeck traveled East for a few days.[1] It seems likely that the date refers to the more fully worked out version, beginning on the third stave, rather than to the one at the top. The initial idea consisted of a succession of eighth notes, the first four of which simply arpeggiate a major-minor seventh chord on C, before articulating the third and fifth of an F-major triad. Brubeck was clearly dissatisfied, because he entered a directive to himself: "Change theme." After the date, and above the revised version, which introduces some chromaticism and is essentially the same tune he recorded later that summer, Brubeck wrote, "This is better." He also noted the "surprise change of key with E♭," beginning in m. 5 (i.e., the passage in flat three). In all cases, the rhythms in the sketch are notated in straight eighth notes rather than the dotted figures of subsequent versions. The passage in A♭ is also rendered in 4/4 rather than its eventual 3/2 meter. Finally, the sketch includes at the bottom an inverted form of the initial motive, which didn't make it into the final composition.

The more than thirty pages of materials pertaining to the composition and performance of "Everybody's Jumpin'" include six that, taken together, match the recording on *Time Out*. (They are not in order, and only the first four pages are numbered, but the remaining two connect seamlessly.) Judging from the scrawly handwriting and the large number of corrections, this document constitutes Brubeck's composing score. The title is given on page 1 as "Everybody's Coming" (see Figure 7.2) and on page 3 (not pictured here) as "Everybody's Jumpin'." Brubeck apparently envisioned it as a potential vocal composition from very early on. At the top of the first page, he wrote, "These scorings could be used for chorus too," and he even added a specific potential performing organization, the "S.M.U. chorus." In this connection, it is worth noting that Brubeck's business papers reveal close connections with Southern Methodist University in Dallas around this time, specifically two concerts there in February 1961 and March 1962.

The initial lines of the lyrics in the first draft are rather drab: "Ev'rybody's comin', ev'rybody's comin'. Sent the invitations out, got the confirmations back." But, interestingly, the exclamations that eventually were sung by Louis Armstrong as "Yes, yes!" originally had religious overtones: "Yes, Lord" and "Praise, Lord." This use suggests the possibility that Brubeck had in mind the sonorities of a gospel choir as backup. Moreover, this early version had a pointedly political tone:

---

1 See Chapter 3, note 39.

FIGURE 7.2. Dave Brubeck, "Everybody's Comin'," composing score, autograph, page 1. Brubeck Collection, Holt-Atherton Special Collections, University of the Pacific Library. © Dave Brubeck.

Nasser is a'comin'
Nehru is a'comin'
Herter is a'comin'
Kruschev [sic] is a'comin'

The individuals named here include Gamal Abdel Nasser (1918–1970) of Egypt, Jawaharlal Nehru (1889–1964) of India, Nikita Khrushchev (1894–1971) of the Soviet Union, and Christian Herter (1895–1966), who served as the US Secretary of State under Dwight Eisenhower, from April 1959 until January 1961—in short, four of the most powerful world leaders of the time. The lyrics then assert optimistically, "Ev'rybody's comin' here / Ev'ry nation will appear / These nobody needs to fear," and they enjoin the listener to "Shout the good news loud & clear."

The last page of his composing score (Figure 7.3) includes the changes for Desmond's and Brubeck's own choruses, along with the following explanation: "Paul & Dave play choruses—After Dave Drum Solo exact melody solo with drum marcking [sic] cadence." This instruction brings to mind Brubeck's remark in a 2003 interview, that "Everybody's Jumpin'" was written "largely with Joe Morello in mind. . . . Joe's the one that's featured on that tune."[2] Following Morello's solo, Brubeck's score directs, "Back to beginning very soft repeat 1st 12 bars." The notated ending encapsulates the essence of what the Quartet recorded, but it is slightly shorter (just ten bars, rather than twelve).

A next stop in the creation of this number is captured in two pages from a yellow spiral manuscript book in a folder that is dated "c. 1959" and marked "Howard and Dave's Sketchbook". The melody provided there matches the lead sheets and recording of *The Real Ambassadors*, but the lyrics are different from the version in the composing score. They are a bit more sophisticated and more overtly oriented toward themes of social justice:

Ev'rybody's coming, ev'rybody's coming
Freedom's cause we're goin' to plead
Ev'ry color, ev'ry creed
Just one day is all we need
Stop this world from sin and greed

2 Dave Brubeck, raw interview audio with Russell Gloyd concerning the album *Time Out,* September 12, 2003 (Brubeck Collection).

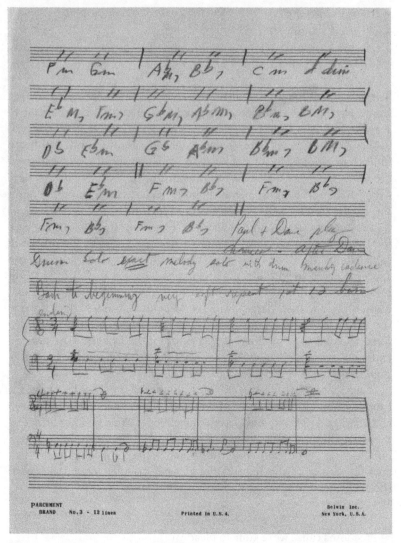

FIGURE 7.3. Dave Brubeck, "Everybody's Comin'," composing score, autograph, page 4.
Brubeck Collection, Holt-Atherton Special Collections, University of the Pacific Library.
© Dave Brubeck.

The list of leaders said to be "a coming" still includes Nasser, Nehru, and Khrushchev. But the US representative has been changed from Herter to "Kennedy," which implies that this pencil draft originated sometime after John F. Kennedy's inauguration on January 20, 1961, and not as early as 1959.

Brubeck's inability to mount *The Real Ambassadors* on Broadway, despite his assiduous efforts, surely ranks as one of the most calamitous setbacks of his career. In the end, the show was performed only once, in a truncated and unstaged version, on September 23, 1962, during the Monterey Jazz Festival in California. A chief reason for the consistently chilly response from Broadway producers was the musical's engagement with issues of civil rights and its critique of governmental policies. In short, its content was considered to be too politically charged.[3]

If one compares the final version of the lyrics for "Everybody's Comin,'" as heard on *The Real Ambassadors* album (Columbia OL 5850) and as found in a manuscript lead sheet in the Brubeck Collection, it seems clear that Dave and Iola Brubeck made some efforts to tone down the show's rhetoric. Instead of the politicians mentioned above, the song introduces the participating musicians:

Ev'rybody's comin'
Ev'rybody's comin'
Ev'rybody's comin' here
Louis Armstrong will appear
Carmen's promised she will sing
Brubeck's combo's gonna swing
Ev'rybody's comin'
Ev'rybody's comin'

Louis is a-comin'
Carmen is a-comin',
Brubeck is a-comin'
Lambert is a-comin'
Hendricks a-comin' and
Ross is a-comin' and

3 See Penny M. Von Eschen, "*The Real Ambassadors*," in *Uptown Conversation: The New Jazz Studies*, ed. Robert G. O'Meally, Brent Hayes Edwards, and Farah Jasmine Griffin (New York: Columbia University Press, 2004), 189–203. An abbreviated version of this material also appears in Penny M. Von Eschen, *Satchmo Blows Up the World: Jazz Ambassadors Play the Cold War* (Cambridge, MA, and London: Harvard University Press, 2004), 79–91.

Trummy's a-comin'
Morello's a-comin' and

Ev'rybody's comin'
Ev'rybody's comin'
Lambert, Hendricks, Annie Ross
Nothing throws them for a loss
Louis play that trumpet call
Come on join us have a ball

Ev'rybody's comin'
Ev'rybody's comin'
Louis is a-comin'
Carmen is a-comin'
Brubeck is a-comin'
Lambert is a-comin'
Hendricks a-comin' and
Ross is a-comin' and
Trummy's a-comin' and
Gene Wright's a-comin' and

Ev'rybody's comin'
Ev'rybody's comin'
Now's the time to sing and shout
Something bells can ring about
Ev'rybody's turning out
Swingers all without a doubt
Louis is a-comin'
Carmen is a-comin'

Brubeck is a-comin'
Lambert is a-comin'
Hendricks is a-comin'
Annie is a-comin'

Ev'rybody's comin'
Ev'rybody's comin'
Ev'rybody's comin'
Ev'rybody's comin'
Let's go!

The nine individuals named include the lead singers Louis Armstrong
and Carmen McRae; the vocal trio of Dave Lambert, Jon Hendricks,

and Annie Ross (known as Lambert, Hendricks & Ross); Dave Brubeck and two members of his combo, Joe Morello and Eugene Wright (Paul Desmond didn't participate in the project); and Trummy Young, a trombonist in the group known as Louis Armstrong and His All Stars.

The remaining manuscript sources include a couple of bass parts and several duplicate lead sheets. There is also a piano-vocal score in an unknown hand, which must have had a role in the live performance in Monterey. For the most part, the lyrics match those in the lead sheets and on the commercial recording. But in the lines where Annie Ross had been mentioned, the name of her substitute—Yolande Bavan—was penciled in, along with another minor adjustment:

. . . Hendricks a-comin' and	. . . Hendricks a-comin' Ba-
Ross is a-comin' and . . .	van is a-comin' and . . .
Lambert, Henricks, Annie Ross	Lambert, Hendricks, and Bavan
Nothing throws them for a loss . . .	Sing you words to think upon . . .

The cause of these modest revisions was Ross's addiction to heroin, and her decision to remain in London in May 1962 to kick the habit.[4] Ross's replacement for the September 1962 concert in Monterey was the twenty-year-old Bavan from Sri Lanka (formerly Ceylon).[5]

"STRANGE MEADOW LARK" AS A SONG

The version of "Strange Meadow Lark" in the publisher's manuscript lead sheet (copyright date of 1961) is in B♭ major, a fourth lower than the recording on *Time Out*. Moreover, it includes the following set of lyrics, credited to Iola Brubeck:

What a strange meadowlark
To be singing oh so sweetly in the park
Tonight!
All alone, meadowlark?
Are you dreaming of the moons that burned so bright?
And of love in flight?

Can't you sleep, meadowlark?
Is there nothing left but whistling in the dark,

---

4 James Gavin, "A Free-Spirited Survivor Lands on Her Feet," *New York Times*, October 3, 1993.
5 "Lambert, Hendricks Add Ceylonese Beauty to Trio," *Jet* 22, no. 6 (May 31, 1962): 65.

So sad?
Is it love, meadowlark?
Were the songs you sang last summer crazy mad?
Think of all you had:

A quiet nest up in the clouds,
Where the soft winds blow,
Far from all the noisy crowds,
Where the earthbound go.
Your wings have brushed against a star.
Boundless are the skies.
You may have flown too high too far.
Love is seldom wise.

Don't you see, meadowlark?
Tho' you try, your call won't turn another lark
In flight.
He has gone, meadowlark.
You can sing your song until the dawn brings light.
Sing with all your might!
Sing away the dark.
Little meadowlark.
Meadowlark, meadowlark.

These words are not especially profound, but they are certainly competent and entirely in keeping with the norms of popular song in jazz around 1960. At the heart of this ballad is an auditory image, the sound of a specific type of bird singing at night. After the first sentence, the balance of the poem is in the second person, addressed to an anthropomorphized meadowlark. The words of the bridge ("A quiet nest up in the clouds," and so forth) evoke nostalgia for budding love during a previous summer. But since then, the lark's mate has flown away, leaving her to sing of her sadness.

This conceit was apparently part and parcel of the original conception of the song, for words along these lines are found in the earliest compositional sketches (see pages 1–3 of Figure 4.5 and Example 4.26). The lyrics, like the musical notation, are in Dave Brubeck's hand. This clue raises the possibility that he may have conceived the basic scenario and even some of the specific language, and Iola subsequently refined this raw material into its ultimate form. Given their unusually close working relationship, however, it is not out of the question that they wrote the song together and that the words in Dave's handwriting were dictated to him by Iola. Either way, the lyrics at this early stage are quite similar to the final version. Page 1 of the sketches has the following words, which are spoken directly to the bird and are intensely nostalgic, as was the case in the first dozen lines of the lead sheet version:

What a strange meadow lark,
What a time to be out there singing.
Don't you know it is time
To be gone, to be swiftly winging
To a far-off land?

Yet you stay, meadow lark,
To your past/home/love you are strongly clinging . . .

At the bottom of page 1 (visible in Figure 4.5, but not transcribed in Example 4.26) are these alternate lyrics, scrawled in Dave's cursive:

What a strange meadow lark,
What a time to be out singing in the dark,
So lonely.
What a strange meadow lark,
All alone, meadow lark,
Don't you know,
Are you grieved for a love that won't return
To you?

This incarnation makes explicit the nocturnal setting, and it intensifies the ballad's emotional content by stressing loneliness and grief.

The lyrics for the bridge on page 3 of the sketches are nearly identical to the final version. The only significant change was the substitution of lines ending with the rhyming words "skies" and "wise," instead of "fall" and "all."

Sketch	Lead sheet
Our wings have brushed against a star,	Your wings have brushed against a star.
And we've watched it fall.	Boundless are the skies.
Did we fly too high too far?	You may have flown too high too far.
Was it worth it all?	Love is seldom wise.

Similarly, page 2 of the sketches reveals that the ending originally included two additional lines ("Waiting in the dark / With a strange meadow lark"), which were subsequently expunged.

On September 9, 1960—fourteen months after the *Time Out* session (July 1, 1959)—the Dave Brubeck Quartet returned to Columbia's 30th Street Studio in New York to record "Strange Meadow Lark" again. They were joined this time by the jazz singer Carmen McRae, who sang a perky rendition of Iola Brubeck's lyrics.[6] This version is rather straightforward. After a five-bar instrumental introduction (piano, bass, and drums only), McRae sings through the entire tune. Near the end of A′, she raises the cadential pitch in m. 45 by a half step ("Sing with all your *might!*"), thereby ushering in a repeat of the bridge. This passage is performed as an instrumental solo—or, more precisely, as a piano solo, since Paul Desmond doesn't participate in this cut at all. McRae re-enters, as expected, at the beginning of A′ and sings straight through to the end.

The key of McRae's recording is neither E♭ major (*Time Out*) nor B♭ major (lead sheet), but F major. Its most distinctive feature, however, is its relatively brisk tempo—around 130 beats per minute, from start to finish. Not only are there no rubato sections—as at the beginning and end of the *Time Out* cut—but Brubeck's style of comping, generally syncopated and frequently staccato, creates a much lighter feel as well. The result of these interpretive decisions is a pleasant but relatively lightweight performance, only about one-third the length of the earlier instrumental version.

Early in 1961, before the Brubeck/McRae album was released, Iola Brubeck tried to interest Dinah Shore in singing her and her husband's songs. Shore was best known as host of *The Dinah Shore Chevy Show,* a popular variety television series that aired on NBC from 1956 until 1963. Iola included with her letter a copy of the Quartet's 1957 album *Jazz Impressions of the U.S.A.* (Columbia CL 984) and a tape recording of Carmen McRae singing three of their tunes, including "Strange Meadow Lark." Iola characterized "Strange Meadow Lark" as a "visual type song, which needs your type of ballad treatment," and she noted, somewhat disapprovingly, that "Carmen was obliged to sing it up tempo to suit the record requirements."

Iola's letter to Shore also contains a tantalizing clue about an aspect of "Strange Meadow Lark" that has remained hidden from view until quite recently. She mentioned "a verse, which she [Carmen McRae] did not use," but "which creates a mood and sets the scene."[7] None of the previous recordings included an extra verse, until the Brubecks' son

6 The Dave Brubeck Quartet, with guest star Carmen McRae, *Tonight Only!* Columbia CL ·1609, 1961, 33⅓ rpm.

7 Iola Brubeck to Dinah Shore, January 20, 1961 (Brubeck Collection).

EXAMPLE 7.1. Dave Brubeck (music) and Iola Brubeck (lyrics), "Strange Meadow Lark," minor-mode introduction (mm. 1–16).

Dan released a compilation of his parents' songs.[8] The arrangement of "Strange Meadow Lark" on this album—in yet another key, C major—begins with a minor-mode introduction (see Example 7.1). The haunting lyrics situate this vignette not only at night ("across a moonlit lake") but in the chilly season of autumn, and the lark's song is portrayed here as a signal of sadness, despair, and heartbreak.[9]

CARMEN MCRAE'S "TAKE FIVE"

Around the same time as the appearance of the "Take Five" instrumental single on pop charts in the United States and the United Kingdom, Brubeck

---

8 The Dan Brubeck Quartet, *Celebrating the Music and Lyrics of Dave & Iola Brubeck,* recorded live at The Cellar, Vancouver, BC, August 2013, Blue Forest Records BFR DB15001, 2015, compact disc. I am grateful to Catherine Brubeck Yaghsizian for calling this recording to my attention and kindly sending me a copy.

9 I appreciate the assistance of Adam Thomas, vocalist in The Dan Brubeck Quartet, and Dan Brubeck himself, in tracking down a chart that includes this introduction. Although the introductory verse apparently originated by no later than 1960, it didn't appear in print until nearly twenty years later, in *Dave Brubeck Anthology, Volume One: Song Book* (Miami Beach, FL: Hansen House, 1979). Many thanks as well to Richard Jeweler for his help in unraveling this mystery.

and others were making plans for a new version with lyrics. During the tour in England, Desmond wrote to his father, Emil Breitenfeld—a keyboardist, composer, and arranger—and invited him to set the tune to words: "Would you be interested in writing a set of sensational lyrics to 'Take Five'? They are desperately needed at the moment. I don't have any particularly interesting ideas myself and everybody is clustering around waving lyrics in my face. Especially Dave, which is a refreshing switch. But if I have one thing fixed firmly dead center in my mind, it's that this is not going to be another Brubeck song sung by Carmen McRae."[10] Desmond's father apparently didn't take him up on the offer, and things progressed in exactly the manner he had feared. Around the same time, Brubeck wrote to Teo Macero (on stationery from a hotel in Manchester, England): "I'm all ready to go with my lyric on 'Take Five,' but Paul is salty because he wants to write one himself. If he doesn't come up with one, I'm hoping to record mine in December. Get Carmen [McRae] and studio time. Tell Carmen to learn melody now."[11]

Brubeck did indeed record his new vocal version of "Take Five" with Carmen McRae, in Columbia's 30th Street Studio on December 15, 1961.[12] But they had already performed it live at Basin Street East three months earlier, and it was that rendition that eventually appeared on the *Take Five Live* album.[13] The words, which are credited to both Dave and Iola Brubeck in the manuscript lead sheet, comprise a typical love song in the form of a soliloquy:

10 Quoted in Doug Ramsey, *Take Five: The Public and Private Lives of Paul Desmond* (Seattle: Parkside Publications, 2005), 210.

11 Dave Brubeck to Teo Macero, undated (Macero Collection, box 7, folder 25).

12 Columbia Records, Artist Job Sheet, Job No. 64991, matrix no. CO 68565 (Sony Music Archives Library).

13 Columbia Records, Artist Job Sheet, Job No. 48583, September 6, 1961 (Sony Music Archives Library). The original "mastering instructions" document (Macero Collection, box 6, folder 21) reveals that Carmen McRae—Dave Brubeck, *Take Five—Recorded Live at Basin Street East* (Columbia CL 2316) was not released until spring 1965 (the ship date is March 22), even though some discographies list an earlier date. Only the single (Columbia 4-42292) appeared early in 1962. The date given at http://www.45cat.com/record/442292 (accessed March 15, 2018) is January 26, 1962. This information is corroborated by Brubeck's remark to his manager about "the single recording of 'Take Five' that Carmen and I have out." Dave Brubeck to Joe Glaser, February 6, 1962 (Brubeck Collection). Moreover, a couple of weeks later a gossip columnist mentioned, "Dave Brubeck's 'Take Five' took off into a hit-record orbit and now remarkably slick, fast lyrics have been added and Carmen McRae's record is worth even more of your ear-bending." Jack O'Brian, "More Courage Than Cohesion," *New York Journal-American*, February 19, 1962.

Won't you stop and take a little time out with me?
Just take five
Only five.
Stop your busy day and take the time out to see
I'm alive.
Just take five.
Though I'm going out of my way,
Just so I can pass by each day,
Not a single word do we say.
It's a pantomime and not a play.
Still I know our eyes often meet.
I feel tingles down to my feet,
When your smile that's much too discreet sends me on my way.
Wouldn't it be better not to be so polite?
You could offer a light.
Start a little conversation now, it's all right.
Just take five.
Just take five.
Just take five.[14]

McRae's interpretation is quite straightforward. The pace is fairly relaxed (about 160 beats per minute). She sings in G minor—a sixth lower than the instrumental original, and the key of the lead sheet.[15] Her only changes to the script are minimal: omission of lines 3 and 6 (which Desmond fills in with saxophone riffs), and two additional iterations of the final line, alternating between high and low octaves. Even with an eight-bar introduction, a sixteen-bar saxophone solo after her first time through the text, and a partial repeat, beginning with the bridge ("Though I'm going out of my way . . ."), the entire cut lasts only a bit over two minutes.

BRUBECK IN FRENCH

In 1965, the singer and songwriter Claude Nougaro (1929–2004)—for all intents and purposes, France's equivalent of Frank Sinatra—recorded as "À bout de souffle" a version of "Blue Rondo à la Turk."[16] After a brief

14 Paul Desmond, "Take Five," lead sheet with text by Dave and Iola Brubeck, undated (Brubeck Collection).
15 A short manuscript in Brubeck's hand, marked "Carmen's bass part," is also in G minor (Brubeck Collection).
16 Originally released in May 1965, as part of a four-song EP, Philips 437.050 BE; then included the next year on an LP, Philips P 77.865 L.

instrumental introduction, the music of the song follows Brubeck's composition rather closely. We hear the entire series of eight-bar rondo refrains and episodes (ABACADA = mm. 1–56), followed by the twenty-two-bar bridge section (mm. 57–78), and the first ten measures of the "hybrid" segment that toggles between 4/4 and 9/8 (mm. 79–88). This passage is followed by a shortened reprise, consisting of three iterations of the refrain, plus half of the first episode: A (mm. 1–8) [B] (mm. 11–12) A (mm. 1–8) A (mm. 1–8).

A much more striking aspect of the song, however, is the sheer number of words that are packed in and delivered in rapid-fire succession.

À bout de souffle	Breathless[17]
Quand j'ai rouvert les yeux	When I reopened my eyes,
Tout était sombre dans la chambre	everything was dark in the room.
J'entendais quelque part comme une sonnerie	I heard a phone ringing somewhere.
J'ai voulu bouger . . .	I wanted to move . . .
Aïe la douleur dans l'épaule droite tout à coup	Ouch! Pain in my right shoulder suddenly
Me coupa le souffle	took my breath away.
Une peur affreuse m'envahit	A dreadful fear engulfed me,
Et mon corps se couvrit de sueur	and my body was covered in sweat.
Toute ma mémoire me revint	It all came back to me:
Le hold-up, la fuite, les copains	*the robbery, the escape, my pals*
Qui se font descendre . . .	*who go down . . .*
J'suis blessé, mais je fonce et j'ai l'fric	*I'm wounded, but I hurry and I have the dough.*
Je glissai la main sous l'oreiller	I slid my hand under the pillow.
La mallette pleine de billets	The briefcase full of cash
Etait là, bien sage . . . deux cents briques! . . .	was there, smart move . . . twenty million francs![18] . . .

17 I'm very grateful to Lois Rosow for providing English translations of "À bout de souffle" and "Le jazz et la java."
18 Presumably "old francs," not the revalued ones of 1960: probably a hundred 1000-franc bills in a "brick" (http://www.languefrancaise.net/bob/detail.php?id=4496) (accessed March 14, 2018).

À bout de souffle	Breathless
Somme toute ça pouvait aller	All in all, it didn't go badly.
Mon esprit se mit à cavaler	My imagination started to run wild.
Sûre était ma planque chez Suzy	My hideout at Suzy's place was safe,
Et bientôt à nous deux la belle vie	and soon it would be the good life for the two of us—
Les palaces, le soleil, la mer bleue, toute la vie . . .	luxury hotels, the sun, the blue sea, all our lives . . .
Une radio s'est mise à déverser	A radio began to pour out
Un air de piano à tout casser	a terrific piano piece.
Je connaissais ce truc	I knew the thing:
C'était le Blue Rondo à la Turk	it was the Blue Rondo à la Turk.
Dave Brubeck jouait comme un fou	Dave Brubeck played like crazy,
Aussi vite que moi mettant les bouts	as fast as me skedaddling.
Soudain, la sonnerie du téléphone	Suddenly the ringing phone—
Mon coeur fit un bond	My heart leapt.
Je pris le récepteur	I took the receiver.
"Allô! C'est Suzy, ça fait deux fois que j'appelle	"Hello! It's Suzy, I've called twice."
—Qu'est-ce qu'il y a?	"What's up?"
—Y a un car de flics au coin de la rue	"There's a cop car on the corner."
Je restai sans voix, j'étais foutu	I stayed speechless; I was screwed.
—Il faut que tu files, me dit-elle	"You have to scoot," she said.
Descends pas, sauve-toi par les toits"	"Don't go down; escape over the rooftops."
Bon Dieu d'bon Dieu, bon Dieu d'bon Dieu	Oh my God, oh my God, oh my God!
Encore les flics, vite le fric	The cops again—[I grabbed] the loot quickly
Et puis l'escalier de service	and then took the service stairs
Quatre à quatre	Four at a time.
Un vasistas était ouvert sur les étoiles	A skylight opened onto the stars,
Et me revoilà faisant la malle	*And here I am clearing out again,*
Parmi les antennes de télé	*among the TV antennas.*

À bout de souffle

Ce pognon, je ne l'aurai pas volé

Trente mètres plus bas dans la rue
Du Colisée c'était la cohue
J'en peux plus, j'en peux plus . . .
J'ai couru comme dans un rêve le long
des cheminées
Haletant, la mallette à la main, je
vacillais . . .
Sur un toit s'amorçait un escalier
d'incendie
S'enfonçant tout au fond d'une cour
Je descendis jusqu'en bas
Et me voici à trois pas d'une sortie sur
la rue
Quelle rue, je ne le savais plus mais tant
pis
Je suis sorti et tout de suite je les ai vus

Quatre flics au bout de la rue
Pas de panique, j'ai reconnu le bar du
Living, j'y suis entré . . .
La boîte était pleine comme un oeuf
Deux ou trois jazzmen faisaient le boeuf
Je brûlais de fièvre, je voyais
Les murs, les bouteilles qui tournaient
Puis quelqu'un m'a saisi par le bras

J'me retournai, Suzy était là
Toute pâle elle me souriait
De nouveau le soleil a brillé
Dans un souffle elle me dit
Viens, j'ai la voiture tout près d'ici
Nous sommes sortis mais devant moi

Breathless

*This dough, I won't [get away with]
stealing it.*

Thirty meters below in the rue
du Colisée there was the crowd.
I can't go any further, I can't do it . . .
I ran as though in a dream along the
chimneys.
Panting, briefcase in hand, I staggered

On a roof a fire escape began,

Sinking to the depths of a courtyard.
I went down to the bottom,
and here I am three steps from an exit
to the street.
Which street I no longer knew, but
never mind,
I went out and immediately I saw
them:
Four cops at the end of the street.
No panic . . . I recognized the Bar du
Living, I entered . . .
The nightclub was chock-full.
Two or three jazzmen jammed.
I was burning with fever; I saw
the walls and bottles spinning—
then someone grabbed me by the
arm.
I turned; Suzy was there.
Her face ashen, she smiled at me.
The sun shone anew.
Very softly she said,
"Come, I have the car near here."
We went out, but right in front of me

À bout de souffle	Breathless
Un poulet a crié "Ne bouge pas!"	a cop shouted, "Don't move!"
Avec la mallette je l'ai frappé	I hit him with the briefcase.
Alors le coup de feu a claqué	Then the gunshot rang out,
Me clouant sur place	nailing me on the spot.
Oh Suzy, t'en fais pas	Oh Suzy, don't worry.
Je te suis, on y va	I'm following you, here we go:
Les palaces, le soleil, la mer bleue	Luxury hotels, the sun, the blue sea,
Toute la vie, toute la vie	all our lives, all our lives,
Toute la vie . . .	all our lives . . .

To sing all these words at a brisk tempo—as essentially a patter song in the jazz idiom—leaves one breathless indeed; hence the title. But *À bout de souffle* is also the name of a 1960 film directed by Jean-Luc Godard, in which a criminal kills a policeman, flees, and then is himself shot by the police. Though it differs in many details, the story in Nougaro's song covers the same basic themes, and it surely ought to be considered as a response to Godard's picture.[19]

"À bout de souffle" was preceded by "Le jazz et la java," which was closely modeled on "Three to Get Ready," but without proper attribution. By contrast with his grim takeoff on "Blue Rondo à la Turk," Nougaro's earlier effort, dating from 1962, is rather lighthearted. It pits a French social dance known as *la java* (essentially a fast and sensual waltz) against American jazz dance, in an imaginary rivalry.[20]

Le jazz et la java	Jazz and Java
Quand le jazz est là	When jazz is around,
La java s'en va	java leaves.
Il y a de l'orage dans l'air	There's [always] a storm brewing,
Il y a de l'eau dans le gaz	a fight on the way,
Entre le jazz et la java	between jazz and java.

19 Graeme Boone, email message to author, February 26, 2015.
20 "Le jazz et la java" appeared on Claude Nougaro, *Le Cinéma,* Philips B 76 559 R, 1962, 33⅓ rpm. A compilation of clips from European films of the 1920s and 1930s, demonstrating the *java* dance, is available on YouTube. Walter Nelson, "On Danse La Java," https://www.youtube.com/watch?v=ikRoyow8Jgw (accessed March 16, 2018).

Le jazz et la java	Jazz and Java
Chaque jour un peu plus	More and more every day
Y a le jazz qui s'installe	there is jazz settling in.
Alors la rage au coeur	So, rage in her heart,
La java fait la malle	java clears out.
Ses p'tit's fesses en bataille	Her little backside wiggling
Sous sa jupe fendue	under her slit skirt,
Elle écrase sa Gauloise	she stubs out her cigarette
Et s'en va dans la rue	and goes out in the street.
Quand le jazz est là . . .	
Quand j'écoute beat	When I listen to the beat of
Un solo de batterie	a drum solo,
V'là la java qui râle	there is java grumbling
Au nom de la patrie	in the name of patriotism.
Mais quand je crie bravo	But when I yell "bravo"
A l'accordéoniste	to the accordionist,
C'est le jazz qui m'engueule	it's jazz that berates me,
Me traitant de raciste	calling me a racist.
Quand le jazz est là . . .	
Pour moi jazz et java	For me, jazz and java,
C'est du pareil au même	it's six of one, half a dozen of the other.
J'me saoule à la Bastille	I get drunk at the Bastille
Et m'noircis à Harlem	and get hammered in Harlem.
Pour moi jazz et java	For me, jazz and java,
Dans le fond c'est tout comme	basically it's the same difference.
Le jazz dit "Go men"	Jazz says, "Go, men";
La java dit "Go hommes"	Java says, "Go, hommes."
Quand le jazz est là . . .	
Jazz et java copains	Jazz and java, buddies—
Ça doit pouvoir se faire	it ought to be possible
Pour qu'il en soit ainsi	to make it so.
Tiens, je partage en frère	Hey look, I share equally:
Je donne au jazz mes pieds	I give my feet to jazz
Pour marquer son tempo	to mark its tempo,

Le jazz et la java	Jazz and Java
Et je donne à la java mes mains	and I give my hands to java,
Pour le bas de son dos	[to caress] her lower back.

According to the information on the album cover, Nougaro penned these lyrics. Brubeck's contribution to the music, however, goes unacknowledged. It is credited instead to the French composer Jacques Datin (1920–1973), who supposedly based it on a classical theme in the public domain: "musique de J. Datin d'après un theme de J. Haydn" (music by J. Datin, after a theme by J. Haydn). Apparently Datin added the sixteen-bar tune in triple meter and in the parallel minor key, which is used for each of the four eight-line stanzas. But Brubeck's composition, including its signature alternation between triple and quadruple meter, constitutes the melody of the refrain, and it clearly formed the song's point of departure.

AL JARREAU'S BRUBECK GRAMMYS

The heyday of jazz singer Al Jarreau began in the mid-1970s, and Brubeck's music played a significant role in his success. He recorded a version of "Take Five" in 1977, and the album on which it appeared won a Grammy in 1978. Four years later, in 1982, Jarreau captured two more Grammy Awards: Best Pop Vocal Performance, Male, for the album *Breakin' Away,* which was also nominated for Album of the Year, and Best Jazz Vocal Performance, Male, for the cut "(Round, Round, Round) Blue Rondo à la Turk." Jarreau's rendition is astonishingly faithful to Brubeck's original, preserving its melody, harmony, and form up through the expected onset of the "hybrid" section (m. 79), where Jarreau launches straight into the blues instead. His improvised scat singing for the next couple of minutes is arguably its highlight. The lyrics for the rest of the song are rather insipid, especially by comparison with the dark and compelling tale told in Nougaro's "À bout de souffle." A representative sample will suffice:

> Round, round, round a melody,
> Round, round, round a harmony,
> Round, round, round a melody,
> Harmony, melody, steadily.
>
> Round, round, round a melody,
> Round, round, round a memory,
> Round, round, round a melody,
> Memory, melody, merrily . . .

Open up an opportunity.
Open up an offer. You will be
Truly happy and content with me.
Measure me, treasure me, pleasure me . . .

Here it comes, our symphony,
Measure by measure, a pleasure,
A melody and harmony,
You and me in harmony,
You and me so happy
We found a new rondo
To end the blue rondo today.

Jarreau's awards for "(Round, Round, Round) Blue Rondo à la Turk" and *Breakin' Away* were sequels to his 1978 Grammy (Best Jazz Vocal Album) for *Look to the Rainbow* (Warner Bros. 2BZ 3052), which was recorded live in Europe and featured his performance of "Take Five." Space limitations allow only a bare-bones treatment of this recording. During the first forty-five seconds of the album version (as opposed to the edited single), Jarreau mimics drum sounds, occasionally interspersing words (for instance, "Could you take a bit of time?" at 0:23). The band enters at 0:48, in the key of D minor. In addition to Jarreau's scat singing, and his otherwise percussive vocal style, the most arresting aspect of this rendition is the twofold modulation upward by half step (to E♭ minor at 2:16 and E minor at 3:03), then back down (to E♭ minor and D minor in rapid succession, at 3:53 and 3:59, respectively). Jarreau sings the original lyrics, though he embellishes them somewhat and his diction is much less distinct than Carmen McRae's.

Whether Paul Desmond was aware of Jarreau's success with his tune is difficult to say. Although it was recorded earlier in 1977, *Look to the Rainbow* was released on May 27—just three days before Desmond's untimely passing. Brubeck, on the other hand, was quite pleased with the renewed attention to his signature tune, and he even performed it with Jarreau twenty years later, at the John F. Kennedy Center for the Performing Arts in Washington, DC, for a national telecast.[21]

21 The television special, "A Celebration of America's Music," was broadcast on January 3, 1998, but recorded at least two months earlier. On November 3, 1997, Brubeck wrote a letter to Jarreau, which begins with the sentence "I still have a great feeling about our performance at the Kennedy Center." A copy of this letter and a videotape of the performance are held in the Brubeck Collection.

CHAPTER 8

RECORDED LEGACY

ONCE THE SEVEN cuts of *Time Out* had been committed to vinyl, there began a long period in which the Quartet revisited and reinterpreted this repertoire. Dave Brubeck continued to perform for more than fifty years after the album was released, and "Take Five" remained his invariable closing number. But the "classic" Quartet and its successors also recorded many new versions of most of the tunes on *Time Out,* with emphasis on the first five ("Everybody's Jumpin'" and "Pick Up Sticks" never received similar attention). Four of these pieces have also been recorded by a variety of other musicians, and several of the cover versions entail radical transformation of Brubeck's original ideas.

The "agenda of projects" for Howard Brubeck, Dave's brother, as it stood a few days after the 1959 performance of Howard's *Dialogues for Jazz Combo and Orchestra* with the Quartet and the New York Philharmonic at Carnegie Hall, included "score and parts for Turkish Rondo for recording," which he labeled as a "big job."[1] There is no evidence that his version of "Blue Rondo à la Turk" ever materialized. Dave Brubeck's longtime manager and producer, Russell Gloyd, told me he was not aware of any arrangement of "Blue Rondo à la Turk" by Howard Brubeck.[2] But it seems clear that, more than a month before the first *Time Out* recording session, Dave and Howard were already planning an album of arrangements for symphony orchestra and jazz combo that would begin with "Kathy's Waltz" and conclude with another selection from the same album, "Strange Meadow Lark." Howard's instrumentation for "Kathy's Waltz" included flute, oboe, and bassoon; pairs of clarinets, horns, trumpets, and trombones; plus strings (six first violins, four second violins, pairs of violas and cellos, and one bass).[3] According to Howard's liner notes for *Brandenburg Gate: Revisited* (Columbia CL 1963), the orchestral version "was first performed by the Cleveland Summer Orchestra in 1959." Therefore, the holograph score preserved in the Brubeck Collection—with the title "Cathy's Waltz," credit line "arranged by H. Brubeck," and instrumentation as just listed—must have been penned sometime during summer 1959.

It wasn't until a couple of years later, however, that Howard's arrangement finally was recorded. In March 1961, Howard sent Teo Macero a "list of material and required instrumentation" (including "Kathy's Waltz") at Dave's request "for possible recording."[4] In his jocular reply, Macero placed the blame for any delay squarely on Dave's shoulders, and set the expectation for a summer recording session:

1 Howard Brubeck to Dave Brubeck, December 17, 1959 (Brubeck Collection).
2 On the other hand, Gloyd conducted the symphonic version by Darius Brubeck, Dave's eldest son, at the Montreal International Jazz Festival in 1987. The Dave Brubeck Quartet, with the Montreal International Jazz Festival Orchestra, *New Wine*, MusicMasters 5051-2-C, 1990, compact disc. Russell Gloyd, email message to author, March 3, 2016.
3 Howard Brubeck to Dave and Iola Brubeck, August 26, 1959 (Brubeck Collection). Howard, who signs here with his family nickname "Peter," mentions that their initial discussions took place at Dave and Iola's home on May 10.
4 Howard Brubeck to Teo Macero, March 14, 1961 (Macero Collection, box 7, folder 17).

Everything seems to be quite clear. Only problem remaining is getting your brother off his fat scrafus. I can't seem to get him into the studio. I need help! help! help! However, I did have a lengthy conversation with Uncle Dave last week and he told me he had talked with you. Let me know when you will come East, as I would like to get some of these things recorded. Dave suggested, though, that we could do the big instrumentals this summer. What do you think about that? Personally, I would like to get them done as soon as possible.[5]

In June, Macero asked the president of Columbia Records for approval to record "several quartet albums and the quartet with a large orchestra."[6] The session took place in August, apparently in the middle of the night.[7] "Kathy's Waltz" was recorded first (under the matrix number CO 67947), followed by Dave's "Summer Song" and Howard's "G Flat Theme." When the album was finally released, more than two years later, in October 1963, "Kathy's Waltz" (still misspelled) was the closing number.

The orchestral arrangement of "Kathy's Waltz" lasts just three minutes, and it consists of a saccharine twelve-bar introduction, followed by five iterations of the thirty-six-bar tune: the head (to which Howard Brubeck added a hectic countermelody), one saxophone chorus, two piano choruses, and the head again. Even though the polymetric procedure is complicated somewhat by the presence of so many additional instruments, Brubeck switches to quadruple meter midway through his first chorus, as usual. Since all previous recordings conclude with a coda, it is worth noting that this rendition dispenses with it and ends with a thud. An undated review in Macero's files, apparently from *Down Beat* and attributed to "J.S.W." (presumably John S. Wilson), awarded *Brandenburg Gate: Revisited* three stars (out of five) and characterized its contents as "very pleasant performances in a sort of superior Roger Williams vein"—which seems about right.[8]

In November 1963, one month after the appearance of *Brandenburg Gate: Revisited*, the Beatles released their second studio album, *With the*

---

5 Teo Macero to Howard Brubeck, March 27, 1961 (Macero Collection, box 7, folder 17).
6 Teo Macero to Goddard Lieberson, June 7, 1961 (Macero Collection, box 7, folder 17).
7 Columbia Records, Artist Job Sheet, Job No. 60257 (Sony Music Archives Library). The time, date, and place of "The Dave Brubeck Quartet and Orchestra—Music arranged and conducted by Howard Brubeck" are given as "11:30 to 2:30 a.m." on August 21, 1961, in the 30th Street Studio. See also the two handwritten "Tape Identification Data" sheets, dated August 21, 1961 (Macero Collection, box 4, folder 19).
8 Macero Collection, box 4, folder 18.

Beatles (Parlophone PMC 1206). What does this have to do with Dave Brubeck? The answer, it seems, is in the eye of the beholder. The last phrase of "Kathy's Waltz" consists of the following scale degrees, in B♭ major: $\hat{4}$ $\hat{3}$ $\hat{2}$ $\hat{3}$ $\hat{4}$ $\hat{5}$ $\hat{6}$ $\hat{7}$ $\hat{8}$. As it turns out, this is the same pattern heard in the opening phrase of the album's third cut, Paul McCartney's "All My Loving" (albeit in E major rather than B♭). As a result, there has been some speculation about a possible connection between the two tunes.[9] The phrase in question, however, is not much more than an ascending scale leading to the tonic, which is hardly a distinctive melodic profile. And it seems exceedingly unlikely that McCartney was listening to Brubeck's *Time Out* at precisely the moment when the Beatles were beginning their meteoric rise to fame. Similarities between these two musical phrases are more than likely an interesting coincidence rather than evidence of Brubeck's influence on the Beatles.

In the period between the recording and release of *Brandenburg Gate: Revisited,* an amusing video of "Blue Rondo à la Turk" aired in July 1962 on the first episode of *The Lively Ones.* This was a musical variety show hosted by Vic Damone, which served as a substitute for the popular sitcom *Hazel* (1961–1966) on the NBC television network during summers 1962 and 1963. In a burst of lighthearted fun, the Quartet is depicted as performing on a "magic carpet" ride over Los Angeles. Adding to the zaniness, a policeman on a motorcycle appears near the end and tries unsuccessfully to give the group a speeding ticket.[10]

On a more serious note, this short film connects the Turkish aspects of the piece with stereotypical notions of exoticism and Orientalism. The mythical magic carpet, and its associations with rapid or instantaneous travel, has its roots in the collection of folk tales known as the *Arabian Nights.* Prince Hussain, son of the sultan of the Indies, is said to have

---

9 For instance, the following comment, "Written in 1963, 'All My Loving' was McCartney's first attempt at writing an MOR [middle of the road] standard, but play 'Kathy's Waltz' from the Dave Brubeck Quartet. You might think a modern jazz group was improvising around 'All My Loving,' but 'Kathy's Waltz' was recorded in 1959." Spencer Leigh, "When It Comes to Songwriting, There's a Fine Line between Inspiration and Plagiarism," *Independent,* July 7, 2010 http://independent.co.uk/arts-entertainment/music/features/when-it-comes-to-songwriting-theres-a-fine-line-between-inspiration-and-plagiarism-2021199.html (accessed March 16, 2018).

More surprising is Dave Brubeck's own claim: "Early on, The Beatles acknowledged me as an influence." Joel Lewis, "Dave Brubeck: Jazz Journeyman," *New Jersey Performing Arts Center* (October 2002): 9 (Avakian Papers, box 18, folder 18).

10 The video is available at https://youtu.be/2htbaJFEAXQ (accessed March 14, 2018). The first few seconds are missing. It begins at m. 5.

visited Vijayanagara in southern India and purchased an expensive tap-
estry whose properties were "singular and marvelous." According to the
broker who managed the transaction, "[w]hoever sitteth on this carpet
and willeth in thought to be taken up and set down upon [an]other site
will, in the twinkling of an eye, be borne thither, be that place nearhand
or distant many a day's journey and difficult to reach."[11] The Quartet
recorded a truncated version of "Blue Rondo à la Turk" for the television show, with only two choruses each for saxophone and piano. Paul
Desmond's artistic response to this cultural stew is reflected in his first
chorus (1:57–2:20), whose melodic content mimics the modal features of
wind music popularly associated with snake charmers in India.

A high-water mark of the Quartet's live performances occurred not
long after this broadcast. "Three to Get Ready," "Blue Rondo à la Turk,"
and "Take Five" were recorded in Carnegie Hall on February 21, 1963,
and released on a double album later that year.[12]

"Three to Get Ready" closed the first half of the concert. In his liner
notes, George T. Simon observed that it displayed "the quartet's relaxed
approach to a number whose polyrhythms would throw almost any
other group of musicians." After performing the piece for several years,
the combo was nonchalant about its metrical challenges. Simon quoted
Brubeck as having said, "We play as if we're in 4/4 time—we're so used to
doing this thing." One sure indicator of the Quartet's self-confidence is
the rapid pace of their performance. The Carnegie Hall rendition is considerably faster than the studio version on *Time Out*. Whereas the earlier
recording settled in at just over 170 beats per minute, the tempo of the
live performance approached 200 beats per minute. Apart from its higher
energy, however, the Carnegie Hall recording sounds quite familiar.
The first five choruses follow the same template of meters and instrumental combinations that were specified in Desmond's manuscript alto

---

11 Richard F. Burton, *Supplemental Nights to the Book of the Thousand Nights and a Night*
    (N.p.: Printed by the Burton Club for private subscribers only, 1887), 3:424–425. This epi-
    sode is discussed in a wide-ranging context in Cathy FitzGerald, "The Magic Carpet Flight
    Manual," *BBC World Service*, originally broadcast on September 24, 2010; available at http://
    www.bbc.co.uk/programmes/po2sbwtq (accessed March 14, 2018).

12 The original double album, The Dave Brubeck Quartet, *At Carnegie Hall* (Columbia C2S
    826), gave the date of the concert as February 22, a Friday. The 2001 compact disc rere-
    lease (Columbia/Legacy C2K 61455) corrected it to the previous night. The Thursday date
    (February 21) is corroborated by numerous documents, including the artist job sheets from
    1963 (Sony Music Archives Library) and the information given at https://www.carnegiehall.
    org/About/History/Performance-History-Search?q=dave%20brubeck&dex=prod_
    PHS&page=2&event=16171 (accessed April 22, 2019).

saxophone part (Figure 4.2). Throughout this opening set of choruses, the eighth notes are swung and the highest pitches in the descending sequence of eighth notes (Example 4.14, mm. 7–8) are accentuated, against the grain of the 3/4 meter. In most cases, the last note of each phrase is clipped rather than sustained. This technique makes room for some flamboyant fills, especially by the drums in the third chorus. The other novelty is the occasional substitution of quarter rests for quarter notes on downbeats, creating a heightened sense of syncopation. Desmond first introduces this idea in the last phrase of the second chorus, then Brubeck perpetuates it through the third chorus and in the last phrase of the fourth, as does Desmond in the fifth. Another nice touch, which elicits audible verbal approval from one of his colleagues, is Desmond's brief quotation of a figure from the Scottish song "Comin thro' the rye" at the beginning of the fifth chorus (at around 0:48).

The live performance context of the Carnegie Hall concert allowed for longer solos. Accordingly, Desmond took seven saxophone choruses—a full two minutes (1:19–3:18)—to match the length of Brubeck's own solo (3:18–5:13). Desmond's improvisation doesn't require intensive scrutiny. As always, it is exceedingly tasteful, intelligent, and well constructed. But his tone sounds especially mellifluous, and the prestigious venue where the concert took place seems to have inspired even greater fluency than usual. Brubeck's improvisation begins with two choruses of single notes in the right hand. At the lead-in to the third chorus (around 3:50), he shifts to block chords and initially stokes his imagination with a chord progression in which is embedded the melody of the old gospel song "When the Saints Go Marching In," which had been popularized in jazz circles by Louis Armstrong and many others. The next two choruses consist of the repetitive block-chord sonorities, and intricate rhythmic patterns, that many critics loved to hate about Brubeck's piano style. The end of his solo returns to a thinner texture, but in these final two choruses the right-hand melody is peppered with syncopated chords in the left hand. After the saxophone and piano improvisations, the Quartet again hews to the formal template of the *Time Out* version. First, the piano and saxophone restate the opening theme, retaining the alternation between 3/4 and 4/4. Then the piano plays the tune in 3/4, as at the very beginning. At the end of the seven-bar extension, with its descending chromatic line, Desmond adds a delicious flourish by embellishing it with two sets of quintuplet sixteenth notes.

The excitement of the Carnegie Hall rendition of "Blue Rondo à la Turk" is reflected in both the brisk tempo and quite a few technical bobbles. Despite its quick pace, this live performance outlasts the studio recording by about five minutes. This is chiefly because of the unusually long blues section. First, Desmond takes eight choruses—twice as many as on *Time Out*. Then Brubeck bests Desmond by doubling his number of choruses to a full sixteen. The last three are especially stirring, on account of the double-time feel (beginning around 9:55), followed by an accelerando that leads to the apex of the improvisatory section and ushers in the reprise.

"Take Five" was played immediately thereafter, as the closing number of the Carnegie Hall concert. The most striking aspect of this rendition is its verve, which stems largely from its accelerated pace. The group maintains a tempo of just over 220 beats per minute. This is a shade faster than the ill-fated first takes discussed in Chapter 5. But the Quartet was clearly quite comfortable with this rapid clip, after having "Take Five" in their repertoire for nearly four years.

The introduction is telescoped from twelve bars to just eight. The drums play alone for four bars, then are joined by the piano and bass for four more. But the head is similar to *Time Out*, consisting of three eight-bar phrases (A B A') played by the saxophone. Desmond's solo, which comes next, is four times longer than the canonical version on the 1959 album. Here he stretches out to a hundred measures (more than two minutes). Though the specific motivic and melodic content is different, it remains within the same modal framework and therefore sounds of a piece with the earlier solo.[13]

After six measures of piano/bass/drums vamp, during which the audience expresses its appreciation with applause, Brubeck weaves his own piano solo. He begins by developing a motive from the end of Desmond's solo, which he stretches into three eight-bar phrases. Then he breaks the mood with a series of virtuosic ascending arpeggios that give shape to the next segment. Brubeck's foray is nearly as long as Desmond's (eighty-six measures), and it seems more exotic on account of his incorporation of new harmonies into the vamp. The presence of an extended piano solo differentiates the Carnegie Hall rendition from the *Time Out* version. So, too, does the abbreviated drum solo (with piano/bass backing, as before), which encompasses only twenty-eight bars, the last four of which serve as preparation ("introduction") for a full reprise of the head. The nine-bar coda also matches the earlier version.

---

13 A transcription of Desmond's solo, by Paul Cohen, is provided in Doug Ramsey, *Take Five: The Public and Private Lives of Paul Desmond* (Seattle: Parkside Publications, 2005), 238–239.

In addition to its important position at the end of the Quartet's iconic performance at Carnegie Hall, the story of "Take Five," especially in the first two decades after its creation, encompasses many fascinating twists and turns. The extraordinary success of this cut was intimately connected with its release as a single. But the production and dissemination of this compact version was an uphill battle, which began immediately after it was recorded and lasted nearly two years. Brubeck later recalled that, on "the day of the session" (presumably either July 1 or August 18, 1959), the president of Columbia Records, Goddard Lieberson, said, "Give me 'Blue Rondo' and 'Take Five' today. I want to take those to the West Coast and try to get a single."[14] Apparently only a promotional single was produced at that time, however.[15] And an internal memo a few months later reveals that Brubeck was none too pleased about the delay. One of the marketing executives at Columbia reported that

> Dave Brubeck has increasingly indicated his desire to participate in the singles record field. He feels that he needs this kind of exposure and promotion in order to broaden his appeal and bring him to new consumers who may not now be buying him. He feels that some of the recent album material could well be attractive on this basis and he is keeping the single record philosophy in mind more and more in planning new projects.
>
> I told him, as Teo [Macero] did before me in earlier discussions, that it's both generally expensive and speculative to release singles on a regular basis. He was given the whole story, but when it's all said and done he still has a burning desire to be part of the single record picture.[16]

Many years later, Brubeck credited Lieberson with breaking the logjam. In his liner notes for a reissue of the album in the late 1990s, Brubeck characterized "Take Five" as "the 'hit' single that finally emerged from *Time Out*." He noted that "*Time Out* had actually been in circulation

14 Owen Goldsmith, "Dave Brubeck," *Contemporary Keyboard* 3, no. 12 (December 1977): 40.
15 The release date of single #4-41479 is given as September 21, 1959, on p. 11 of the liner notes for The Dave Brubeck Quartet, *The Columbia Studio Albums Collection, 1955–1966*, 19 compact discs, Sony/Legacy, 2011. A typed publicity statement, undated but obviously from 1959, describes the record as follows: "This new single, 'Blue Rondo à la Turk' and 'Take Five,' is part of a new album by the Dave Brubeck Quartet titled *Time Out*, which is soon to be released." Macero Collection, box 7, folder 4.
16 Stan Kavan to Bill Gallagher, February 18, 1960 (Macero Collection, box 7, folder 16).

as an LP for more than a year before the sales department, urged by Columbia's president, Goddard Lieberson, decided to release a single for radio and jukebox play. It zoomed to #1 on the charts!"[17]

The "Take Five" single was released in May 1961.[18] Its rise was meteoric indeed. By the end of May, a sales manager in St. Louis was already asking the record company for "some new jazz singles, especially for jukeboxes," on the strength of the success of "Take Five."[19] Six weeks later, one of Brubeck's booking agents was crowing about the fact that "Dave's single release 'Take Five' is one of the top, most-played records in the city of Chicago."[20] In mid-August, Lieberson requested, and Brubeck agreed to, financial concessions designed to give the "Take Five" single a "big push" that month, with the goal of catapulting it into the "smash hit" category.[21] The strategy was quite effective, and by early November the record was selling between two and three thousand copies every day.[22] Moreover, it crossed over to the pop charts, entering the Billboard Hot 100 at position #64 on September 11, remaining on the list for twelve weeks (through November 27), and peaking at #25 (October 9).[23]

A promotional flier from the end of 1961 claimed that "Take Five" had sold nearly a quarter of a million copies since it was released "several months ago."[24] A few months later, sales had reached "over one million."[25] And by 1967, it had "sold astronomically—an estimated two million over the past seven years."[26]

17 Dave Brubeck, "Time Out Is Still In," liner notes for The Dave Brubeck Quartet, *Time Out*, Columbia/Legacy CK 65122, 1997, compact disc.

18 Columbia Records, Artist Contact Card, "Dave Brubeck," page 18 (Sony Music Archives Library).

19 Memo from Tom Berman to "Dave K.," regarding the previous week's sales, May 31, 1961 (Macero Collection, box 7, folder 4).

20 Paul Bannister (Associated Booking Corporation, Chicago) to Iola Brubeck, July 6, 1961 (Brubeck Collection).

21 Goddard Lieberson to Dave Brubeck, August 16, 1961 (Macero Collection, box 7, folder 17).

22 Teo Macero to Dave Brubeck, November 7, 1961 (Macero Collection, box 6, folder 22).

23 "Jimmy's Charts—Artists beginning with D" http://www.racpro.com/grid.php?pid=5&asc ii=68&from=asccom&page=3 via "Internet Pop Song Database Billboard Top 40 Hot 100 Charts Hits Lyrics" http://www.song-database.com/ (accessed March 15, 2018).

24 "Since 'Take Five'" (Macero Collection, box 7, folder 5).

25 "Isle Progressive Jazz Fans Welcome Brubeck at Shell," *Honolulu Star-Bulletin*, March 23, 1962.

26 Leonard Feather, "The End of an Era in Modern Jazz," *Los Angeles Times*, July 30, 1967.

Meanwhile, in October 1961, Coronet Records was preparing to release the "Take Five" single in Australia.[27] And the next month, in connection with a British tour that began at London's Royal Festival Hall on November 18, Fontana's issue reached the Top Ten. It entered at #8 (November 9), peaked at #6 the following week (November 16), and remained in the top tier of the charts for a total of five weeks (until December 7).[28] Brubeck was delighted with the record's success, of course, but he also found it to be rather puzzling, in light of the album's chilly reception in the past: "One of the stupidest programmings I ever did—and I learned a lesson from it—was to play at the Royal Festival Hall in London our *Time Out* album with maybe one standard. . . . We were on about twenty-five minutes. We boobed."[29] The cut's subsequent favor with the public was not only personally satisfying, but it also improved jazz's standing in the musical world. As Brubeck explained, "A hit can be tremendously beneficial to a particular artist. But at the same time, it is also beneficial to jazz in general in that it constitutes another step forward in its acceptance on a national scale. Every time a jazz record becomes a hit, jazz wins a few more friends and followers."[30]

The extraordinary success of "Take Five" naturally led to calls for a sequel. Desmond's relatively unfamiliar "Take Ten" was one result. This was the title track for an album that was recorded at Webster Hall in New York in June 1963.[31] The other musicians were Jim Hall (guitar), Connie Kay (drums), and for this cut only, Desmond's bandmate from

27 Kenn Brodziak (Managing Director, Aztec Services, Melbourne) to Dave Brubeck, October 10, 1961 (Brubeck Collection).

28 "take five | full Official Chart History | Official Charts Company," http://www.officialcharts. com/search/singles/take%20five/ (accessed March 15, 2018).

29 Ian Dove, "Nobody Wanted to Know about 'Take Five' in London, Says Dave Brubeck," *New Record Mirror*, November 1961.

30 Keith Goodwin, "It's Great to Be in the Top Ten—Declares Dave Brubeck," unidentified clipping, England, November 1961 (Brubeck Collection). The following year, Ralph Gleason, who had long been quite critical of Brubeck, publicly (and somewhat surprisingly) acknowledged his seminal role in expanding jazz's audience: "Dave Brubeck, . . . whether or not you dig him and whether or not he has had a direct influence as a jazz stylist upon other jazz musicians, has been a major force in broadening public acceptance of jazz. Thousands of radio stations have played Brubeck albums and single hits like 'Take Five' that would never in a million years have played a jazz record knowingly. Thousands of people who profess a dislike for jazz have met it through Brubeck and ended up liking it. There are many hard core jazz musicians who publicize their distaste for Brubeck who have a long way to go before they do as much as he has done for the music they love." Ralph J. Gleason, unidentified clipping, August 16, 1962 (Brubeck Collection).

31 Paul Desmond, *Take Ten,* RCA Victor LSP-2569, 1963, 33⅓ rpm.

the Dave Brubeck Quartet, Eugene Wright (bass). Although there were undoubtedly high hopes all around for another hit, Desmond's description in the liner notes is decidedly bland: " 'Take Ten' is another excursion into 5/4 or 10/8, whichever you prefer. Since writing 'Take Five' a few years back, a number of other possibilities in the 5 & 10 bag have come to mind from time to time. 'Take Ten' is one of them." The same absence of a creative spark is evident in the music, too. It is nearly a carbon copy of "Take Five"—but with guitar instead of piano, and a half step lower, in D minor rather than E♭ minor. The introduction is layered, as in "Take Five": four bars of drums alone are followed by four more in which the bass and guitar join in to start the vamp. Next, the head is played on the saxophone. It runs to thirty-two bars, but only because the first eight-bar phrase is repeated, producing the form AABA. After Desmond's modal solo (twenty-one bars), the head is played again, but without the repeat (ABA, like "Take Five"). And it ends with a brief coda (also like "Take Five"). A contemporary review of the *Take Ten* album judges it to be "uncertain ground"—and now, more than fifty years on, that seems like a generous appraisal.[32]

Though Desmond was unable to replicate his triumph with "Take Five," he left a valuable legacy nonetheless—and he did so almost off the cuff. A profile that originally appeared in *The New Yorker* (September 16, 1991) recounts a conversation between Desmond and his attorney, Noel Silverman, in spring 1977. Silverman "suggested to [Desmond] three or four months before he died that he make a will." After discussing other details, Silverman "asked [Desmond] about the rest of his estate, the income from records and from songs like 'Take Five,' and he said, 'Give it to the Red Cross, they're a good outfit.' "[33] According to Gioia, as of 2012 the American Red Cross had received more than six million dollars, and the organization had "reciprocated by naming a training room in its Washington, D.C. headquarters after the alto saxophonist."[34]

The year 1967 marked the end of the line for the "classic" Quartet (with Desmond, Wright, and Morello), which performed their final concert in Pittsburgh on the day after Christmas. A recording of this crucial event wasn't released until more than forty years later, in 2011, under the title *Their Last Time Out* (Columbia/Legacy 88697 81562 2), a punning

32 *Punch*, February 5, 1964.
33 Whitney Balliett, "An Insouciant Sound," in *American Musicians II: Seventy-Two Portraits in Jazz* (New York: Oxford University Press, 1996), 440.
34 Ted Gioia, *The Jazz Standards: A Guide to the Repertoire* (New York: Oxford University Press, 2012), 418–419.

reference to the group's most famous album, the subject of the present book. The concert ended with "Take Five," as always. The only other number from *Time Out* that made it onto their set list was "Three to Get Ready," which they played toward the beginning, after "St. Louis Blues."

Perhaps the most remarkable thing about the Quartet's "last" performance of "Three to Get Ready" is that it was so unremarkable. Like any specific outing, it has its unique moments. There are a few brief patches of polytonality in Desmond's saxophone solo—that is, moments when he plays in a different key from that of the piano and bass. This is routine for Brubeck, of course, but less common for Desmond. Brubeck's piano solo becomes quite dissonant and rather free in the last several choruses (especially around 3:25–3:33 and 3:57–4:28), but there is nothing unprecedented here. The choruses at the beginning, before the saxophone and piano solos, include some fresh harmonies and chromaticism in Brubeck's piano part, and a cornball drum and cymbal riff at the end of the third chorus (0:41–0:44) elicits a chuckle from the live audience. But otherwise we hear many of the same gestures and ideas as in previous recordings, including Desmond's use of a snippet from a Scottish song at the end of the fourth chorus (0:58–1:00).[35] Additionally, the order of events (apart from the five saxophone choruses and eight piano choruses) is identical to the *Time Out* version from more than eight years earlier.

Another live performance, recorded at the Interlochen Arts Academy in Michigan on March 10, 1976, held special significance for Brubeck and his colleagues.[36] During the eight years following the "classic" Quartet's final performance in Pittsburgh, the individual musicians pursued a variety of projects of their own choosing. But in 1976, to mark the twenty-fifth anniversary of the group's formation, Desmond, Morello, and Wright joined Brubeck for a reunion tour. During the month from mid-February through mid-March, they performed a series of concerts in the Mid-Atlantic, the South, New England, and the Midwest. This turned out to be the last opportunity for such an event. The next year, Desmond was diagnosed with lung cancer, and he passed away on May 30, 1977.

The unique features of the 1976 recording of "Take Five" center principally on Desmond's extensive solo. The introduction conforms to the

---

35 In the present context, given that this concert took place between Christmas and New Year's Day, Desmond was more likely alluding to a different Scottish song, "Auld Lang Syne," which shares this motive with "Comin thro' the rye."

36 The Dave Brubeck Quartet, *25th Anniversary Reunion*, A&M Records CD 0806, 1988, compact disc.

pattern of the Carnegie Hall performance—eight bars, in which Morello plays the first half alone, and then is joined by Brubeck and Wright. This is followed by the usual twenty-four-bar head (8+8+8). The moment Desmond plays the last note of this tune, however, he launches into a three-minute improvisational extravaganza that quotes or alludes to Beethoven, Broadway, Khachaturian, and early jazz—four rather strange bedfellows.

These four passages summarize Desmond's approach to the use of preexistent material in his solos. The first, to which he turns almost immediately (beginning at 0:58), is a nearly literal quotation of the main theme in the first movement of Beethoven's Sixth Symphony. Comparison of this solo (Example 8.1a) with the Beethoven melody (Example 8.1b) reveals that Desmond transposed it down a step from F major to E♭ major, and altered the rhythm to fit into 5/4 meter (and to provide a modicum of swing, by introducing some syncopation). Otherwise, the intervallic content is identical. The reference in the second passage (Example 8.1c, beginning at 2:37) is more oblique. It doesn't come clearly into view until the last half dozen pitches, when it becomes evident that Desmond is alluding to "The Surrey with the Fringe on Top" from the musical *Oklahoma!* (1943) by Rodgers and Hammerstein. The third quotation (Example 8.1d, beginning at 2:56) is also somewhat veiled. Its repetition of the seventh scale degree, coupled with chromaticism and a descent to the fifth scale degree, was apparently inspired by the "Sabre Dance" from Khachaturian's ballet *Gayane* (1942) (Example 8.1e), which was wildly popular, beginning in the late 1940s. Finally, the ascending melodic

EXAMPLE 8.1A. Paul Desmond, "Take Five," excerpt from alto saxophone chorus (Desmond) at live concert in Michigan on March 10, 1976, with allusion to Beethoven theme, transcription.

EXAMPLE 8.1B. Main theme from first movement of Beethoven's Sixth Symphony.

EXAMPLE 8.1C. Paul Desmond, "Take Five," excerpt from alto saxophone chorus (Desmond) at live concert in Michigan on March 10, 1976, with allusion to Rodgers and Hammerstein theme, transcription.

EXAMPLE 8.1D. Paul Desmond, "Take Five," excerpt from alto saxophone chorus (Desmond) at live concert in Michigan on March 10, 1976, with allusion to Khachaturian theme, transcription.

EXAMPLE 8.1E. Theme from "Sabre Dance" from Khachaturian's *Gayane.*

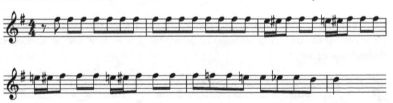

EXAMPLE 8.1F. Paul Desmond, "Take Five," excerpt from alto saxophone (Desmond) chorus at live concert in Michigan on March 10, 1976, with allusion to "When the Saints Go Marching In," transcription.

fragment at the beginning of the first three pairs of measures in Example 8.1f (beginning at 3:27) is redolent of "When the Saints Go Marching In," the gospel tune that became a jazz standard largely through the influence of Louis Armstrong, beginning in the late 1930s.

The latter three examples are typical of Desmond's improvisatory procedures and not especially surprising. The Beethoven quotation, on the other hand, gives one pause, because of its remarkable fidelity to the original melody and its forthright presentation at the very beginning. Given the performance venue—an arts academy more famous for classical music than jazz—one wonders whether a student orchestra there might perhaps have been studying Beethoven's Sixth Symphony at that time, and Desmond was moved thereby to include its theme in his solo. Interlochen is also a place of great natural beauty (even in March), so it is possible that Desmond chose this tune on account of the Pastoral Symphony's evocation of rural life—especially given Beethoven's annotation of the first movement, "Awakening of cheerful feelings upon arrival in the countryside."

Brubeck's two-minute piano solo (3:57–6:00) remains in the major mode, but it oscillates from E♭ up to E♮ and back, and it also incorporates some polytonality toward the end. Eight bars after Brubeck reinstates the E♭-minor vamp (beginning at 6:00), Morello commences his drum solo, which is accompanied by the piano and bass. During the last twenty seconds (beginning at 8:03), Brubeck begins introducing some substitute chords and intensifying the dynamic level, in preparation for the return of the head, which is rounded off by the usual nine-bar coda.

For the Quartet's 1976 reunion concert at Interlochen, "Three to Get Ready" also was on the program again, this time with the expanded title "Three to Get Ready and Four to Go." Considered against the backdrop of the 1959, 1963, and 1967 recordings discussed so far, the 1976 version is strikingly different (see Table 8.1). The first three share the same formal template; only the lengths of the saxophone and piano solos vary from one performance to the next. The *25th Anniversary* rendition begins, like the other three, with the tune played on the piano in triple meter (but Brubeck swings the eighth notes here, as opposed to his deadpan presentation on *Time Out*). The first surprise comes already with the introduction of alternation between 3/4 and 4/4 in the second chorus (the differences are bolded in Table 8.1). In the past, the fills in the 4/4 measures had always been played by the saxophone. But in the *Reunion* performance, the piano plays both the 3/4 tune and the 4/4 fills. Moreover, it had previously been a fixed pattern that the chorus with the drum fills (number 3) had preceded the chorus with the bass fills (number 5), and

TABLE 8.1.   Dave Brubeck, "Three to Get Ready," comparison of recordings from 1959, 1963, 1967, and 1976

Time Out (1959)	Carnegie Hall (1963)	Their Last Time Out (1967)	25th Anniversary Reunion (1976)
Chorus 1: piano—3/4	Chorus 1: piano—3/4	Chorus 1: piano—3/4	Chorus 1: piano—3/4
Chorus 2: saxophone, piano—3/4 and 4/4	Chorus 2: saxophone, piano—3/4 and 4/4	Chorus 2: saxophone, piano—3/4 and 4/4	**Chorus 2: piano—3/4 and 4/4**
Chorus 3: piano, drums—3/4 and 4/4	Chorus 3: piano, drums—3/4 and 4/4	Chorus 3: piano, drums—3/4 and 4/4	**Chorus 3: piano, bass—3/4 and 4/4**
Chorus 4: piano, saxophone—3/4 and 4/4	Chorus 4: piano, saxophone—3/4 and 4/4	Chorus 4: piano, saxophone—3/4 and 4/4	**Chorus 4: piano, drums—3/4 and 4/4**
Chorus 5: saxophone, bass—3/4 and 4/4	Chorus 5: saxophone, bass—3/4 and 4/4	Chorus 5: saxophone, bass—3/4 and 4/4	**Chorus 5: piano, saxophone—3/4 and 4/4**
Choruses 6–8: saxophone solo—3/4 and 4/4	Choruses 6–12: saxophone solo—3/4 and 4/4	Choruses 6–10: saxophone solo—3/4 and 4/4	Choruses 6–11: saxophone solo—3/4 and 4/4
Choruses 9–15: piano solo—3/4 and 4/4	Choruses 13–19: piano solo—3/4 and 4/4	Choruses 11–18: piano solo—3/4 and 4/4	Choruses 12–19: piano solo—3/4 and 4/4
Chorus 16: piano, saxophone—3/4 and 4/4	Chorus 20: piano, saxophone—3/4 and 4/4	Chorus 19: piano, saxophone—3/4 and 4/4	
Chorus 17, plus 7-bar extension—3/4	Chorus 21, plus 7-bar extension—3/4	Chorus 20, plus 7-bar extension—3/4	Chorus 20, plus 7-bar extension—3/4

the saxophone was the instrument that alternated with the bass in the latter chorus. But here the bass is featured first (in chorus 3, where Eugene Wright plays some wild multiple-note glissandos at around 0:40), then the drums (chorus 4), and the bass is paired with the piano rather than the saxophone. The upshot of all this is that Desmond doesn't enter until the fifth chorus (1:04–1:21). And when he does, he unexpectedly *sings* his first fill—the opening of "Auld Lang Syne" on a neutral syllable—to howls of laughter. After the six choruses of Desmond's saxophone solo and the eight of Brubeck's piano solo, there is another departure from the norm. The head usually returns in its 3/4–4/4 guise. But that section is omitted here, and it moves instead directly to the final 3/4 section, with the customary seven-bar extension.

Ten years after the reunion of the "classic" Quartet, a newly constituted Quartet—with Brubeck's old friend Bill Smith on the clarinet, his son Chris Brubeck on the electric bass, and Randy Jones on drums—made a pair of sharply contrasting recordings of "Blue Rondo à la Turk" within a few months of each other. In November 1986, they recorded this tune in San Francisco for an album titled *Blue Rondo*.[37] Their sound is quite different from the earlier combo, owing primarily to the substitution of the clarinet for the alto saxophone and the use of an electric instead of an acoustic upright bass. Beyond this, the tempo is slightly slower, which yields a more controlled (less manic) and therefore more accurate rendition than in the past. Smith and Brubeck are both in fine form, and they take six choruses each in the blues section.

The reprise matches the shortened version heard consistently in the recordings from the late 1950s and early 1960s. But the 1986 version differs from the earlier renditions in one important respect. After the conclusion of Brubeck's solo, the reprise had always been preceded by a passage in which two-bar segments in 4/4 alternate with two-bar segments in 9/8 (2+2+2+3), for a total of ten measures—a shortened "hybrid" section. In the 1986 recording, this passage occupies the usual ten measures, but it remains in 4/4 throughout. As a result, the reintroduction of the Turkish *aksak* rhythm is postponed until the beginning of the reprise.

The following summer, the same Quartet joined forces with the Montreal International Jazz Festival Orchestra for a performance of a symphonic version of "Blue Rondo à la Turk." The arrangement was made by Dave Brubeck's eldest son, Darius.[38] It has the energy and urgency of a chase scene in a movie—a fact worth noting

37 The 1987 Dave Brubeck Quartet, *Blue Rondo*, Concord Jazz CCD-4317, 1987, compact disc.
38 The Dave Brubeck Quartet with the Montreal International Jazz Festival Orchestra, *New Wine*, recorded at the Festival International de Jazz Montréal, July 3, 1987, MusicMasters 5051-2-C, 1990, compact disc. Darius Brubeck's original pencil score is in the Brubeck Collection. According to Darius's handwritten note (May 1, 2007), it was written in Wilton, Connecticut, before he and his wife moved to South Africa in 1983. Indeed, it must have been somewhat earlier than that, as the arrangement began showing up on concert programs in the late 1970s—for instance, the Cincinnati Symphony Orchestra on June 3–4, 1977.

in light of Claude Nougaro's vocal arrangement, which was discussed in Chapter 7. The material up until the beginning of the blues follows the usual order of events, but with a broader palette of timbres. After Smith's five choruses on the clarinet, Brubeck takes eight on the piano. Brubeck's wide-ranging three-minute solo is marked in particular by a high degree of dissonance, some double-time passages, and occasional nods to the stride-piano style. As in the 1986 combo recording, the ten-bar segment immediately following the blues choruses doesn't deviate from 4/4. The beginning of the reprise is three times as long as usual—ABA (mm. 1–24) instead of just A (mm. 1–8)—presumably in order to maximize the effect of the orchestral colors on the home stretch. The extra beat at the very end, with a concluding flourish, serves a similar purpose.

The *Blue Rondo* album also includes a fresh interpretation of "Strange Meadow Lark" in which Dave is joined by Chris on the electric bass and trombone.[39] This arrangement entails essentially two run-throughs of the entire tune, and the Brubecks divide the labor more or less equally.

When Brubeck's new Quartet performed "Three to Get Ready" in Moscow in 1987, they modified its format yet again.[40] The usual five choruses before the individual solos are telescoped into just four. First, Dave plays the head in 3/4 meter on the piano. Then the piano alternates with each of the other three instruments. Dave plays the 3/4 bars and the fills in the 4/4 measures are allocated to the clarinet, drums, and bass in successive choruses. The set of solos that follow deviates even more extensively from the beaten path. In all of the previous versions (see Table 8.1), just two instruments took solos, saxophone and piano, always in that order. Only the number of choruses (and their content, of course) varied between performances. In the present case, however, Smith kicks things off with five meticulously crafted choruses on the clarinet. Dave then takes over and stretches out to no fewer than a dozen piano choruses (more than three and one half minutes), including some remarkably virtuosic passagework at the beginning and a stunning level of intensity toward the end. The real surprise, though, is that Chris then sneaks in an electric bass solo, four choruses in length, before the recapitulatory final two choruses.

Several years later, Dave Brubeck recorded a solo piano version of "Strange Meadow Lark," which he characterized as "quite reminiscent of

39 The other two members of the Quartet do not participate in this cut.
40 Dave Brubeck, *Moscow Night*, Concord Jazz CCD-4353, 1988, compact disc.

the original [1959 *Time Out*] recording with a few new twists and turns."[41] The layout of this rendition does indeed hew rather closely to its predecessor. Brubeck plays the fifty-two-bar version of the tune twice. The cut is then rounded out with an A' section consisting of the first ten-bar phrase, followed by the slightly extended version of that same phrase with which it customarily ends. The chief novelty of this solo recording is Brubeck's extensive use of an up-tempo stride-piano idiom, a style not normally associated with ballads. It begins in the bridge, the first time through, and continues until the onset of the concluding section (A').

COVER VERSIONS, BOTH STRANGE AND WONDERFUL

There are nowhere near as many covers of "Three to Get Ready" as there are of "Take Five." But the former has caught the ear of a variety of musicians who have concocted new versions of the tune, some of which are amusing or surprising. For instance, the Nashville saxophonist Boots Randolph (1927–2007) recorded "Three to Get Ready" in 1964, on the heels of his 1963 hit "Yakety Sax."[42] His version is quite short (just over two minutes), including one chorus each for the saxophone, electric guitar, and piano, in addition to the head (a 3/4 chorus and a 3/4–4/4 chorus) at the beginning and end.

The previous year "Three to Get Ready" was also recorded in Paris by the Hungarian jazz guitarist (and violinist) Elek Bacsik (1926–1993).[43] Bacsik was a younger cousin of the much better known guitarist, Django Reinhardt (1910–1953). His rendition is even more compact than Randolph's, lasting just under two minutes. It is noteworthy for its almost exclusive focus on the electric guitar, including multitracking in some of the choruses. Even more surprising, however, is that Bacsik plays only the twelve-bar 3/4 version of the tune, and never introduces alternation between triple and quadruple meter, thereby disregarding the piece's very essence. He does follow Brubeck's model, though, in extending the tenth and final chorus. But rather than simply adding a few measures, Bacsik's recording includes a repeat and fade ending.

41 Dave Brubeck, liner notes dated July 1994, *Just You, Just Me*, Telarc CD-83363, 1994, compact disc.

42 Randolph's recording of "Three to Get Ready" appears on *Hip Boots!*, Monument SLP 18015, 1964, 33⅓ rpm. "Yakety Sax" was famously used as the theme music for *The Benny Hill Show*, a British comedy series in the 1970s and 1980s.

43 Elek Bacsik, *Guitar Conceptions*, Fontana 680-240 ML, 1963, 33⅓ rpm.

Around forty years later, in 2003, "Three to Get Ready" received an astonishing performance, which upon closer inspection shouldn't have been surprising at all. The avant-garde saxophonist and composer Anthony Braxton (1945–) recorded Brubeck's tune in Portugal during a European tour.[44] In some respects, Braxton's rendition couldn't be more different from the version on *Time Out*. He plays the head in a very high register, on his sopranino saxophone—first, all in 3/4 meter, and then, alternating between 3/4 and 4/4, with drum fills in the quadruple measures. Immediately thereafter, he launches into an extended solo, running to fifteen choruses over the span of nearly five minutes. Braxton's masterful and virtuosic improvisation is followed by nine guitar choruses and six for the bass, in both cases supplemented by the percussionist playing on a glockenspiel from time to time. .

Braxton's edgy and agitated style is a far cry from Paul Desmond's mellifluous saxophone tone, and the Braxton Quartet might seem to have little in common with Brubeck and his groups. But Braxton began playing and listening to jazz in earnest around 1959, and one of his favorite albums was Brubeck's *Jazz at the College of the Pacific* (Fantasy 3-13, 1954), which begins with "All the Things You Are," a standard by Jerome Kern and Oscar Hammerstein II.[45] Fifteen years later, in 1974, Braxton recorded this tune with Brubeck.[46]

Just two out of the dozens of cover versions of "Take Five" must suffice to illustrate the tune's extraordinary pliability. Taking full advantage of its status as a "hit" in 1961, George Cates—Lawrence Welk's musical director—recorded it on his album, titled (not surprisingly) *Take Five* (Dot Records DLP-25400). This flat-footed arrangement is (also not surprisingly) quintessential elevator music, complete with ambient female vocal lines ("oohs and aahs") and a half-step modulation upward at its midpoint. When asked about the phenomenon of lesser-known

44 Anthony Braxton, *23 Standards (Quartet)*, Leo Records CD LR 402/405, 2004, four compact discs. Kevin O'Neil, guitar; Kevin Norton, percussion; Andy Eulau, percussion; Anthony Braxton, saxophones.

45 Ronald M. Radano, *New Musical Figurations: Anthony Braxton's Cultural Critique* (Chicago and London: University of Chicago Press, 1993), 50–51. For a lively account of Braxton's early years, including the influence of Brubeck and Desmond, see George E. Lewis, *A Power Stronger Than Itself: The AACM and American Experimental Music* (Chicago and London: University of Chicago Press, 2008), 145–148.

46 Dave Brubeck, *All the Things We Are*, Atlantic SD 1684, 1976, 33⅓ rpm. Braxton plays alto saxophone with Brubeck, Jack Six (bass), and Roy Haynes (drums) on the Brubeck standard "In Your Own Sweet Way," and this group is expanded to a quintet with Lee Konitz (alto saxophone) on "All the Things You Are." Both tracks were recorded on October 3, 1974.

groups trying to capitalize on his achievements, Brubeck was remarkably gracious: "I had a cover job on ['Take Five'] by George Cates, and the same thing is likely to happen again. It's a natural reaction. . . . If other musicians can find success through playing my numbers in a more simplified manner, can they be blamed for finding a short cut?"[47]

A very different and much more engaging arrangement is the mambo version of "Take Five" on the 1985 album *Mambo Diablo* (Concord Jazz Picante CJP-283) by Tito Puente and His Latin Ensemble. The hallmarks of this rendition are its high energy—largely attributable to the expanded percussion section (including timbales, congas, and bongos)—and the prominence of brass instruments (trumpet, flugelhorn, and trombone) alongside the saxophone, piano, and bass. It is surprising to hear, however, that the meter has been altered here from the irregular 5/4 to conventional common time.

The best-known cover of "Blue Rondo à la Turk" is Keith Emerson's "Rondo." It first appeared in 1967 on *The Thoughts of Emerlist Davjack*, the inaugural album of the psychedelic rock band The Nice.[48] A few years later, on August 29, 1970, the progressive rock band Emerson, Lake & Palmer played "Rondo" at the Isle of Wight Festival, their *de facto* debut, and the tune subsequently became a staple of their repertoire. The group never recorded a studio version, but the live renditions available on the Internet—not only the Isle of Wight performance, but appearances at Royal Albert Hall in London (October 1992), in Kurtowice, Poland (June 1997), and at the High Voltage Festival in Victoria Park in London (July 2010), for instance—all meld Brubeck's "Blue Rondo à la Turk" with classical favorites, such as the last movement of J. S. Bach's Italian Concerto, Aaron Copland's *Fanfare for the Common Man*, "America" from Leonard Bernstein's *West Side Story*, and even "O Fortuna" from Carl Orff's *Carmina Burana*.

In all cases, Brubeck's composition is adapted in a highly idiosyncratic manner. The first episode and second refrain of the rondo are always omitted, with the resultant form A (mm. 1–8)—C (mm. 25–32)—A (mm. 33–40)—D (mm. 41–48)—A (mm. 49–56), with respect to the original. The last eight measures of the composed section (before the

47 June Harris, "I Don't Want to Go Commercial, Says Dave Brubeck," *Disc*, November 25, 1961.

48 The Nice, *The Thoughts of Emerlist Davjack*, Immediate IMSP 016, 1967, 33⅓ rpm. The name in the album title was formed by combining portions of the names of the band members: Keith *Emer*son, David O'*List*, Brian *Dav*ison, and Lee *Jack*son. "Rondo" is credited to "Emerlist Davjack," with no mention of Brubeck's name.

EXAMPLE 8.2. Emerson, Lake & Palmer, "Rondo," mm. 1–16, transcription.

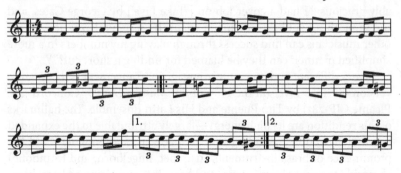

twelve-bar passage that alternates between 4/4 and 9/8) are augmented to twice their regular length, for a total of sixteen. And, oddest of all, the rhythm is shoehorned into 4/4 throughout, effectively neutralizing the piece's raison d'être (see Example 8.2).

This cavalier treatment notwithstanding, Emerson conceived his "Rondo" as a tribute to Brubeck, one of his musical heroes. Emerson first met Brubeck in 2003, when the Quartet performed at a venue on the southern coast of England, near the town where Emerson grew up. After their paths crossed again six years later, at a concert in California, Emerson recalled that Brubeck had signed a publication of his transcribed solos with the gracious words, "For Keith, with many thanks for your 4/4 version [of "Blue Rondo à la Turk"] which I can't play." Emerson also revealed that his fascination with Brubeck's piece originated during his teen years, around the time when it was first released: "When I was 15 years old [1959] I was going through further education in Sussex, England. My mother and father earned little and my meager earnings from a newspaper and grocery round were put towards a stereo record player. That Christmas, my present from Mum and Dad was a single 45 vinyl record, 'Take Five.' On the B-side was 'Blue Rondo à la Turk.' I played the hell out of it. In 1968 [sic], I recorded a 4/4 version of 'Blue Rondo' and played the hell out of it in live performance."[49]

"Strange Meadow Lark" was the first of the *Time Out* tunes to attract attention from other musicians. In March 1962, Brubeck wrote about it in a letter to Pieter Sweens. He told the Dutch journalist that he was flattered by his interest in the piece, and said that Iola had written lyrics

49 Keith Emerson, "Meeting Mr. Brubeck Again," http://www.keithemerson.com/MiscPages/2009/20090924-DaveBrubeck.html (accessed March 14, 2018).

for it "several years ago." He also mentioned that Carmen McRae had recorded it, and that her version was "in more of an up tempo." His opinion was similar to Iola's, and he expressed it diplomatically: "Although I like Carmen's version very much, the original conception was for a ballad, more like the instrumental on *Time Out*."

Reading between the lines, it appears that Sweens had declared his interest in performing the piece, a prospect that delighted Brubeck. It also prompted Brubeck's intriguing remark: "I'd love to hear it someday given full treatment with strings and woodwinds. . . . Willie Ruff is currently working on an arrangement of 'Strange Meadow Lark' multitracking four French horn parts."[50] Ruff was the horn-playing half of the Mitchell-Ruff Duo, along with pianist Dwike Mitchell. According to Mitchell's obituary, the Duo was propelled "to world fame in 1959, when Mr. Ruff, who had a part-time teaching job at the Yale School of Music, arranged for them to accompany the Yale Russian Chorus on a summer visit to the Soviet Union."[51] Ruff was on Brubeck's radar because he had interviewed Ruff on the FM radio station WJZZ (Bridgeport, Connecticut) in 1960. Later that year, Brubeck recommended that Radio Free Europe invite Ruff on the air, noting that Ruff was the first modern jazz musician to play in Russia, and that he spoke four languages, including Russian.[52]

In a file of business correspondence in the Brubeck Collection labeled "Other 1961" is a sheet of paper, mostly in Brubeck's hand, with Willie Ruff's name at the top and a list of thirteen song titles, including "Meadow Lark." This note suggests that the arrangement Brubeck mentioned to Sweens in 1962 may have formed part of a larger project. When I asked Ruff about it, he credited Russell Garcia, described in his obituary as "an influential figure in the West Coast music scene during the 1950s and '60s"[53] (and who coincidentally was born in Oakland, California, where the Brubecks were living in 1959): "Sadly, nothing ever came of the recording. It was done in Europe and the arranger Russell Garcia did a terrific job, but it was one of those projects that got lost in the pipeline."[54]

---

50 Dave Brubeck to Pieter Sweens (Naarden, The Netherlands), March 14, 1962 (Brubeck Collection).

51 Paul Vitello, "Dwike Mitchell, Zealous Jazz Pianist, Dies at 83," *New York Times*, April 18, 2013.

52 Dave Brubeck, interview with Martin Bush, Jazz Gallery, Greenwich Village, New York, December 9, 1960 (typescript, Brubeck Collection).

53 Dennis McLellan, "Russell Garcia Dies at 95; Arranger, Composer and Conductor," *Los Angeles Times*, November 24, 2011.

54 Willie Ruff, email message to author, May 29, 2013.

Interest in "Strange Meadow Lark" was even more widespread in the jazz community in the early 1960s. In connection with a proposed "Brubeck and Friends" album—featuring collaborative performances with musicians such as Charles Mingus, Benny Goodman, Tony Bennett, Gerry Mulligan, Jimmy Rushing, Louis Armstrong, and Carmen McRae—Brubeck wrote to Teo Macero in September 1963, "Perhaps Miles [Davis] and I could do one track in the studio, as Miles has told me he would like to do 'Strange Meadow Lark.' "[55] This recording apparently never came together. But a memo in Iola Brubeck's hand provides additional evidence that Davis was indeed interested in the tune (see Figure 8.1). Dated August 6, 1962, and with the heading "Music Promotion," it has a list of six tunes, including "Strange Meadow Lark," that were "sent to Miles Davis at his request."[56]

Fifty years later, in 2012, two other jazz masters—pianist Chick Corea and vibraphonist Gary Burton—joined forces for a new interpretation of "Strange Meadow Lark" on their album *Hot House* (Concord Jazz 0888072333635). This pair of musicians has been collaborating for decades, and they work here hand in glove. The order of events in their seven-minute recording is clear cut. They play the A and B sections three times in a row. The first time through A is in tempo rubato. Corea takes the first ten bars—which he spices up with a variety of complex and dissonant sonorities—then Burton joins (and Corea plays a fragmentary bass line) for the next ten. The raised fifth scale degree in the melody two measures before the bridge signals a shift to regular time, in an easygoing tempo (around ninety-four beats per minute). After they play the B section together, they each take a thirty-six-bar chorus (A = 10 + 10; B = 8 + 8) in which both continue to play but one or the other dominates (Corea first, then Burton). At the end of the vibraphone chorus, there is a return to the tempo rubato for a single statement of A', followed by an imaginative ending, beginning around 6:16. This dreamy passage begins with an E♭ pedal articulated by the piano, which dissolves into C major, then is complicated at the last moment by an F♯ augmented triad.

On May 11, 2013, about five months after Dave Brubeck's passing, a celebration of his life was held at the Cathedral of St. John the Divine in New York. The program included a number of spoken tributes, and family and friends performed thirteen of Brubeck's compositions. On this solemn occasion—when a vast throng gathered to pay their final

55 Dave Brubeck to Teo Macero, September 11, 1963 (Macero Collection, box 7, folder 19).
56 Iola Brubeck, "Music Promotion" memo (Brubeck Collection).

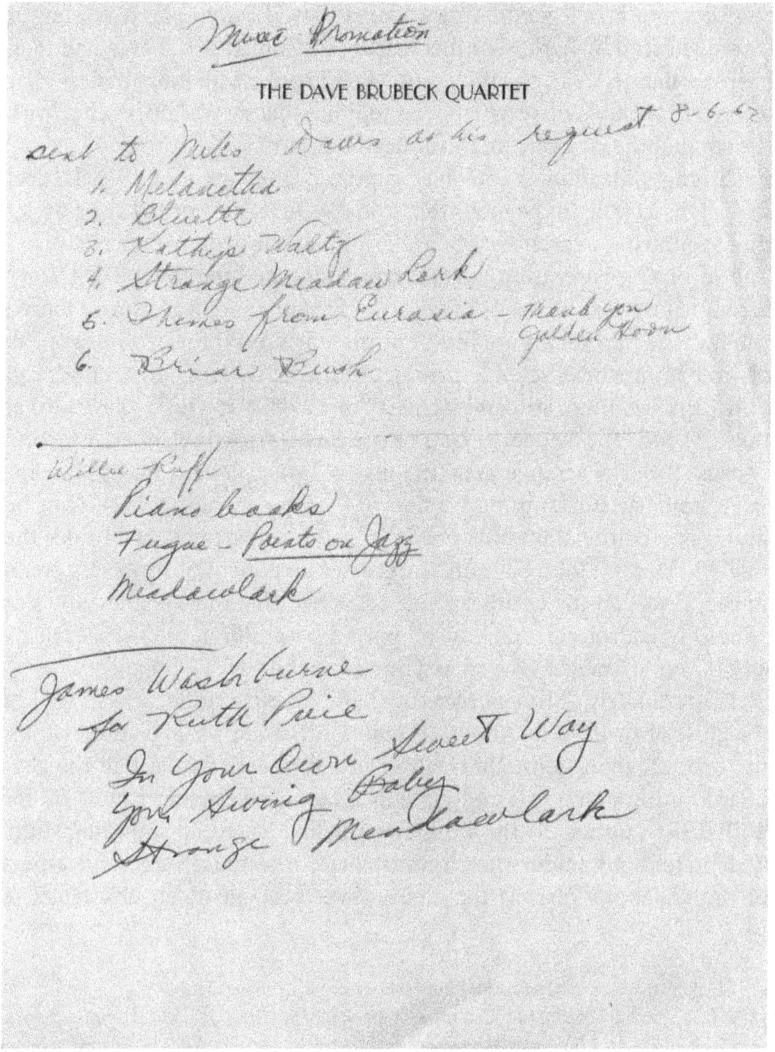
Music Promotion

THE DAVE BRUBECK QUARTET

sent to Miles Davis at his request 8-6-62

1. Melanctha
2. Bluette
3. Kathy's Waltz
4. Strange Meadow Lark
5. Themes from Eurasia – Thank you Golden Horn
6. Briar Bush

Willie Ruff

Piano books

Fugue – Points on Jazz

Meadowlark

James Washburne

for Ruth Price

In Your Own Sweet Way

You Swing Baby

Strange Meadowlark

FIGURE 8.1. Iola Brubeck, handwritten "Music Promotion" memo, August 6, 1962. Brubeck Collection, Holt-Atherton Special Collections, University of the Pacific Library. © Dave Brubeck.

respects to a jazz legend—Chick Corea played a solo piano version of "Strange Meadow Lark." For this reason, I assumed that Corea had long been acquainted with the tune. But when I spoke with him about it after a concert a couple of years later, he told me that he was unfamiliar with the song until Gary Burton introduced it to him.[57]

"Strange Meadow Lark" has captured the attention of classical musicians as well. In the 1990s the Brodsky Quartet recorded an arrangement for string quartet by Michael Thomas, the group's first violinist.[58] The recording is pleasant but unsurprising. The tune is played straight through, just once, in the original key of E♭ major and in a leisurely tempo rubato. The harmonies are lush, but there is no improvisation to speak of, except for a brief set of harmonics in the first violin part around 2:20 of the three-minute cut, and a cheeky birdlike chirp (high glissando) at the very end. The bridge, in fact, is modeled closely on Brubeck's second chorus (Brodsky arrangement, 1:13–1:55 = *Time Out* version, 5:57–6:28).

A similarly unassuming version of "Strange Meadow Lark" can be found in a compilation of twenty-five piano solos, published under the title *Nocturnes*.[59] John Salmon, the greatest exponent of Brubeck's piano music, recorded the entire set and described them in his liner notes as "small, lyrical pieces that can be played by children and savoured by adults," comparable to the more famous nocturnes of Chopin.[60]

Unfortunately, "Strange Meadow Lark" doesn't fare nearly so well in the guise of an art song. About a year before Salmon's solo piano sessions, the operatic tenor John De Haan recorded it, with Brubeck at the keyboard.[61] Although it was undoubtedly an exciting crossover moment for both artists, ultimately this bittersweet ballad ended up sounding stuffy and pretentious under the circumstances. The most successful aspect of the collaboration was the eighty-three-year-old Brubeck's sensitive

57 Chick Corea, interview with author, Atlanta, Georgia, October 3, 2015.
58 It first appeared on *Brodsky Unlimited: A Compilation of the Quartet's Favourite Encores* (Teldec Classics 2292-46015-2, 1991)—alongside works by Shostakovich, Falla, Gershwin, Copland, Prokofiev, Debussy, Ravel, and Elgar—and it was later included on *Best of Brodsky Quartet* (Teldec Classics 3984-28404-2, 1999).
59 Dave Brubeck, *Nocturnes*, edited and proofread by John Salmon (Miami, FL: Warner Bros. Publications, 1997), 33–35.
60 Dave Brubeck, *Nocturnes*, with John Salmon (piano), recorded at the University of North Carolina at Greensboro, February 6, 20, and 27, and April 17, 2005, Naxos 8.559301, 2006, compact disc.
61 Dave Brubeck, *Songs*, with John De Haan (tenor) and Dave Brubeck (piano), along with Jane Giering-De Haan (soprano) and Cliff Jackson (piano), recorded at the University of Miami, January 9–11, 2004, Naxos 8.559220, 2005, compact disc.

comping and imaginative introduction (nearly one minute of the entire 4:45 cut).

On the other hand, Andrew Rathbun's a cappella arrangement of "Strange Meadow Lark" for the San Francisco-based choral ensemble Chanticleer is an aural feast of bold harmonies and fresh sonorities.[62] Had Brubeck lived to hear it, he would surely have been pleased no end, on account of its impeccable musicianship and the group's connections with the Bay Area, where he grew up.

---

62 Chanticleer, *Someone New*, Chanticleer Records CR4010, 2013, compact disc.

CHAPTER 9

METRICAL EXPERIMENTATION

A FUNDAMENTAL CHARACTERISTIC of Dave Brubeck's *Time Out* album is that it eschews common meter, which had long formed the temporal basis for jazz. This recording project was preceded by many years of interest in diverse approaches to meter and rhythm, but it was Brubeck's first opportunity to explore them in a systematic way.

"Blue Rondo à la Turk," the first selection on *Time Out,* is the album's keystone in many respects. Its prevailing meter is an asymmetrical version of 9/8. The opening composed section (before the improvised blues) consists of numerous iterations of a four-bar pattern. In the first three measures of each phrase, the eighth notes are grouped 2+2+2+3.[1] Each

---

1 "Blue Rondo à la Turk" is presented as an exemplar of non-isochronous meter in Justin London, *Hearing in Time: Psychological Aspects of Musical Meter,* 2nd ed. (New York: Oxford

segment is then rounded off with a fourth measure in the more usual compound triple meter (three groups of three eighth notes).

Placing the tune with the most unusual and challenging meter as the initial cut was a bold statement of Brubeck's artistic intent. The familiarity and accessibility of "Blue Rondo à la Turk" has perhaps blunted its effect somewhat, so many decades after its creation. But it remains a sui generis composition not only in the wider world of jazz standards but even within the more narrowly circumscribed group of Brubeck's time experiments.

The second cut, "Strange Meadow Lark," on the other hand, is the only selection that retains the old-fashioned common meter that Brubeck was pushing back against. Yet Brubeck felt that this tune belonged on *Time Out*, even though it didn't share the experimental approach to musical time of the other pieces. If nothing else, its presence on the album demonstrates that Brubeck hadn't completely rejected traditional meter in jazz. The juxtaposition of "Blue Rondo à la Turk" (the most adventuresome cut) and "Strange Meadow Lark" (the most conventional) underscores this point.

"Take Five," the third and final cut on Side One, is of course the most famous metrical experiment on *Time Out*. The five quarter notes in each measure are stressed with a primary accent on beat 1 and a secondary accent on beat 4. This stress sets up a pattern of alternating groups of three and two beats: $5/4 = 3/4 + 2/4$. This template is absolutely unvarying from start to finish, through the entire cut (nearly five and one-half minutes). In addition, the primacy of a pattern with three quarter notes at the beginning of every measure contributes to the sense that this is actually a variant of the jazz waltz, in which the even-numbered "measures" are truncated by one beat.[2]

There is no question that "Take Five" was enormously popular and has been widely imitated. But was it a pioneering effort, and was it influential? With regard to 5/4 in particular, it has been observed that Max

University Press, 2012), 123–125. See also Evelyn Lamb, "Uncommon Time: What Makes Dave Brubeck's Unorthodox Jazz Stylings So Appealing?" *Scientific American*, December 11, 2012, http://www.scientificamerican.com/article/uncommon-time-dave-brubeck/ (accessed March 14, 2018).

2 The syncopated rhythm in the first part of each measure, as opposed to straight quarter notes on beats 4 and 5, is also characteristic of the jazz waltz. It is surely for this reason that "Take Five" was included (along with "Kathy's Waltz," another number from *Time Out*) in an anthology of jazz waltzes published in the Soviet Union. *Dzhazovye val'sy dlya fortepiano*, compiled by Yurii Chuganov (Moscow: Sovetskii Kompozitor, 1985), 32–36.

Roach employed this meter, too. In fact, Ingrid Monson suggested that its extensive use in the 1960 *Freedom Now Suite* may have been intended as a wry commentary on "Take Five."[3]

A related issue, even more pressing in the present context, concerns the relationship between "Take Five" and "As Long as You're Living" from Roach's *Quiet as It's Kept*.[4] The latter is a twelve-bar blues that moves at a brisk clip (about 185 beats per minute). The tune was composed by two of the band members, Tommy Turrentine (trumpet) and Julian Priester (trombone), and it was recorded at Capitol Studios in New York on July 21, 1959—just three weeks after "Take Five" and only about a mile away from Columbia's 30th Street Studio. One critic has noted that Roach's recording "sounded more natural and swinging" than Brubeck's (I tend to agree), and he even went so far as to allege that "Brubeck got credit for making sound hard what Roach got no credit for making sound easy."[5] This is a complicated claim, yet what is clear, however, is that other jazz musicians—such as Max Roach, but also the trumpet player Booker Little, who worked with Roach in the late 1950s and early 1960s—were actively exploring unusual time signatures around the same time as Brubeck was. In 2001, Brubeck recalled that, some forty years earlier, he had spoken with Roach at a jazz festival "about using different time signatures." Brubeck maintained that "neither one of us knew the other was doing it until that day," and he stated flatly, "I didn't influence Max and he didn't influence me."[6]

The secret of the success of "Take Five" resides in its unique amalgamation of complexity and simplicity. A German jazz critic pointed out the contrast between Brubeck and Roach in this regard: "Brubeck's pieces in odd meters were a sensation above all because he knew how to shape all his rhythmic innovations in such a tremendously concise manner and thereby to popularize them—unlike Max Roach, for instance, who attained such complexities with his deviations from the canonical common time that only insiders could follow

---

3 Ingrid Monson, *Freedom Sounds: Civil Rights Call Out to Jazz and Africa* (New York: Oxford University Press, 2007), 178–179.

4 Max Roach Plus Four (Roach—drums, Tommy Turrentine—trumpet, Julian Priester—trombone, Stanley Turrentine—tenor saxophone, Bob Boswell—bass), *Quiet as It's Kept*, Mercury MG 20491, 1959, 33⅓ rpm.

5 Kevin Whitehead, *Why Jazz? A Concise Guide* (New York: Oxford University Press, 2011), 83–84.

6 Darius Brubeck, "Jazz 1959: The Beginning of Beyond" (MA thesis, University of Nottingham, 2002), 135 n. 17, 239–240.

him."[7] Ted Gioia echoed this point of view, characterizing Brubeck's combination of "an odd meter with a simple, memorable vamp" in "Take Five" as a mixture of "the eccentric and the simple," and noting that this was one of his "most salient and effective stylistic devices."[8] Similarly, Alyn Shipton discerned that, "for all the perceived problems musicians had with the piece in 1959, apart from the mental gear-change needed to think and play in five beats to the bar instead of four, 'Take Five' is extremely simple—its complexity coming entirely from Desmond's deceptively straightforward-sounding solo."[9] Even Billy Joel articulated his admiration in terms of Brubeck's uncanny ability to balance experimentation with accessibility: "The way Brubeck messed around with time signatures appealed to the musician in me. It was, 'This is impossible, this should not be allowed to happen,' but he made it work in a melodic, musical way."[10]

As for the influence of "Take Five" on later musicians, perhaps the most generous—and specific—claims have been made by Ted Gioia:

As soon as one leaves the inner cliques of jazz, where his name is seldom mentioned, one sees Brubeck's impact everywhere. The background music between news flashes on TV, a few seconds of filler, bounces around in a Brubeckian 5/4 before disappearing. Jethro Tull, the long-lived rock group, hits the charts with "Living in the Past," a lilting tune with a "Take Five" breakdown of 5/4 into a waltzy three-step followed by the two hard hits on beats four and five. The TV show "Mission Impossible" grabs listeners with the same Brubeck-derived rhythm. Although the jazz world may be sparing in its praise, the music community at large accepted Brubeck as an innovator long ago, as did the listening public.[11]

---

7 "Da waren dann Brubecks Stücke in ungeraden Metren eine Sensation, vor allem deshalb, weil er es verstand, alle seine rhythmischen Neuerungen so enorm griffig zu gestalten und dadurch zu popularisieren—im Unterschied etwa zu Max Roach, der mit seinen Abweichungen vom kanonisierten Viervierteltakt zu solchen Komplexitäten gelangte, daß ihm nur noch Insider folgen konnten." Ulrich Olshausen, "Swingender Akademiker: Dave Brubeck—Zwischen Kritik und Anerkennung," *Musik + Medizin* 3 (1979): 46.

8 Ted Gioia, *West Coast Jazz: Modern Jazz in California, 1945–1960* (Berkeley: University of California Press, 1998), 91.

9 Alyn Shipton, *A New History of Jazz*, rev. ed. (New York: Continuum, 2007), 513.

10 Hank Bordowitz, *Billy Joel: The Life and Times of an Angry Young Man*, rev. ed. (Milwaukee, WI: Backbeat Books, 2011), 11.

11 Gioia, *West Coast Jazz*, 68.

There is really no doubt that the Brubeck tune was the inspiration for the *Mission: Impossible* theme. Its composer, Lalo Schifrin, said as much: "I suppose the Dave Brubeck Quartet's 'Take Five' was in my heart, but the 5/4 tempo just came naturally. It's forceful, and the listener never feels comfortable."[12] And in 1966, the very year when the television series first aired, Brubeck lauded Schifrin as "a great new writer" and noted that "he's doing so many fine things."[13]

The situation with Jethro Tull is not as straightforward. Tim Smolko, who has investigated their music quite thoroughly, points out that Ian Anderson, the group's frontman, "was writing interesting, unconventional songs even early in his career, and went on to write dozens of songs in unusual meters." To attribute the time signature of his 1969 hit "Living in the Past" to Brubeck's influence, then, is "a bit of an overstatement."[14] On the other hand, Anderson specifically mentioned Brubeck when he was asked about the origins of "Living in the Past," shortly before a tour of Australia in December 2014. He recalled that, during Jethro Tull's first tour of the United States in 1969, his manager asked him to "quickly whip upstairs to your room and write a hit single we could record next week in New York." Anderson said he "decided to write the most uncommercial, three-and-a-half-minute song I could muster from the title 'Living in the Past.' " Its 5/4 meter "was commercially a no-no, because you couldn't really dance to it." Much to his surprise, it became a hit, and he noted, "It was the second and probably the last time that a tune in 5/4 time signature would make it into the Top Ten of the charts. The first, of course, [was] Dave Brubeck's famous 'Take Five.' "[15]

Side Two of *Time Out* consists of two pairs of tunes. The members of each set initially seem quite different from one another. On closer inspection, however, it becomes clear that they share deep affinities. Although the last two cuts are in very different styles, they also have much in common with each other. According to Brubeck, both "Everybody's Jumpin' " and "Pick Up Sticks" were written with his drummer, Joe Morello, in mind. Another significant similarity is that both numbers

12 Marc Myers, "Sounds of Suspense: Cultural Conversation with Lalo Schifrin," *Wall Street Journal*, November 12, 2012.

13 Leonard Feather, "Dave Brubeck, Composer," *Down Beat* 33, no. 13 (June 30, 1966): 20.

14 Tim Smolko, email message to author, July 20, 2016. See Tim Smolko, *Jethro Tull's "Thick as a Brick" and "A Passion Play": Inside Two Long Songs* (Bloomington: Indiana University Press, 2013).

15 Interview with Ian Anderson, *Tom Magazine*, October 7, 2014. http://www.tommagazine. com.au/2014/10/07/ian-anderson/ (accessed March 15, 2018).

exist in two versions with distinct titles ("Pick Up Sticks"—"Watusi Drums" and "Everybody's Jumpin'"—"Everybody's Comin'"). The metrical shifts in "Everybody's Jumpin'"—three four-bar units (4/4, 3/2, 4/4), plus four additional measures of 3/4 and four of 2/4—contrast with the stable and consistent 6/4 ostinato undergirding "Pick Up Sticks."

The other two cuts on Side Two, "Three to Get Ready" and "Kathy's Waltz," both juxtapose triple and quadruple meter. In "Three to Get Ready" the contrasting time signatures are used in alternation, whereas in "Kathy's Waltz" they occur simultaneously.

The metrical structure of "Three to Get Ready" was part and parcel of its recording process. During the evening session on June 25, 1959, the Quartet recorded two additional takes of "Three to Get Ready." The second recording has not been preserved among Brubeck's personal materials. There exists only a short clip in which Teo Macero announces it as follows: "Remake. 3/4—4/4. Take two." This is nearly identical to the way he had announced the first take of the remake, although previously he had also included the matrix number (CO 62556). In both announcements, however, Macero referred to the tune not by its familiar title, but rather by its meter signatures, "3/4—4/4." Macero's shorthand version makes explicit the alternation between groups of three and four beats throughout the tune. On the other hand, this oscillation is only implied in the final title, which is extracted from the well-known children's rhyme:

One for the money,
Two for the show,
Three to get ready,
And four to go!

Brubeck's obsession with polymeter manifested itself in the fabric of his family life. His daughter, Catherine, recalled sitting with her brothers at a big oval table in their home, practicing how to tap two beats against three. She said that her father was teaching them and they were listening. "Other dads go out and throw a baseball," but he taught his children polymeters. "It's a weird way to hear the world," she mused. "I don't hear it that way. Probably most people don't."[16]

By the time Brubeck recorded "Kathy's Waltz," he had plenty of experience with performing in more than one meter at a time, and especially

16 Catherine Brubeck Yaghsizian, interview with the author, November 12, 2013.

with the juxtaposition of triple and quadruple meter. In the liner notes to his *In Europe* album, Brubeck mentioned two other tunes with a similar procedure. He said he was relieved to hear Paul Desmond suggest that the Quartet play "Wonderful Copenhagen" "as a waltz against 4/4 as we did on 'Someday My Prince Will Come' in the Disney album."[17] Around the same time, Brubeck confessed that he really didn't know how all this worked. After a live performance of "Someday My Prince Will Come" on Radio Free Europe in 1960, he said to the interviewer (who thought it "sounded magnificent"): "We were playing three rhythms [i.e., meters] at once and we stayed in those three rhythms for, I would say, three to four minutes at a time." The Quartet started out with a waltz, then "went into four-four and then we superimposed every possible [rhythm]—I couldn't tell you what we were doing [in] the last set—against those things. Those were the two basic rhythms. I think we were playing some five, some seven patterns—you never know what you've done afterwards."[18]

Though Brubeck himself had difficulty explaining his improvisational procedure, another jazz musician has taken a stab at it. Since analytical descriptions of Brubeck's recordings are relatively few and far between, it is worth quoting Eddie Meadows's account of "Kathy's Waltz" at some length:

> Brubeck superimposed the 3/4 and 4/4 in his improvisation. He also displayed flowing melodic lines, but his scale choices were primarily major scales, with occasional blue notes thrown in for contrast. Near the end of his first improvisation, he added more flow to his right-hand lines and then followed with stacked chords containing flatted fifths and sevenths, realized in a style reminiscent of both ragtime and honky-tonk piano styles. The improvisation is imbued with developmental techniques that echo concepts sometimes used by Euro-American classical music composers. Specifically, this portion of the improvisation is permeated with sequences and the creation and development of a motif that eventually evolves into a section in which the 3/4 and 4/4 meters are superimposed. This was achieved by drummer Joe Morello, who kept a 3/4 rhythm while Brubeck played 4/4 ideas on top of every two 3/4 meters, thereby producing a 4 against 6 contrast. Wright contributed to the cross-rhythm feel by playing single

17 The Dave Brubeck Quartet, *In Europe*, Columbia CL 1168, 1958, 33⅓ rpm.
18 Martin Bush, transcript of interview with Dave Brubeck at the Jazz Gallery in Greenwich Village, December 9, 1960 (Brubeck Collection).

notes on counts 1 and 3 of each of Brubeck's 4/4 measures, effectively functioning simultaneously as the downbeat of Morello's 3/4 rhythm. Brubeck added two more layers to these rhythmic innovations by simultaneously performing a 4/4 in his right hand and a 3/4 waltz pattern in his left hand.[19]

Although "Kathy's Waltz" functioned as a vehicle for Brubeck's polymetric experimentation, it simultaneously was grounded in the conventions associated with a popular social dance. *Grove Music Online* unhelpfully defines jazz waltz as "a term which might be applied to any jazz piece in 3/4 time."[20] The definitive history of the waltz in jazz has yet to be written, but it surely ought to include as important landmarks Fats Waller's "Jitterbug Waltz" (1942), with its distinctive use of the Hammond organ, and Sonny Rollins's "Valse Hot" (1956). Max Roach, who played drums in Rollins's "Plus 4" combo, went on shortly thereafter to release an entire album of *Jazz in 3/4 Time* (EmArcy MG 36108, 1957). The liner notes to Roach's project, which originated just two years before *Time Out*, claim on the one hand that "the concept of a jazz waltz is not new," but on the other hand, that "it remains a relatively old phenomenon." There should be no thought, then, that Brubeck was blazing a new trail with "Kathy's Waltz."[21] Even the notion of dedicating a waltz to a female relative had been anticipated by another pianist, Bill Evans, who first recorded his famous "Waltz for Debby" (his niece) in 1956.[22]

With regard to his work with unusual meters and rhythms on *Time Out*, Dave Brubeck's metrical experimentation didn't appear out of nowhere in 1959. By then, he had been interested in such matters for more than two decades. And Brubeck's fascination with the temporal aspects

19 Eddie S. Meadows, *Bebop to Cool: Context, Ideology, and Musical Identity* (Westport, CT: Praeger, 2003), 268–269.

20 "Jazz waltz," *Grove Music Online*, accessed March 16, 2018, http://www. oxfordmusiconline.com/grovemusic/view/10.1093/gmo/9781561592630.001.0001/omo-9781561592630-e-2000602900.

21 Brubeck himself made no such claim. In a 1995 interview, he said, "When I first used waltz time, I'd never heard any other jazz players use the waltz. And then I found Fats Waller's 'Jitterbug Waltz,' and so he beat me. But I didn't know it. So I thought I was the first. . . . Dangerous to think you're ever first. [*Laughs*] You'll find somebody long before you who did it." Paul Zollo, *Songwriters on Songwriting*, 4th ed. (Cambridge, MA: Da Capo Press, 2003), 52.

22 Bill Evans, *New Jazz Conceptions*, Riverside RLP 12–223, 1956, 33⅓ rpm. The album *Waltz for Debby* by the Bill Evans Trio appeared five years later (Riverside RLP 399, 1961).

of jazz didn't cease with *Time Out*. Rather, it was the first in a series of five such projects in the oeuvre of the "classic" Quartet. Brubeck wasn't the only jazz musician, or the first, to move beyond common meter. But his enduring legacy, it seems, rests on his unique ability to pursue this progressive musical agenda while simultaneously achieving broad popular appeal.

CHAPTER 10

TIME MARCHES ON

TIME OUT DIDN'T materialize out of thin air. Its experiments with meter and rhythm were the product of many years of reflection and trial and error, and during the long gestation of the project, the Quartet collaborated with Leonard Bernstein and the New York Philharmonic, Brubeck became involved in issues of civil rights, and Dave and Iola Brubeck worked doggedly to bring *The Real Ambassadors* to fruition.

BERNSTEIN PLAYS BRUBECK PLAYS *BERNSTEIN*

Time Out's official release date was in mid-December 1959, immediately after the Dave Brubeck Quartet performed Howard Brubeck's *Dialogues for Jazz Combo and Orchestra* with the New York Philharmonic in Carnegie Hall. However, Brubeck's association with the Philharmonic and its music director, Leonard Bernstein, continued and intensified shortly thereafter.

On Saturday, January 30, 1960, Brubeck was back in New York, to record his brother's *Dialogues* with Bernstein and the New York Philharmonic.[1] The idea of a project along these lines had been in the air for quite some time. During the previous summer, while the Quartet was recording *Time Out*, Brubeck's attorney communicated with his counterpart at Columbia Records about "the possibility of Dave's making records with his Quartet and a symphony orchestra, with strings, and/or a choral group." A few weeks after their July 13 phone conversation, the record company's representative committed to paper his "understanding as to how such special recordings should be handled," and the copy in Teo Macero's files includes a handwritten annotation indicating that its content had been approved by a letter from Brubeck's representative on August 12.[2] The next month, the president of Columbia Records, Goddard Lieberson, told Macero in a memo that Brubeck had come in to see him, and that Brubeck "wondered if somebody was following through on the possibility of recording with Leonard Bernstein and the Philharmonic."[3] Macero told Lieberson that he and John McClure, another producer with whom he had discussed the project, were "not anticipating any real problem in this matter," although they had not yet had the opportunity to discuss it with Bernstein himself.[4]

Although the Quartet had performed the *Dialogues* with this same orchestra just a few weeks earlier, apparently the late January recording session was rather dicey. Brubeck's pencil entries into his personal daytimer provide a rare glimpse of his frame of mind and the hectic pace of his life. He left home in California at 7:00 a.m. on Friday, January 29, in order to catch an 8:45 flight from San Francisco to New York.

---

1 Columbia Records, Artist Job Sheet, Job No. 50577, January 30, 1960 (Macero Collection, box 6, folder 7).

2 Jerome Talbert (Columbia Records) to James R. Bancroft, August 3, 1959 (Macero Collection, box 7, folder 15).

3 Goddard Lieberson to Teo Macero, September 17, 1959 (Macero Collection, box 6, folder 6).

4 Teo Macero to Goddard Lieberson, September 23, 1959 (Macero Collection, box 6, folder 6). McClure's first project with Bernstein, the historic recording of Shostakovich's Fifth Symphony at Boston's Symphony Hall, was just a few weeks in the future (October 20, 1959). He subsequently produced about 200 recordings with Bernstein, over a thirty-year period. The reason McClure and Macero were unable to speak with Bernstein at that time was that the orchestra was in the midst of an extensive two-month tour of Europe, including three weeks in the Soviet Union. See William Yardley, "John McClure Dies at 84; Produced Classic Records," *New York Times*, June 24, 2014.

Upon his arrival, he took a taxi directly from the airport to Columbia's 30th Street Studio, for a 7:00 p.m. appointment, which he characterized as a "very swinging session with J[immy] Rushing."[5] According to Brubeck, the next day's session began at 2:00 p.m. and ran until 5:40, with ten minutes off every twenty minutes. He noted that he "had to play safe" because it was disorienting to hear the "two different beats" of his drummer Joe Morello and the orchestra, and he "often got turned around." It was, in short, "a real nightmare with a happy ending." As if that weren't enough for a single weekend, on Sunday Brubeck had a late morning breakfast with the president of his booking agency, Joe Glaser; recorded a retake with Rushing and started a new session of tunes from the Broadway musical *Beg, Borrow or Steal* in the afternoon; then met with the choreographer Dania Krupska (1921–2011) in the evening, to discuss the possibility of using Brubeck's "Dziekuje (Thank You)" for an original ballet.[6]

The four movements of Howard Brubeck's *Dialogues for Jazz Combo and Orchestra* amount to twenty-two minutes of music, and therefore

5 This was the first of three recording sessions (the others were on February 16 and August 4) that led to the release of *Brubeck & Rushing: The Dave Brubeck Quartet Featuring Jimmy Rushing* (Columbia CL 1553) at the end of the year. Brubeck and the famous blues singer Jimmy Rushing (1901–1972) traveled together on the European tour of the Newport Jazz Festival in September and October 1959 (a copy of the itinerary is preserved in Macero Collection, box 41, folder 17). In October, Brubeck's manager, Mort Lewis, sent a note to the Columbia Records producer Irving Townsend, reminding him "to discuss with Jimmy Rushing the possibility of what tunes he would like to do with Dave." And Lewis followed up with Townsend in December, as follows: "After our return from our European tour with Jimmy Rushing, I wrote you that Dave is most anxious to make an LP with Jimmy. Both Dave and Jimmy have discussed the idea and are very favorably inclined to it." Mort Lewis to Irving Townsend, October 26, 1959 (Macero Collection, box 5, folder 5); Lewis to Townsend, December 26, 1959 (Brubeck Collection).

6 "Executary, January [1960]" (Brubeck Collection). The music for *Beg, Borrow or Steal* was by Brubeck's friend Leon Pober (1920–1971). It was a Broadway flop, which ran at the Martin Beck Theatre for only four days (February 10–13, 1960). See Steven Suskin, *The Sound of Broadway Music: A Book of Orchestrators and Orchestrations* (New York: Oxford University Press, 2009), 336; and Corinne J. Naden, *The Golden Age of American Musical Theatre, 1943–1965* (Lanham, MD: Scarecrow Press, 2011), 49. Brubeck had high hopes for the show back in January, however, and he wanted to capitalize on its potential success by recording some of its tunes. On February 13, Brubeck noted its swift demise in his daytimer and remarked dolefully, "All that work for nothing." On the other hand, the conversation with Dania Krupska led to the composition of Brubeck's *Points on Jazz* and its performance by the American Ballet Theatre in 1961. See Ethan L. Rogers, "Convergent Styles: A Study of Dave Brubeck's *Points on Jazz*" (DMA thesis, Louisiana State University, 2017).

they fit comfortably on the A-side of an LP. The original idea for the B-side was more of the same—namely, a group of Howard's arrangements for jazz combo and orchestra of tunes by Dave. The day after Lieberson's memo to Macero, Howard wrote to Macero himself and provided a list of pieces and their instrumentation, in preparation for "the recording sessions for the album with Dave and backgrounds." He specified that Dave "would like to do the 'Brandenburg Gate' on the album with the *Dialogues*," but also listed "Dziekuje (Thank You)," "In Your Own Sweet Way," "Summer Song," and "Kathy's Waltz," plus another composition of his own, titled "G Flat Theme."[7]

Three months later, this plan was still in play, along with an alternative. A few days after Christmas, Mort Lewis wrote to Macero, outlining his and Dave's thinking concerning LPs with Columbia in 1960. The flip side of the Bernstein and New York Philharmonic disc could be some of Howard's arrangements, or it could be "just the Quartet, which both you and Dave feel would be such a good idea."[8] By the second week of January, Brubeck and Lewis were "concerned about the other side of the Bernstein LP," because the matter had not yet been settled.[9]

The solution didn't come until the evening immediately after the Quartet and orchestra recorded the *Dialogues*. The album's liner notes soberly report the facts. Paul Desmond suggested that the Quartet could play some tunes from Bernstein's Broadway shows, and Brubeck liked the idea. Bernstein then sat down at the piano, played selections from *On the Town* (1944), *Wonderful Town* (1953), *Candide* (1956), and *West Side Story* (1957), and the Quartet made their selections.[10]

A more colorful account, which conveys the same information but also captures a sense of Bernstein's larger-than-life exuberance, is found among Macero's personal papers:

What about the other side? How did that come into being? Plain and simple: time, for one thing—excitement about another man's work, for another.

---

7 Howard Brubeck to Teo Macero, September 18, 1959 (Macero Collection, box 7, folder 15). Most of these arrangements appeared later on *Brandenburg Gate: Revisited* (Columbia CL 1963), which entered our discussion in Chapter 8.

8 Mort Lewis to Teo Macero, December 29, 1959 (Macero Collection, box 7, folder 15).

9 Mort Lewis to Teo Macero, January 10, 1960 (Macero Collection, box 7, folder 16).

10 Liner notes, the New York Philharmonic with the Dave Brubeck Quartet conducted by Leonard Bernstein, *Bernstein Plays Brubeck Plays Bernstein*, Columbia CL 1466, 1960, 33⅓ rpm.

Before we had finished recording *Dialogues for Jazz Combo and Orchestra*, I asked Lenny if he would have some time to discuss the work or works which we could put on the other side of the album.

"Dave," commented Lenny, "we can discuss it in a cab on the way uptown, as I have to leave immediately for a dinner date." "O.K."

We finished recording ahead of schedule, so I asked Lenny if he would be leaving soon. "Yep!" was what I got. But that "yep" ended almost two hours after the session. It seems that the second side of the LP was soon to be decided without my help and without my even being aware of it.

Paul Desmond, an important member of the Brubeck Quartet, said to Lenny, unbeknownst to me, "Hey, Lenny, what about playing some of your songs on the other side of the album?" "Yeah," replied Dave. Lenny started walking slowly for the piano, and before long we had the idea for the second side. Lenny played on and on, playing through most of his Broadway shows . . . I guess, every piece he has ever written. What a memory! If I only had thought of recording this, it would have been a classic. Lenny playing jazz and at the same time, finding ideas for this song and that. Everyone, including Dave and myself, was awed at this man. This lasted about two hours. I think Lenny arrived a little late for his dinner date.[11]

Brubeck set to work right away. By the next weekend, the Quartet was rehearsing his arrangements of two tunes from *West Side Story*, and he stayed up until late at night working on two more. Several days later, Dave wrote in his daytimer that the rehearsal went okay, and he was especially pleased with the "rhy[th]mic figure in 'Maria.'"[12] The next day, the Quartet recorded "Tonight," "I Feel Pretty," "Maria," and "Somewhere" from *West Side Story*, all of which were selected for the album.[13] The other tune, "A Quiet Girl" from *Wonderful Town*, was recorded three days later.[14]

The decision to favor *West Side Story* was, as always, a shrewd business calculation. Not only was it Bernstein's most current musical, but it

11 "Brubeck-Bernstein 'Dialogues for Jazz Combo & Orchestra,'" unpublished typescript (Macero Collection, box 6, folder 6).

12 "Executary, February [1960]," entries for February 7 and 13 (Brubeck Collection).

13 Columbia Records, Artist Job Sheet, Job No. 50577, February 14, 1960, 2:30–5:30 p.m. (Macero Collection, box 6, folder 7).

14 Columbia Records, Artist Job Sheet, Job No. 50577, February 17, 1960, 2:30–5:30 p.m. (Macero Collection, box 6, folder 7).

had recently enjoyed a highly successful twenty-one-month run at the Winter Garden Theatre on Broadway (September 26, 1957 through June 27, 1959). Even more importantly, it was set for a return engagement, which coincided with the album's release in August 1960.[15] All parties were eager to derive as much financial benefit as possible from the show's timeliness and popularity.

The first inkling of the album's checkered reception came several months before its official release. Columbia Records pressed a special copy of the *Dialogues for Jazz Combo and Orchestra* for a panel discussion of "jazz and the classics" at the University of Minnesota. Brubeck had been invited to participate as a panelist, but his travel schedule didn't permit it. While simultaneously thanking Brubeck profusely for going to the trouble of arranging for a prepublication copy, the program consultant informed him euphemistically that "the reaction of the panel to the recording was mixed." He then attempted to soften the blow by painting an optimistic picture: "The general consensus was that, although this recording was not the full and perfect achievement of synthesis between jazz and classical music, it certainly is one of the best attempts to date and is a 'step in the right direction.'" He concluded with the wish that Brubeck's "unusual combination of popularity and significant contributions to the development of jazz as an art form will continue for many years to come."[16]

It seems unlikely that Brubeck lost much sleep over this judgment of his recording of the *Dialogues*. But the fraught question of his role in the synthesis of classical music and jazz known as Third Stream was clearly on his mind around that time. When asked for his thoughts about Third Stream, in an interview for Radio Free Europe later that year, Brubeck complained that he was "always left out of the people who have contributed to this." He noted that he had been attempting to meld the two since the 1940s and asserted that his Quartet "is as important in this Third Stream as any group and shouldn't be omitted at all."[17] It must have been deeply dispiriting, then, when Gunther Schuller—who coined the term Third Stream in a lecture at Brandeis University in 1957—later said, "The mainstream of jazz today is terribly limited. It's too uncomplicated, both

---

15 The show returned to the Winter Garden Theatre from April 27 through October 22, 1960. It then continued for several more weeks at the Alvin Theatre, from October 24 through December 10.

16 Ronald N. Loomis to Dave Brubeck, May 19, 1960 (Brubeck Collection).

17 Dave Brubeck, interview with Martin Bush, Jazz Gallery, Greenwich Village, New York, December 9, 1960 (typescript, Brubeck Collection).

rhythmically and tonally. Mr. Brubeck was a great hope to us in the late forties and early fifties in doing something about this; but today, he is only a commercial jazz player. His so-called experimentations with time changes are merely superficial."[18]

The published reviews of *Bernstein Plays Brubeck Plays Bernstein*, and specifically of Howard Brubeck's *Dialogues*, varied greatly from one to the next. The blurb in *Cash Box* characterized the *Dialogues* as "a successful experiment in combining the forms of jazz and classical music" and said it "remains of high interest to students of this blossoming serious art."[19] The reviewer in *Down Beat*, on the other hand, awarded the album only three-and-a-half stars (out of five). He felt that the *Dialogues* was "one of the most ambitious and one of the least successful" of the attempts to merge jazz and classical music. Moreover, Howard Brubeck's orchestral scoring reminded him of the saccharine sounds of "a Nelson Riddle background being performed by a hip pit band."[20]

The negative assessment in *Down Beat* must have been especially difficult for Dave to absorb, because he had assumed considerable financial risk on his brother's behalf. According to Dave's attorney, their initial investment in the composition and orchestration of the *Dialogues* amounted to "more than five thousand dollars," as of June 1960.[21] And matters went from bad to worse in the coming months. In February 1961, Iola Brubeck confided in their old friend and sometime musical collaborator, the clarinetist Bill Smith, as follows: "The Bernstein album is selling fantastically well, but so far Dave has not made a penny off of it. He is still paying off the Philharmonic, which was counted as an advance against royalties."[22]

It is doubtful that Brubeck ever recouped the costs of this expensive project. But it was a stroke of genius, in terms of general publicity and prestige, to have hitched his wagon to Bernstein's musical. On October 18, 1961—just eight months after Iola Brubeck's glum missive to Bill Smith—United Artists released *West Side Story* as a feature film, and it subsequently garnered the Academy Award for Best Motion Picture.

---

18 Ralph Thomas, "Brubeck vs. Schuller: Two Approaches to Modern Music," *Toronto Sun*, 1964 (Brubeck Collection).
19 *Cash Box*, August 13, 1960 (Macero Collection, box 7, folder 10).
20 Bill Mathieu, review of *Bernstein Plays Brubeck Plays Bernstein*, *Down Beat*, 1960.
21 James R. Bancroft to Alfred B. Lorber (Columbia Records), June 29, 1960 (Brubeck Collection).
22 Iola Brubeck to Bill Smith, February 19, 1961 (Brubeck Collection).

Within five days, Columbia's marketing department had designed and produced a sticker "to be affixed to every *Bernstein Plays Brubeck Plays Bernstein* album . . . in the field," with the additional instruction that their sales force should include the album "as an integral part of all 'West Side' promotions and displays."[23] More significantly, and not surprisingly, they eventually redesigned the cover and renamed the album *The Dave Brubeck Quartet Plays Music from Leonard Bernstein's "West Side Story,"* to highlight its connection with the film.[24]

CANCELLATION OF BRUBECK'S SOUTHERN TOUR

In April 1959, Brubeck recorded an album of standards, meeting one of Columbia Records' conditions for approval of the *Time Out* project. *Gone with the Wind* (Columbia CL 1347) borrowed the title of Margaret Mitchell's famous novel, set in Georgia during the American Civil War and the Reconstruction Era. The novel was published in 1936, and adapted for the screen three years later. Columbia's promotional materials for January 1960 stressed that Brubeck's upcoming February "tour of top Southern colleges" provided "a perfect chance to plug both *Time Out* and the Dixie-flavored *Gone with the Wind*."[25] And the prospects for commercial success with the latter album seemed so good that a sequel, titled *Southern Scene* (Columbia CL 1439), was already in the works.[26]

The plans for an extensive tour in the South date back to September 1959, not long after the third and final recording session for *Time Out* (August 18), and they brought to the surface once again the ugly racial tensions that had bedeviled the Quartet ever since Eugene Wright joined the group in January 1958. Just a few months after the high-profile cancellation of a concert at the University of Georgia in March 1959, in a stupefying display of racism and greed, a staff member at Brubeck's own booking agency attempted to pressure him into using a white bass player for the impending tour:

---

23 "Spreading the (West Side) Story," copy for newsletter, October 23, 1961 (Macero Collection, box 7, folder 10).

24 "Album Cover Copy," February 7, 1962 (Macero Collection, box 7, folder 10).

25 "Time Out for *Time Out*," *Insight*, January 20, 1960, p. 6 (Macero Collection, box 7, folder 5).

26 Its ten tracks were recorded in New York on September 10 and 11, 1959, and Hollywood on October 29. Columbia Records, Artist Job Sheet, Job No. 50294, September 10, 1959, 10:00 a.m.–1:00 p.m. and 2:00–5:00 p.m.; Columbia Records, Artist Job Sheet, Job No. H-135383, October 29, 1959, 10:00 p.m.–1:00 a.m. (Sony Music Archives Library). The job sheet for September 11 has not been preserved.

A couple of weeks ago I wrote to you about playing 25 colleges and universities in the South and Southwest during the month of February, sponsored by a newly formed organization. The chairman of this organization just called me and wanted to know if you had any colored boys in your group, which you do. My purpose in writing you is to see if you could arrange to have an all-white group to play these colleges and universities, because they will not accept you as a mixed group. Please let me hear from you immediately, as 25 dates for $1,500 per concert are not to be sneezed at. This should be considered seriously, as college concerts are the backbone of your income.

At the bottom of the page, handwritten in large letters and underlined, is an additional notation that was intended to heighten the urgency of this request: "You need this."[27]

Brubeck's response was negative, of course, as it had always been in the face of such incidents—including his refusal to play in South Africa under apartheid in 1958, and his rejection of what would have been "the biggest TV booking" of his career.[28]

The attrition of the Southern tour dates apparently occurred in three stages. On the day after Christmas, Iola Brubeck informed Eugene Wright that the Quartet would "be in Oakland until about January 28th, at which time we leave for the tour of Southern colleges, which is scheduled to last until February 20."[29] It is unclear when the first wave of cancellations took place, but a letter from Brubeck's booking agent (a different one) eleven days later included a detailed itinerary that encompassed those dates, but included only fourteen scheduled appearances out of the original twenty-five.[30] According to Ralph Gleason's newspaper account the following week, the number then sank to ten, "as schools dropped out, when they learned the Brubeck quartet was not an all-white group." Brubeck then asked his "booking agency, Associated Booking Corporation in New York, to send a wire notifying the schools that the Brubeck quartet is interracial. That's when the final cancellations came in."[31] In the end,

27 Bob Bundy to Dave Brubeck, October 6, 1959 (Brubeck Collection).
28 "Jazz Pianist Brubeck Turns Down $17,000 from S. Africa," *Oklahoma Eagle*, October 30, 1958; "Why Brubeck's Band Won't Play in Georgia," *New York Post*, February 24, 1959 (Brubeck Collection).
29 Iola Brubeck to Eugene Wright, December 26, 1959 (Brubeck Collection).
30 Larry Bennett to Dave Brubeck and Mort Lewis, January 6, 1960 (Brubeck Collection).
31 Ralph J. Gleason, "Racial Issue 'Kills' Brubeck Jazz Tour of the South," *San Francisco Chronicle*, January 12, 1960 (Brubeck Collection).

only three schools survived this contractual white flight: Jacksonville (FL) University, Vanderbilt University, and the University of the South.[32]

The documentary evidence suggests a rapid chain of events. The telegram to the final ten colleges and universities went out during the weekend of January 9 and 10, 1960.[33] On Monday, January 11, Brubeck's manager Mort Lewis was notified that "all the schools in the South turned down the mixed group for concerts except three."[34] As of midweek, an agent at the Chicago office of the Associated Booking Corporation was "pulling [out] all [the] stops to fill [the] February dates," and he felt sure they would "come out OK."[35] On the same day, the president of the booking agency expressed his support for Brubeck's stance. He noted that it made him "very happy," that he greatly appreciated the "way you and Mort express yourselves," and he signed his message as "your greatest friend and admirer."[36] Brubeck was undoubtedly aware that his agent was speaking largely in his own self-interest. He must therefore have been immeasurably prouder of an unsolicited message of appreciation that arrived at nearly the same time, from officials representing the West Coast branch of the National Association for the Advancement of Colored People (NAACP): "We are anxious to express our deep admiration of your courageous stand against submitting your band to the pressures of immoral racial discrimination. We do not underestimate the financial loss incurred, nor do we overestimate the very valuable and tangible contribution that you have made to the fight for human rights. Again we commend you for a very inspiring stand and we echo your sentiments that prejudice is indeed 'morally, religiously, and politically wrong.'"[37]

For several days thereafter, members of the Brubeck organization handled this situation with kid gloves. Lewis's letter to a university in Ohio mentioned that the cancellations had "caused considerable confusion."[38]

---

32 It appears that the Jacksonville date may have remained intact because of a misunderstanding. At all events, Brubeck wrote in his daytimer for February 1, 1960, "Should call Teo [Macero] and [Joe] Glaser. School was told we were all-white group [and that we] would send substitute for $2,225.00, Chris Connors." "Executary, February [1960]" (Brubeck Collection).

33 Gleason, "Racial Issue 'Kills' Brubeck Jazz Tour."

34 "'Matter of Money' Cancels Brubeck," *Oakland Tribune,* January 13, 1960 (Brubeck Collection).

35 Fred Williamson to Mort Lewis, telegram, January 13, 1960 (Brubeck Collection).

36 Joe Glaser to Dave Brubeck, telegram, January 13, 1960 (Brubeck Collection).

37 Tarea Hall Pitman et al. to Dave Brubeck, telegram, January 13, 1960 (Brubeck Collection).

38 Mort Lewis to Ruth Williamson (Wittenberg University), January 14, 1960 (Brubeck Collection).

One of the booking agents referred to the turn of events as "your unfortunate situation."[39] Even Brubeck himself veered in the direction of understatement when he told an old friend, "we have encountered several difficulties in our proposed tour through the South."[40] By the following week, however, Brubeck was prepared to state bluntly what had taken place. He told a composition teacher at the Juilliard School of Music in New York, who had invited him to speak to his class, that his "February college concert tour was scuttled by the 'white supremacists.'"[41] The next day, the same booking agent who several months earlier had tried in vain to persuade Brubeck to tour with an all-white group sent him a revised itinerary. It is notable for its brevity—containing only the three residual Southern dates, plus four in the Midwest, and a week in New York City—and also for its businesslike tone and prudent lack of commentary.[42]

The kudos also continued to roll in. An editor at Doubleday, who had recently approached Dave and Iola about the possibility of writing a book, signaled his approval in a follow-up letter: "The newspaper stories about your refusal to back down on the Southern tour are very inspiring. You had fans before; you have just enlarged the group."[43] As had been the case the previous week, these sentiments may well have been sincere, but they were hardly unalloyed praise, under the circumstances. Two other responses were surely much closer to Brubeck's heart. The Dining Car Cooks and Waiters' Union, Local 456, in Oakland—which had "organized black food service workers on the railroads" and had been "led by black journalist and activist William McFarland"[44]—were quick to give credit where credit was due: "We were instructed by our membership meeting yesterday to communicate their sentiments to you relative to your cancellation of your southern tour this spring. Your decision to stick with principle rather than succumb to the bigots is a clear demonstration of your desire for true democracy. It is our firm conviction that no man should be deprived of the right to earn a living in an

39 Paul Bannister to Mort Lewis, January 14, 1960 (Brubeck Collection).
40 Dave Brubeck to Bob Thornton, January 15, 1960 (Brubeck Collection).
41 Dave Brubeck to Charles Jones, January 18, 1960 (Brubeck Collection). Jones (1910–1997) taught at Mills College in California until 1946, just as Brubeck began his graduate studies there, and he was a close associate of Brubeck's teacher, Darius Milhaud. See Anthony Tommasini, "Charles Jones, a Composer, 86" [obituary], *New York Times*, June 10, 1997.
42 Bob Bundy to Dave Brubeck, January 19, 1960 (Brubeck Collection).
43 Samuel S. Vaughan to Dave Brubeck, January 19, 1960 (Brubeck Collection).
44 Chris Rhomberg, *No There There: Race, Class, and Political Community in Oakland* (Berkeley and Los Angeles: University of California Press, 2004), 233 n. 32.

occupation for which he is qualified because of race. We congratulate you on your stand."[45] Equally touching was the eyewitness testimony of Brubeck's twelve-year-old son Darius, who reported in his junior high school newsletter: "Within the last month, my father, by refusing to substitute a white bass player for his colored bass man, caused quite a stir in the papers across the country. I was not at all surprised when I heard of Dad's refusal to compromise on his stand for integration. My father is a man of principle, whose actions match his words."[46]

The public face of this episode was documented in the pages of *Down Beat* magazine, among other places. About a month after the cancellations, Ralph Gleason published "An Appeal from Dave Brubeck," which drew upon the story he broke in the *San Francisco Chronicle* (see note 31, this chapter), and other sources, to provide a detailed account of the proceedings. Brubeck's plea was a clarion call to upset the status quo in the South: "All we want is that the authorities accept us as we are, and allow us—and all other integrated jazz groups—to play our music without intimidation or pressure."[47] Gleason hadn't always seen eye to eye with Brubeck, but he was strongly and unambiguously supportive of Brubeck's recent statements and actions. The following month Gleason's entire "Perspectives" column amounted to a high-profile expression of admiration. Gleason called attention to "Dave Brubeck's laudatory action in refusing to alter his group to conform to the racial prejudices of the South" and noted that, in so doing, Brubeck had "tossed away a $40,000 tour." He respected this decision, along with "people in all parts of the country," because "[n]othing carries as much weight in our culture as a gesture which costs one money." Gleason concluded with a shout-out to principled action: "My hat, if I wore one, would be off to Dave Brubeck right now. He's done a great thing for all of us and we—members of all races—owe him a debt of gratitude."[48]

At least one prominent voice took issue with such congratulatory rhetoric. Norman Granz was a well-known record producer and impresario, whose most important contribution was the organization of concerts in Los Angeles as early as 1944, and concert tours through 1957, under

45 Eugene V. Blandin (president) and T. W. Anderson (secretary-treasurer) to Dave Brubeck, January 21, 1960 (Brubeck Collection).

46 Darius Brubeck, "Announcing Dave Brubeck," *Montorreodor* [Montera Junior High] 1, no. 2 (February 1960): 1 (Brubeck Collection).

47 Ralph J. Gleason, "An Appeal from Dave Brubeck," *Down Beat* 27, no. 4 (February 18, 1960): 12.

48 Ralph J. Gleason, "Perspectives," *Down Beat* 27, no. 6 (March 17, 1960): 43.

the title "Jazz at the Philharmonic." He famously insisted not only on featuring racially integrated bands but also on performing for multiracial audiences. Granz's beef, which *Down Beat* presented as "a divergent view," was that Brubeck didn't go far enough. Granz knew that Brubeck meant well, but he also felt that "playing before a mixed audience . . . is far more important than [having a] mixed group." Brubeck's efforts fell short, because "only by enforcing vigorously the legal rights of everyone in an audience can true integration be achieved, and not by holding up as an example the mixing of musicians."[49]

While Granz, a white man, struggled unsuccessfully to suppress his criticism of Brubeck's perceived shortcomings, a black reporter for an African American newspaper was quick to laud Brubeck's courageous actions: "Dave Brubeck may not realize it, but he did something that should have been done years ago when he refused to bend to Southern prejudice . . . If Brubeck's stand doesn't serve as a step to be taken by other mixed groups who face segregation in the South, it should become a yardstick by which to measure their consciences."[50]

It would be nice to think that Brubeck's resistance somehow moved the needle concerning this aspect of institutional racism. But his business correspondence reveals that it was an ongoing concern. A letter from Brubeck's manager to a booking agent, in the aftermath of the cancellation of the February dates, requested that a venue for a July concert in Virginia Beach be notified "that we have a mixed group (Negro bass player), so that if he wants to cancel the contract, let it be now."[51] A few days later, the agent informed Brubeck that "these promoters are well aware that you carry a mixed group, which is agreeable." Moreover, he assured him that "Eugene Wright will be received with the proper respect as a member of your group."[52]

By the time the Quartet played the July date in Virginia, Brubeck had discovered a solution to the problem of their accommodations on the road. On May 16, 1960, the group performed at the University of Oklahoma, and they apparently had to lodge in two different places. An entry in Brubeck's daytimer reads, "Stayed at Lockett Hotel, so

49 Norman Granz, "The Brubeck Stand: A Divergent View," *Down Beat* 27, no. 15 (July 21, 1960): 24.

50 George E. Pitts, "Give Brubeck Credit for a Slap at Bias," *Pittsburgh Courier*, February 13, 1960 (Brubeck Collection).

51 Mort Lewis to Jack Archer (Associated Booking Corporation), April 21, 1960 (Brubeck Collection).

52 Jack Archer to Dave Brubeck, April 25, 1960 (Brubeck Collection).

segregation."[53] The next night, all four members of the Quartet were accommodated at the Holiday Motel in Tulsa. Brubeck noted that it was the only place where they could stay together, and felt that they "should make more future reservations nationwide with them."[54] A few weeks later, Brubeck attempted to do just that. In preparation for an upcoming concert in West Virginia, he wrote to the organizer, "As you know, one of our members is a Negro and we would prefer to stay in a hotel or a motel which will accommodate the entire group. If there is a member of the Holiday Motel chain in Wheeling, I have found them to be excellent motels for us because of their interracial policy."[55]

Brubeck again erred on the side of caution late in the year, when the Brubeck organization was finalizing the details for a February 1961 concert at Virginia State, a historically black college in Petersburg. The booking agent told Iola Brubeck that he had in his possession a letter from Dr. Thomas Bridge, an African American music educator at the school, stating, "We are aware DAVE BRUBECK is a mixed group, and are proud to present him at our college." The agent noted, "This being a Negro college, they were well aware of this fact before the date was ever consummated." But he thanked her for calling it to his attention, as he "would certainly not want any last-minute mix-ups."[56]

THE REAL AMBASSADORS *PROJECT AND ITS DENOUEMENT*

Brubeck devoted much more time and energy in 1959 to the promotion of what he hoped would be a Broadway musical, *The Real Ambassadors*, than to the creation of *Time Out*. Although there were occasional flares of interest in the early 1960s—such as the prospect of producing the show at some small venues in New England, or discussions about recasting it as a "spectacular" for network television—the only concrete results were

53 "Executary, May [1960]" (Brubeck Collection). Apparently, the Lockett Hotel in Norman practiced discrimination somewhat selectively. At all events, five years earlier, in 1955, this establishment had hosted an integrated board meeting of the United Packinghouse Workers of America (UPWA). See Moses Adedeji, "Crossing the Colorline: Three Decades of the United Packinghouse Workers of America's Crusade against Racism in the Trans-Mississippi West, 1936–1968" (PhD diss., North Texas State University, 1978), 188.

54 "Executary, May [1960]," entry for May 17 (Brubeck Collection).

55 Dave Brubeck to Thomas G. Slokan (Oglebay Institute, Wheeling, West Virginia), June 8, 1960 (Brubeck Collection).

56 Jack Archer to Iola Brubeck, November 8, 1960 (Brubeck Collection). In 1963, Bridge and a fellow violinist, Joe Kennedy, were the first black musicians to join the Richmond Symphony. "Joe Kennedy Jr." [obituary], *Richmond Times-Dispatch*, February 1, 2002.

an album of its tunes, released in August 1962, and an unstaged concert version performed the next month at the Monterey Jazz Festival.

Apart from the "experimental takes" that were recorded in July 1959, the first glimmer of what eventually became *The Real Ambassadors* album is found in a May 1960 letter from Brubeck to his favorite promoter in England. Among other details, Brubeck declared that he planned "to work with Columbia in the recording of a complete show album of 'World Take a Holiday'" (its original title), and to start as soon as possible that summer.[57] The idea of making this recording apparently originated with Franklin Heller, a television director and friend of the Brubecks.[58]

As things turned out, it wasn't until July 1961 that the project began to pick up steam. A series of letters between Iola Brubeck and the president of their booking agency reveals that this momentum came about largely at her initiative.[59] An internal memorandum to the president of Columbia Records reported that, as of mid-July, Brubeck was "planning to record portions of the score together with Armstrong and Carmen McRae for release as an album" and that he was "negotiating with Joe Glaser for Armstrong's services in connection with this album."[60] And the same day, Brubeck told a film producer, "We are proceeding with the plans for an LP with Louis Armstrong. . . . There is tremendous excitement at Columbia about the show album with Louis and Carmen McRae."[61]

The Real Ambassadors was recorded in five sessions during September (12, 13, and 19) and December (12 and 19) of 1961.[62] To hear Armstrong's (and

---

57 Dave Brubeck to Harold Davison (London), May 18, 1960 (Brubeck Collection).

58 At all events, that is what Heller told the president of the CBS News Division, when trying to interest him in making a documentary about *The Real Ambassadors*: "Briefly, the background is that Dave Brubeck and his wife wrote what they hoped to be a Broadway show for Louis Armstrong. When they found it impossible to get Armstrong for an extended run, it was my good fortune to be able to suggest to them that they get it out of their systems and make it as a record." Franklin Heller to Richard Salant, May 23, 1963 (Brubeck Collection). Heller was best known as the director of more than 600 episodes of the popular television quiz show "What's My Line?" between 1950 and 1967.

59 Iola Brubeck to Joe Glaser (Associated Booking Corporation), July 2, 1961; Joe Glaser to Iola Brubeck, July 5, 1961; Iola Brubeck to Joe Glaser, July 7, 1961; Joe Glaser to Iola Brubeck, July 11, 1961 (Brubeck Collection).

60 Walter L. Dean (attorney) to Goddard Lieberson, July 14, 1961 (Macero Collection, box 6, folder 10.

61 Dave Brubeck to Bob Roberts (London), July 14, 1961 (Brubeck Collection). Roberts served as executive producer for "All Night Long," a British drama in which Brubeck and Charles Mingus made cameo appearances.

62 Klaus-Gotthard Fischer, "Discography," in Ilse Storb and Klaus-Gotthard Fischer, *Dave Brubeck, Improvisations and Compositions: The Idea of Cultural Exchange*, trans. Bert

---

Brubeck's) agent tell it, Armstrong was pleased with the results. On the day of the third session, he wrote to Iola, "I speak to Louis at least three or four times a day and he is really and truly very enthused and happy about the recording session."[63] And he reiterated a couple of weeks later that "Louis really and truly enjoyed recording your and Dave's wonderful music and score."[64] Understandably, the feeling was mutual. Dave's brother Howard reported to the album's producer that "Dave seems excited and pleased over the recordings with Louis et al."[65]

The album wasn't released until the following August, presumably in order to coincide with the show's live performance in Monterey, to be discussed presently.[66] By mid-October, it had already sold "considerably more than a thousand" copies.[67] *The Real Ambassadors'* reputation was cemented with a five-star (excellent) review in *Down Beat,* which noted that its "very strength lies in its complete success in blending popular appeal with melodically and lyrically valid ideas."[68]

In April 2014, an unstaged version of *The Real Ambassadors* was performed in New York in the context of Jazz at Lincoln Center's Dave Brubeck Festival.[69] As Brubeck's manager, Russell Gloyd, remarked at the time, Dave and Iola's labor of love had finally made it to Broadway, more than fifty years after their determined efforts in pursuit of this dream—and, unfortunately, just shortly after their passing.[70]

Thompson (New York: Peter Lang, 1994), 239–243. This information is corroborated by several letters and business documents in the Macero Collection and the Brubeck Collection.

63 Joe Glaser to Iola Brubeck, September 19, 1961 (Brubeck Collection).

64 Joe Glaser to Iola Brubeck, October 6, 1961 (Brubeck Collection).

65 Howard Brubeck to Teo Macero, October 9, 1961 (Macero Collection, box 7, folder 17).

66 Typed sheet of sales figures for selected Columbia jazz albums through the third quarter of 1964 (Macero Collection, box 7, folder 19).

67 Michael J. Maloney (attorney) to Dave Brubeck, October 17, 1962 (Brubeck Collection).

68 Leonard G. Feather, review of *The Real Ambassadors, Down Beat* 29, no. 27 (October 25, 1962): 35–36.

69 At present, the best overview of *The Real Ambassadors* is found in Penny M. Von Eschen, *Satchmo Blows Up the World: Jazz Ambassadors Play the Cold War* (Cambridge, MA, and London: Harvard University Press, 2004), 79–91. Much of this material also appeared in Penny M. Von Eschen, "The Real Ambassadors," in *Uptown Conversation: The New Jazz Studies,* ed. Robert G. O'Meally, Brent Hayes Edwards, and Farah Jasmine Griffin (New York: Columbia University Press, 2004), 189–203.

70 Iola Brubeck was aware of the plans for the festival in New York, but she died about a month beforehand, on March 12. Dave had passed away more than a year earlier, on December 5, 2012. See Peter Keepnews, "Iola Brubeck, Collaborator and Wife of Jazz Pianist, Dies at 90," *New York Times,* March 14, 2014; Ben Ratliff, "Dave Brubeck, Whose Distinctive Sound Gave Jazz New Pop, Dies at 91," *New York Times,* December 5, 2012.

When Brubeck agreed to appear at the fifth annual Monterey Jazz Festival, it seems that a performance of *The Real Ambassadors* was not yet in the cards. The contract stipulates only that the Quartet should play "one concert between 9:00 p.m. & 12:00 midnight daily" on September 22 and 23, 1962.[71] About three months in advance of the festival, Brubeck's attorney began circulating tapes of the 1961 recording sessions, before Columbia had released the album. He sent them to the jazz critic Ralph Gleason and told him that only "about ten people in the whole world have heard the tapes, including no one at Columbia!" He also mentioned that he had given one to the promoter Jimmy Lyons, "so he can think about Monterey feasibility."[72] By the end of June, the decision to present *The Real Ambassadors* evidently had been made, and Iola Brubeck gave free rein to her angst about the details in a remarkable handwritten letter to Lyons. She promised to send him a complete set of lyrics, so he could arrange for the preparation of cue cards, and remarked that she "can only pray" that the principal cast members were learning their parts. Moreover, she implored him not to promise more than could be delivered:

Please, Jim, be careful in your announcements regarding the show that you make it extremely clear that this is a *concert* version, or *excerpts* from the score—*not* a full mounted production! If the rumor persists, everyone will expect to see a Broadway show, which, of course, they will not—and cannot. With such short rehearsal time it will be a miracle to get *through* it! Do *not* build it up as *the big event!* It just cannot be with so little time. Please, in ads and press releases, refer to it as a "concert version" of *The Real Ambassadors.*[73]

The general unease about the upcoming presentation in Monterey was shared as well by the star of the show, Louis Armstrong. About one month out, the booking agent for both Armstrong and Brubeck told the latter that Armstrong was "quite upset" when he heard they were going to do eight numbers together, rather than just one or two. Despite his protestations that "neither of you have ever done the numbers, haven't done them together, and haven't had an opportunity to rehearse," the show went on as planned.[74]

---

71 Contract Blank, Associated Booking Corporation, May 7, 1962 (Brubeck Collection).
72 Mike Maloney to Ralph Gleason, June 20, 1962 (Brubeck Collection). Lyons was an old friend of Brubeck's and the founder of the Monterey Jazz Festival.
73 Iola Brubeck to Jimmy Lyons, July 30, [1962] (Brubeck Collection).
74 Joe Glaser to Dave Brubeck, August 20, 1962 (Brubeck Collection).

All indications are that the concert was a resounding success. Ralph Gleason seems to have been profoundly touched by Armstrong's performance:

> Louis Armstrong . . . wound up the Monterey Jazz Festival Sunday night [September 23, 1962] with an eloquent, moving rendition of excerpts from Dave and Iola Brubeck's "The Real Ambassadors." Louis' golden horn blew the notes out into the cold night air, and his rough voice turned sweet to sing the lyrics that told of love and human dignity, and hope and inspiration. . . . It was a difficult chore to bring off the amalgam of jazz humor, religiosity, and social comment, but the gentle charm of Louis Armstrong was equal to the job. When the performance was finished, Iola Brubeck was in tears . . . and Ambassador Satch [Armstrong] was smiling from ear to ear. The audience gave them all a standing ovation, complete with cheers. It was a deep, emotional moment.[75]

The show's undeniable triumph squelched the scruples Brubeck's booking agent held about Armstrong's role. In fact, within two weeks he was already corresponding with Brubeck's attorney about the possibility of forming an equal partnership between the two musicians for a package show under the title *The Real Ambassadors,* a concept that never played out. The same letter also includes a startling paragraph that indicates quite clearly that a previously unknown recording of the Monterey performance was made by a Las Vegas musician named Jack Eglash. Apparently Brubeck's attorney had inquired about whether Glaser had any knowledge of this situation. Glaser's response is almost comical in its defensiveness:

> To say I am surprised and bewildered to think that Jack Eglash of the Vegas Musicians Union would take it for granted he had the right to tape or record the Brubeck show is putting it mildly. I personally had put myself on record in writing with Jack Eglash as well as with the headquarters of the American Federation of Musicians that we were definitely and positively not giving Eglash the right to tape or record Louis

---

75 Ralph J. Gleason, "A Symbolic Finale at Monterey," *San Francisco Chronicle,* September 24, 1962. Gleason also contributed a similarly ebullient review to *Variety* magazine. See Ralph J. Gleason, "Brubecks' 'Ambassadors' Wows 'Em as Monterey Jazz Fest Pulls 87½G," *Variety* (September 26, 1962), 49, 52.

Armstrong's and Dave Brubeck's appearance. To think he did it without permission is unbelievable, but I guess there is nothing you can do about a situation of this kind that presents itself with a fellow like him who assumes because he is a union representative he can get permission to do anything, especially as I repeat he was given to understand in writing he had no right to do this and I see no reason why he should take it for granted that he can get out records on Dave, especially when Dave is under contract to Columbia Records.[76]

Eglash died in 2006, but his son Ryan more recently indicated that this recording may still exist in the archives of the Musicians Union of Las Vegas.[77]

CRITICAL AND POPULAR RECEPTION OF TIME OUT

Throughout his long life, Dave Brubeck never tired of telling the story about how *Time Out* reached the pinnacle of success against all odds. But once the album appeared, in the early months of 1960, its critical reception was mixed.

Closest to home, a critic in the Bay Area recalled the concert at the Woodminster Amphitheater in Oakland during the previous summer, when Brubeck presented some of his new material publicly for the first time. He noted that, while the performance was "not flawless," it nevertheless "gave promise of most interesting things to come." He viewed *Time Out* as the fulfillment of that promise, adding that, despite its bold time experiments, "there is not a bar which fails to swing—though it swings in a new fashion."[78] Around the same time, Ralph Gleason selected *Time Out* as "Album of the Week" in his syndicated column, characterizing it as "the most venturesome album Brubeck has made in several years and frankly . . . also the most musically provocative."[79]

These were the type of review that Brubeck was accustomed to. It therefore must have come as quite a shock when Ira Gitler assigned only two stars ("fair," out of a possible five) to *Time Out* on the national stage, in his

---

76 Joe Glaser to Mike Maloney, October 5, 1962 (Brubeck Collection).
77 Ed Koch, "His Music Will Be Missed" [obituary], *Las Vegas Sun*, February 15, 2006. Ryan Eglash, email messages to author, August 24 and September 1, 2014.
78 C. H. Garrigues, "Brubeck Swings to a Tricky Oriental Beat," *San Francisco Examiner* [January/February 1960] (Brubeck Collection). The clipping is undated, but an ad on the same page for a concert on February 12 provides a terminus ante quem.
79 Ralph J. Gleason, "Competition Will Weed Inferior Talent, Says Kenton," *Boston Globe*, January 31, 1960.

review for *Down Beat* magazine. The essence of Gitler's critique was that the music on this album didn't feel like authentic jazz. He disputed Steve Race's claim in the liner notes that this was a "jazz milestone," saying instead that it seemed "more like drawing-room music." His most damning complaint was that Brubeck "has been palmed off as a serious jazzman for too long"—and Gitler took this opportunity to attempt to reverse that trend. He eviscerated each number, with the exception of "Strange Meadow Lark," the album's "best track." "Blue Rondo à la Turk" was bombastic and its theme was "far from jazz." Joe Morello's drum solo in "Take Five," "over the omnipresent vamp," sounded "like the accompaniment for a troupe of trampoline artists." The theme of "Three to Get Ready" was "again alien to jazz." "Everybody's Jumpin'" was "a bore." And the ostinato in "Pick Up Sticks" nearly drove him to distraction. Gitler excoriated Brubeck: "If he wants to experiment, let him begin with trying some real jazz."[80]

Yet despite Gitler's harsh judgment, the album was extremely successful. An executive at Columbia said that the company considered *Time Out* to be "the jazz album which has received greatest public acceptance in the last five years." Its total sales in the United States at the beginning of 1961 were 50,000.[81] An internal Columbia document shows that it continued to sell briskly, for a grand total of 183,576 copies by the year's end.[82] During the first week of March 1962, both *Time Out* and *Time Further Out* sold nearly as well or better than the soundtracks for the blockbuster musicals *West Side Story, Camelot,* and *My Fair Lady.* Total sales for *Time Out* had by then reached 225,000.[83] The next sales milestone was 500,000, which was reached by May 1963 and for which the album was awarded a gold record.[84] In February 1965, Teo Macero estimated that its sales "must be close to three-quarters of a million," and he crowed, "It's fantastic.

---

80 Ira Gitler, review of *Time Out, Down Beat* 27, no. 9 (April 28, 1960): 37–38.

81 Stanley West to Dave Brubeck, January 18, 1961 (Brubeck Collection).

82 "Dave Brubeck Sales Study 1961" (Macero Collection, box 7, folder 17).

83 "Columbia Sales Figures, March 2, 1962," document in Iola Brubeck's hand (Brubeck Collection). During the week of March 2, *Time Out* sold 20,000 copies and *Time Further Out* 17,000, while the figures for *West Side Story, Camelot,* and *My Fair Lady* were 21,000, 18,000, and 15,000, respectively. See also the Columbia Records promotional flyer for *Time Further Out,* which apparently dates from around the same time: "At this writing the album [*Time Out*] is heading for A QUARTER OF A MILLION COPIES!" and it was occupying "the NUMBER 2 position on the *Billboard* album chart." Reproduced in the liner notes for the rerelease of the Dave Brubeck Quartet, *Time Out,* Columbia/Legacy 88697 39852 2, 2009, three compact discs.

84 The Recording Industry Association of America (RIAA) database has April 19, 1963 as the date of certification. "Gold & Platinum—RIAA" https://www.riaa.com/gold-platinum/?tab_active=default-award&se=dave+brubeck#search_section (accessed March 16, 2018).

When the returns come in, it's selling just like a single, not an album."[85]
Time Out was certified platinum (more than 1,000,000) in 1997, and it
attained double platinum status (2,000,000) in 2011.[86]

Despite the indisputable commercial success of *Time Out*, Gitler never
changed his opinion in later years. When Hedrick Smith interviewed him
for the documentary *Rediscovering Dave Brubeck* (2001), Gitler characterized his reaction to the album as "very mixed." Smith asked whether,
"looking back on it," he still came down in the same place, and Gitler
said, "I think I do." When questioned about any subsequent personal
encounters with Brubeck, Gitler told a story of meeting him "on the way
to Detroit for a jazz festival." Gitler said that Brubeck "was very nice
about it [Gitler's review of *Time Out*] and we had a nice discussion about
that and other things." Gitler had also panned a recording by Cannonball
Adderley. At the festival in Detroit, they staged a tongue-in-cheek photo
op, with Brubeck "brandishing his fist" at Gitler and Adderley "actually
choking him."[87]

THE FOUR SUBSEQUENT "TIME" ALBUMS

The spectacular commercial success of the "Take Five" single in the
weeks and months following its May 1961 release boosted the sales of

Shortly thereafter, the album's producer informed Brubeck's attorney that "Dave is to get
a gold record for having sold 500 thousand copies of 'Time Out.' This presentation will be
tied in with the release of the 'Carnegie Hall' album." Teo Macero to Michael Maloney, May
2, 1963 (Macero Collection, box 7, folder 19). It is unclear when Brubeck received the phys-
ical memento. About seven years later, Macero advised Columbia's director of publicity that
"Dave Brubeck would like to have a gold record for 'Time Out,' the same as I received some
time ago." Teo Macero to Bob Altschuler, March 3, 1970 (Macero Collection, box 7, folder 25).
The gold record must have come into Brubeck's possession within the next few years, but
he was apparently under the mistaken impression that the album's sales were twice as high
as they actually were. Brubeck wrote to a marketing executive at Columbia, "I have heard
that you get a gold record if you sell 500,000 copies of a single LP. Is that true? I had always
thought that it was a million, which was when I received a gold record for TIME OUT." Dave
Brubeck to Bruce Lundvall, December 3, 1974 (Macero Collection, box 6, folder 14).

85 " 'Brubeck Deserves Success,'" *Melody Maker,* February 6, 1965, 6.
86 "Dave Brubeck's 1959 Jazz Masterpiece Time Out Certified Double Platinum by RIAA,"
PRNewswire, December 6, 2011 http://www.prnewswire.com/news-releases/dave-
brubecks-1959-jazz-masterpiece-time-out-certified-double-platinum-by-riaa-135117793.
html (accessed March 16, 2018).
    The RIAA database (see n. 84, this chapter) has April 28, 1997 as the date of the previous
    certification.
87 "PBS: Rediscovering Dave Brubeck, With Hedrick Smith" http://www.pbs.org/brubeck/
theMusic/criticIraGitler.htm (accessed March 16, 2018).

Time Out and, unsurprisingly, engendered plans for sequels. As early as May 1, Iola Brubeck mentioned to the famous cartoonist Arnold Roth that Dave was "engrossed in writing a new 'Time Out' type album."[88] Beginning almost immediately thereafter, and continuing through early June, the Quartet recorded the tunes that eventually comprised *Time Further Out* (Columbia CL 1690).

TIME FURTHER OUT (1961)

Much of this album's intent can be discerned from its cover. On the right side of the front, against a stark white background, is a list of "Titles and Tempos"—that is, names of the nine tunes and their meter signatures (see Table 10.1). One of its organizing features is an upward progression from 3 through 9 in the numerator and a shift from 4 (quarter notes) to 8 (eighth notes) in the denominator. According to Brubeck's liner notes, *Time Further Out* was "conceived as a blues suite."[89] The arrangement of its constituent parts in such a scheme amounts to a systematic (and somewhat pedantic) exploration of ideas that had been approached more haphazardly (or spontaneously) in *Time Out*.

The apparent goal of listing the "tempos" was to demonstrate that jazz could be created across a spectrum of different time signatures, ranging from waltzlike 3/4 to compound meters such as 9/8. Although the point is well taken, it couldn't be achieved without fudging the numbers a bit. Most notably, the penultimate cut, "Bru's Boogie Woogie," is supposedly in 8/8, paving the way to the 9/8 of "Blue Shadows in the Street." In truth, however, there is no appreciable difference between the putative 8/8 of the boogie-woogie and the 4/4 of "Charles Matthew Hallelujah," except that the former is a bit faster (around 210 beats per minute, versus 160). The meter signature 8/8—as opposed to eighth-note motion in 4/4—seems to have been conceived in the interest of filling out the entire sequence of numerators from 3 to 9. The original bass part, in Brubeck's own hand, though, was notated in 4/4.[90]

Like *Time Out*, the cover of *Time Further Out* is adorned with modern art, this time by the Catalan Spanish painter Joan Miró (1893–1983). The latter album carries the subtitle "Miró Reflections," and it

---

88 Iola Brubeck to Arnold and Caroline Roth, May 1, 1961 (Brubeck Collection). Roth had created cover art for the 1956 release of the *Dave Brubeck Octet* album on the Fantasy label.

89 Dave Brubeck, liner notes, The Dave Brubeck Quartet, *Time Further Out*, Columbia CL 1690, 1961, 33⅓ rpm.

90 The manuscript page bears the title "Bru's Boogey Blues" (Brubeck Collection).

TABLE 10.1. List of "Titles and Tempos" on *Time Further Out*

It's a Raggy Waltz	3/4
Bluette	3/4
Charles Matthew Hallelujah	4/4
Far More Blue	5/4
Far More Drums	5/4
Maori Blues	6/4
Unsquare Dance	7/4
Bru's Boogie Woogie	8/8
Blue Shadows in the Street	9/8

features a 1925 painting known as "The Sun."[91] Brubeck had originally hoped to use Miró's piece for *Time Out*, but he was unable to obtain permission before the release date. Xenia Cage subsequently helped to track down Miró on his yacht in the Mediterranean, and in June 1961 Pierre Matisse, son of Henri Matisse and owner of the painting, granted permission for it to appear on the cover of *Time Further Out*.[92]

COUNTDOWN: TIME IN OUTER SPACE (1962)

The title and content of Brubeck's next "time" project clearly refer to the Space Race between the Soviet Union and the United States. Moreover, *Countdown: Time in Outer Space* was dedicated to John Glenn (1921–2016), the astronaut who became the first American to orbit the Earth

---

91 This work is now held by the National Museum of Modern Art in Paris. See no. 168 in the Joan Miró Online Imagebank http://successiomiro.com/catalogue/1/4 (accessed March 16, 2018).

　　See also Brenda Lynne Leach, *Looking and Listening: Conversations between Modern Art and Music* (Lanham, MD: Rowman & Littlefield, 2015), 65–73 (Chapter 6, "Dave Brubeck and His Reflections on Miró: Music and Art across Time").

92 Cage, an artist herself, frequently visited the painter Jean Jackson, who had a cottage next door to the house in Connecticut where the Brubeck family resided temporarily in 1960. See Darius Brubeck, "Jazz 1959: The Beginning of Beyond" (MA thesis, University of Nottingham, 2002), 125; also Dave Brubeck, "Time Further Out: 1995" (typescript liner notes for rerelease, Brubeck Collection), and Pierre Matisse to Iola Brubeck, June 16, 1961 (Macero Collection, box 6, folder 22).

on February 20, 1962, about two months before the album appeared. It is therefore surprising to discover that most of its tunes originally had nothing to do with space exploration. Indeed, the album almost certainly wasn't originally conceived as a tribute to Glenn, but rather was gradually reshaped in this direction as a marketing strategy.

Though *Countdown: Time in Outer Space* was released six months after *Time Further Out*, it shares much of the DNA of the earlier album. In fact, "Castilian Blues" from *Countdown* was recorded in the same May 1961 session as "It's a Raggy Waltz," the first cut on *Time Further Out*.[93] Notations on a scruffy sheet of paper in Brubeck's own hand indicate that three other tracks on *Countdown* ("Eleven Four," "Three's a Crowd," and "Castilian Drums") also were castoffs from *Time Further Out*.[94]

The earliest glimpse of the incipient album is provided by a pencil draft in Brubeck's hand, with the heading "Master for L.P. after Miró." At this point, the project did not yet have a title of its own. But Brubeck clarified at the bottom of the page that "this will be the second 'time' album after the [one with] 'Far More Blue' [i.e., *Time Further Out*]." Eight of the eleven cuts that populated the album when it was released are listed here, albeit with different titles in several cases. "Waltz Limp" was originally titled "Show Me Chopin." The tune in 7/4 that eventually came to be known as "Three's a Crowd" is given as "Baby Needs Shoes." "Danse Duet" originated as "Pas de Deux." And the album's first track, "Countdown," had the provisional title "Boogey Woogey with Tymp," because Joe Morello plays timpani rather than a drum kit at the beginning.[95]

One cannot fail to notice on this sheet the absence of any references to astronautics, both for the album as a whole and for the individual tracks. In a handwritten letter to Teo Macero, dating from the latter part of 1961,

---

93 Columbia Records, Artist Job Sheet, Job No. 60076, May 3, 1961 (Macero Collection, box 5, folder 11). Early takes of "Far More Blue" (*Time Further Out*) and "Castilian Blues, Part II" (later renamed "Castilian Drums" on *Countdown*) were also recorded in that same session.

94 Macero Collection, box 6, folder 22. On one side of the sheet from a pad of ruled paper, Brubeck wrote a series of track titles for *Time Further Out*, with their timings and his editorial comments (e.g., "Maori Blues—3:53 OK as is"). "Castilian Blues" and "Castilian Drums" (listed as "Castilian Blues," parts 1 and 2) were entered alongside parts 1 and 2 of "Far More Blue," before Brubeck struck them, with the comment "both Castilians out!!" On the back of the page, Teo Macero wrote an instruction to "pull" these tunes, along with "Eleven Four" and "Three's a Crowd." All four of them subsequently were incorporated into *Countdown: Time in Outer Space*.

95 Macero Collection, box 5, folder 11. The same folder also contains a typed sheet that includes a transcription of these notes, under the additional heading "Brubeck."

Brubeck first refers to the project as "Time and Space."[96] Another undated sheet in Macero's hand lists ten tracks, including the eight mentioned earlier, plus "Someday My Prince Will Come" and "Fast Life," under the title "Time in Space," with the expanded "Time Out in Space" (a nod to the popular *Time Out* album) entered in the margin.[97] At this juncture, the title of the tune with timpani had morphed into "Timp Boogie." As of early November 1961, Iola Brubeck wrote out the same ten song titles for "Time in Space," but she indicated further that "Fast Life," "Waltz Limp," "Three's a Crowd," and "Danse Duet" were from Dave's ballet *Maiden in the Tower*.[98] An internal memo the next month documents Dave Brubeck's wish that the album be titled "Time Out in Space" (the formulation noted above).[99] His request obviously was approved, because it is listed that way on the album cover copy from the following week. In addition, the eleventh and final tune, "Back to Earth," was added by hand to the typed form.[100] Just over a month later, the project took its final shape, with "Timp Boogie" renamed "Countdown," and the album title altered to *Countdown: Time in Outer Space*.[101] By this time, John Glenn's expedition was just a few weeks in the future, and at some point before its release in April the decision was made to add to the cover the words "The Album is Dedicated to Lieut. Col. John H. Glenn, Jr."[102]

96 Dave Brubeck to Teo Macero, undated but on stationery from The Midland Hotel, Manchester, England, after his trip to the United Kingdom in July, for the filming of "All Night Long" with Charles Mingus (Macero Collection, box 7, folder 25).

97 Macero Collection, box 5, folder 11.

98 Macero Collection, box 5, folder 11.

99 Teo Macero to Dave Kapralik (Columbia Records), December 13, 1961 (Macero Collection, box 5, folder 11).

100 Macero Collection, box 5, folder 11.

101 Album Cover Copy, January 31, 1962 (Macero Collection, box 5, folder 11).

102 On the assumption that John Glenn probably owned a copy of the album dedicated to him, which was recorded by the most famous and successful jazz combo of its time, and in hopes that additional relevant documentary evidence might exist as well, I contacted the archivist at the Ohio Congressional Archives, The Ohio State University, which holds the John H. Glenn Archives. He told me that he was "unable to locate any information— letters, newspaper clippings, or a copy of the LP—pertaining to Dave Brubeck or his *Countdown: Time in Outer Space* project in the John Glenn Archives." Moreover, he found this lack of material to be "rather surprising . . . given the status of Dave Brubeck and the amount of other music pertaining [to] John Glenn's Friendship 7 space flight held in the collection." Jeffrey W. Thomas, email message to author, May 21, 2014. Shortly thereafter, when Senator Glenn's executive assistant was kind enough to ask the man himself, she told me that "he did not recall anything about it [Brubeck's album]." Kathy Dancey, phone conversations with author, May 21 and July 29, 2014. It is hard to know what to make of

In addition to continuing the exploration of meters uncommon in jazz, this third "time" album shared with its predecessors the use of modern art on its cover. The painting was selected by the art department at Columbia Records.[103] According to the annotation printed on the cover, "Orange and Black Wall" by the American abstract expressionist Franz Kline (1910–1962) dates from 1959, was in the collection of Mr. and Mrs. Robert C. Scull, and was made available courtesy of the Sidney Janis Gallery in New York. The piece later came into the possession of Caroline Wiess Law, who bequeathed it to the Museum of Fine Arts in Houston, where it hangs today.[104]

TIME CHANGES (1964)

The cover of the next LP in the series also featured a painting by an artist of the same ilk. But the abstract expressionist painting by Sam Francis (1923–1994) apparently was created specifically for Brubeck's album.[105] In addition, *Time Changes* was a kind of pre-celebration of the World's Fair in New York, which ran for a year, beginning in April 1964. It was recorded between late November 1963 and early January 1964, and its February release was timed to take advantage of the anticipation surrounding this high-profile exposition. "World's Fair," a breezy and sometimes rather dissonant piece in 13/4 (3+3+4+3), was written for a promotional film for Clairol called "Hair Styles and Fair Styles." As a result of his work on this project, Brubeck was invited to a dinner at the "Top of the Fair" restaurant, where it was filmed, to hobnob with several hundred "women columnists and editors for women's columns, fashion columns, television, radio stations and magazines . . . from all over America," as well as "an additional 40 or 50 editors from the Metropolitan area who represent the syndicated magazines and newspapers."[106] Mutual backscratching of

---

this, except to conclude that the dedication of *Countdown: Time in Outer Space* apparently was far more important to Brubeck and the marketing executives at Columbia Records than it was to John Glenn.

103 Stanley West to Dave Brubeck, November 1, 1961 (Brubeck Collection). See Dave's handwritten note to Iola at the bottom.

104 "Orange and Black Wall | The Museum of Fine Arts, Houston" https://www.mfah.org/art/detail/30412 (accessed March 16, 2018).

105 See "Sam Francis: A Dave Brubeck Album Cover—Sam Francis Foundation" http://samfrancisfoundation.org/2012/08/28/sam-francis-dave-brubeck-album-cover/ (accessed March 16, 2018).

106 Allan Stanley (Dolphin Productions, New York) to Dave Brubeck, December 27, 1963 (Brubeck Collection).

this kind was entirely typical of the highly commercialized environment within which Brubeck's albums were produced. "Unisphere," the album's obligatory offering in 5/4 meter, was named after the gigantic, twelve-story stainless steel model of the Earth that was built to symbolize the Fair's theme of "Peace through Understanding."[107] After *Time Changes* had been in circulation for six months and the exposition was well under way, in August 1964 Brubeck gave a concert at the World Fair's Singer Bowl in Flushing, New York, opening for Duke Ellington.[108]

The entire B-side of the album is devoted to *Elementals*, Brubeck's more than a quarter-hour composition for jazz combo and orchestra. This was Dave's opportunity to write and record a work of his own, along the lines of his brother Howard's *Dialogues*, discussed earlier in this chapter. Dave Brubeck clearly poured himself into the project (the manuscript materials in the Brubeck Collection are vast), and it must have been quite a blow, when he sought its publication, to receive word that "a reviewing committee has determined that it is not suited to our publication needs."[109]

Elementals was composed during summer 1963. In a mid-June letter to Dave's mother, Iola mentioned that "Dave is still working on the piece for the Rochester [New York] Symphony. He is supposed to *finish* it tonight to mail to the copyist, so he is struggling at orchestration in the studio downstairs. It will be performed with the Quartet and Orchestra on August 1."[110] The August 1, 1963 appearance at the Eastman Theatre had been in the works for several months, at least.[111] The conductor for the concert and the subsequent recording was Rayburn Wright (1922–1990), an Eastman School of Music graduate who was an arranger for Radio City Music Hall, ran a summer Arrangers Workshop, and later became a professor at Eastman. According to a letter from Wright to Teo Macero, the orchestra read through *Elementals* for the first time on July 17, and Wright was planning for a recording session on August 2, the day after the concert, for an album to be titled *Brubeck at Eastman*.[112] When Macero wrote to the

---

107 Among Brubeck's sketches for this composition, dated November 9, 1963, is an annotation indicating that his brother "Howard said this is not in 5 but in 10." Nevertheless, both pages are consistently notated in 5/4 (Brubeck Collection).

108 The contract for the August 5, 1964 performance is preserved in the Brubeck Collection. The information about Ellington is in a cover letter from Bob Bundy (Associated Booking Corp.) to Dave Brubeck, July 16, 1964 (Brubeck Collection).

109 Publications Department, G. Schirmer, Inc. to "Mr. David W. Brubeck," June 15, 1981 (Brubeck Collection).

110 Iola Brubeck to Bessie Brubeck, June 19, 1963 (Brubeck Collection).

111 The contract is dated February 26, 1963 (Brubeck Collection).

112 Ray Wright to Teo Macero, July 21, 1963 (Macero Collection, box 7, folder 8).

University of Rochester requesting permission to make the recording, the provost informed him that the university had an exclusive contract with Mercury Records, on behalf of Howard Hanson (1896–1981), the long-time director of the Eastman School, and that "any recording of University of Rochester music groups by recording companies other than Mercury is prohibited."[113] The recording of *Elementals* for *Time Changes* finally took place several months later, in December and January.[114]

The critical reception of *Elementals* was mixed, but generally tilted in the negative direction. The reviews were occasionally ebullient, such as one that appeared in *The Sacramento Bee*: "*Elementals* is a tremendous piece of music—brilliant, powerful and unfailingly beautiful, and a striking and rare success in the history of attempts to introduce a true brotherhood between the techniques of symphonic and jazz composition."[115] But more frequently, they were critical of the curiously episodic nature of Brubeck's piece. One of the most pointed critiques was the following terse but vivid description by the British poet Philip Larking (1922–1985): "*Elementals,* showing the Quartet struggling like flies in the syrup of an Eastman School of Music Orchestra, is no more than a series of gestures in the direction of atmosphere—menace, romance, Stan Kenton, Latin America, and a kind of seaside bandstand noise that accompanies Paul Desmond."[116] Even Desmond himself had misgivings about the project. In a letter to his father during summer 1963, he mentioned that he would be going "up to Rochester tomorrow for three days, to do a piece of Dave's for quartet and orchestra. It should be nice, but even so, it's not really worth it. You have to rehearse for a month, and then you play it for an audience that would rather hear 'Take Five' in the first place. But as they say, it's a living."[117]

---

113 Teo Macero to Jack End (Public Relations, University of Rochester), July 23, 1963; McCrea Hazlett (Provost, University of Rochester) to Teo Macero, July 26, 1963 (Macero Collection, box 7, folder 8).

114 In Dave Brubeck and Sally Slade's letter to Mike Maloney (Brubeck's attorney), Sally (Brubeck's assistant) noted that Dave is "somewhat excited as well as worried" about the upcoming recording. "Has asked for luck to be wished on him by all and sundry." December 6, 1963 (Brubeck Collection).

115 William C. Glackin, "The Bigger Brubeck: Dave Has Fine Time with Symphony," *Sacramento Bee*, June 21, 1964 (Brubeck Collection).

116 Philip Larkin, *All What Jazz: A Record Diary 1961–1971*, rev ed. (London: Faber & Faber, 1985), 117. Originally published on July 18, 1964.

117 Paul Desmond to Emil Breitenfeld, undated [July 1963] (Paul Desmond Papers, Holt-Atherton Department of Special Collections, University of the Pacific Library).

Time In was the final installment in the series that began with *Time Out*, and it was the end of the road for the metrical and rhythmic experimentation of the "classic" Quartet. The album maintained continuity with its four predecessors in ways that will be summarized below. But it also reflected important changes in Brubeck's mindset and priorities. The first cut on the B-side, "Travellin' Blues," is a straight-ahead example of its genre, whose lyrics by Iola and Dave Brubeck gave voice to the weariness associated with the jazz musician's life on the road, and formed the backdrop for Dave's monumental decision to disband the Quartet:

I've traveled 'cross the country.
I've sung with lots of bands.
I've played in those big cities
That book those one-night stands.
I'm lonely and I'm weary.
I know the scene so well.
The blues have come to get me
And to drag me down to hell.
But I keep trav'lin',
What have I got to lose?
I just keep trav'lin',
Unrav'lin' all my blues.[118]

The last cut on the A-side, "Forty Days," is also a vector toward the future. It is an instrumental version of a movement from Brubeck's *The Light in the Wilderness: An Oratorio for Today* (1968), the first in a series of sacred works he penned following the Quartet's breakup in 1967.[119] According to a promotional brochure for the 1969–1970 season, Brubeck "first decided to write the oratorio during World War II service as an infantryman, and began work in earnest in 1965 when older brother and fellow composer Howard Brubeck lost an only son." Its world premiere was given

---

118 Manuscript and published lead sheets preserved in the Brubeck Collection. This is the first of four stanzas. The version on *Time In* is instrumental only. But the vocal rendition had been recorded by Carmen McRae already in September 1961 and released in 1965 on *Carmen McRae—Dave Brubeck, Take Five—Recorded Live at Basin Street East* (Columbia CL 2316).

119 See H. G. Young III, "The Sacred Choral Music of Dave Brubeck: A Historical, Analytical, and Critical Examination" (PhD diss., University of Florida, 1995).

at the Ecumenical Concert of the Cincinnati Symphony Orchestra on February 29, 1968.[120]

The recording sessions took place in September and October 1965, and the title of the album changed a couple of times before it was released the following July. Initially, it was conceived as a celebration of the Quartet's longevity, which was unusual among jazz combos in the 1950s and 1960s. A document prepared for a March 1966 meeting at Columbia Records lists the title as "Fifteenth Anniversary Album," marking a decade-and-a-half since Brubeck's swimming accident in Hawaii in 1951, which led to the formation of the Quartet, when Paul Desmond rejoined his former musical collaborator.[121] According to the minutes, it was decided at that meeting to borrow the title of its concluding track, "Cassandra," for the entire album.[122] The final title wasn't settled until May, as is evident from an internal document in which the typed word "Cassandra" was crossed out and the phrase "Time In" was added by hand.[123] This change came about as a result of a discussion between a marketing executive at Columbia and the album's producer. The former told several colleagues, "I have discussed this title ['Cassandra'] with Teo Macero and we concur that the best title for this album is 'Time In.' Teo feels certain that Brubeck will agree to retitle one of the more commercial selections in the album 'Time In.'"[124] Indeed, that is exactly what happened. The cut that ultimately became known as "Time In" was changed from "Spider."[125]

The other defining characteristic of the project, which took shape even later (not until June 1966), was the recruitment of eight prominent jazz critics—mostly longtime friends and allies—to write the liner notes. Jimmy Lyons, Ralph J. Gleason, Barry Ulanov, Leonard Feather, John Hammond, John S. Wilson, George Wein, and George T. Simon each contributed a brief write-up about one of the tracks. This material

120 *Music and Drama Associates* [New York, 1969] (Macero Collection, box 7, folder 13).

121 "Title Meeting," March 16, 1966 (Macero Collection, box 7, folder 1).

122 Office Communication, Columbia Records, Marc Pressel to Bob Cato, March 16, 1966 (Macero Collection, box 7, folder 1).

123 Columbia Records, Album Cover Copy and Mastering, May 11, 1966 (Macero Collection, box 7, folder 2).

124 Bruce Lundvall to Marc Pressel [cc: Kavan, Norton, Macero, Harrison], May 16, 1966 (Macero Collection, box 7, folder 1).

125 Moreover, it previously had been changed from yet another title, "Poly-Rhythm." See the Artist Job Sheet, Job No. 98408, dating from November 16, 1965 (for the October 13 recording session) and other data sheets up through the June 16, 1966 Album Cover Copy and Mastering sheet (third revision) in Macero Collection, box 7, folder 2.

was framed by laudatory statements from the president of Columbia Records, Goddard Lieberson, and the album's producer, Teo Macero, marking the Quartet's extraordinary fifteen-year tenure. Behind the scenes, Lieberson had grown so frustrated with Brubeck's demands that just one year earlier he had contemplated allowing Brubeck's contract to expire.[126] But now, all was forgiven, and Lieberson was willing to publically trumpet his praise: "After fifteen years, Dave Brubeck remains one of our great performing artists. . . . Dave Brubeck, almost more than anyone else, has proven that an artist can speak for himself as well as for a very wide public. He is original without being merely temporarily bizarre, and that is why he survives fads and follies."[127]

BLUES AND WALTZES IN THE FOREFRONT

The four sequels to *Time Out* favor three main types of music. First of all, nearly half of the tunes (sixteen out of thirty-five) are blues of one kind or another (including boogie-woogie), whether this style is reflected in their titles or not. Since *Time Further Out* is a blues suite, as was mentioned earlier, it includes "Bluette," "Far More Blue" (perhaps a not-so-subtle dig at Miles Davis's *Kind of Blue*), its companion piece "Far More Drums," "Maori Blues," and "Blue Shadows in the Street," plus "Bru's Boogie Woogie" and another boogie-woogie that celebrated the birth of Brubeck's sixth child, "Charles Matthew Hallelujah." In addition, "Unsquare Dance" in 7/4 meter follows the twelve-bar blues pattern. *Countdown: Time in Outer Space* is not infused as heavily with the blues, yet it still begins with the boogie-woogie "Countdown" and ends with another blues-related tune, "Back to Earth," in addition to "Castilian Blues," its alter ego "Castilian Drums," and "Three's a Crowd" (whose original manuscript in the Brubeck Collection bears the title "7/4 Blues"). The blues are represented by "World's Fair" on *Time Changes*, and by "Travellin' Blues" and "He Done Her Wrong" on *Time In*. Though the presence of the blues on these albums is in itself unremarkable, the relatively high proportion of such tunes is surprising, given its near

126 Goddard Lieberson to Walter Dean [cc: Glancy, Gallagher, Macero, Davis], March 19, 1965 (Macero Collection, box 7, folder 21): "It seems to me we have allowed them [Brubeck and his lawyer] to successfully mix apples and pears in their discussions with us. . . . When an artist makes additional demands involving copyright, and if those demands make him unprofitable no matter how well he performs as a record seller, I don't see that we gain much by resigning him."

127 Goddard Lieberson, liner notes, Dave Brubeck, *Time In*, Columbia CL 2512, 1966, 33⅓ rpm.

absence on *Time Out* (blues appear only in the middle portion of "Blue Rondo à la Turk").

The second musical thread that runs through all of the "time" albums is the waltz. It began with "Kathy's Waltz" on *Time Out*, which was examined in Chapter 4. Although *Time Further Out* emphasizes the blues, the waltz has pride of place as the album's first cut ("It's a Raggy Waltz"), and "Bluette" is also in waltz time. *Countdown: Time in Outer Space* makes more room for this genre, including "Why Phillis Waltz" (by Eugene Wright) and "Waltz Limp," as well as "Someday My Prince Will Come" from the Walt Disney film *Snow White and the Seven Dwarfs* (1937), which the Quartet previously had recorded on *Dave Digs Disney* (Columbia CL 1059, 1957). Triple meter is the abiding preoccupation of *Time Changes*, appearing in "Iberia," "Shim Wha" (by Joe Morello), "Cable Car," and "Theme from Elementals"—although, strictly speaking, only the latter selection is a waltz. The title track of *Time In* is also in a fast three, while "Lost Waltz" from the same album begins with just forty-five seconds of triple meter before breaking into rapid quadruple time for the rest of the cut. Because of this intensive and consistent activity, as well as numerous examples on other albums, Brubeck came to believe that he was "the one who introduced this concept [the jazz waltz] to his contemporaries."[128]

The third and final strand that unites *Time Out* and its sequels is the use of asymmetrical and other "odd" meters. The Quartet's most famous excursion into this territory was, of course, the 5/4 of Paul Desmond's "Take Five." And each of the other albums includes at least one tune in this meter as well: "Far More Blue" and "Far More Drums" on *Time Further Out*; "Countdown," Castilian Blues," and "Castilian Drums" on *Countdown: Time in Outer Space*; "Unisphere" on *Time Changes*; and "Forty Days" and "He Done Her Wrong" on *Time In*. Meters other than 5/4 include the 7/4 (2+2+3) of "Unsquare Dance" and "Three's a Crowd," Desmond's "Eleven Four" (generally 5/4 + 6/4, but in reverse order toward the end), and the complex thirteen (3+3+2+2+3) of "World's Fair."

---

128 Dave and Iola Brubeck to author, February 4, 2007: "The Dave Brubeck Quartet was playing 'Alice in Wonderland' in the early fifties and [it was] later taken up by Bill Evans. 'Someday My Prince Will Come' dates to that era, also. Miles [Davis] heard the Quartet's version when both his group and the DBQ were sharing the bill at the Black Hawk in San Francisco and other clubs during the '50s. Later, Miles recorded an LP for Columbia called 'Some Day My Prince Will Come' [Miles Davis Sextet, Columbia CL 1656, 1961]. Dave believes that he is the one who introduced this concept to his jazz contemporaries. Before him, of course, Fats Waller had composed the 'Jitterbug Waltz.'"

Dave Brubeck had a series of three five-year contracts with Columbia Records, beginning on July 1, 1954, and ending fifteen years later in 1969. The high drama associated with Brubeck's initial signing was recounted in Chapter 1. Ten years on, in 1964, Brubeck and his legal team were slowing the process down again. In fact, the "1964" contract wasn't executed until more than a year later. The negotiations began in a timely fashion, with the plan for Columbia's representative to meet with Brubeck's attorneys in early March, "to finalize the terms for a new contract with Dave Brubeck."[129] In June, a contract was prepared, "for a period of five years commencing July 1, 1964."[130] Two months later, Columbia's representative wrote a cordial letter to Brubeck's attorney, expressing his hope that "you will soon be able to give us your comments on the contract which I sent you for Dave."[131]

When the matter still was unresolved at year's end, the representative asked one of his colleagues to "consider the possibility of applying some subtle or not so subtle pressure to speed the process along."[132] Some weeks later, Brubeck's own impatience was on clear display in a letter he wrote to Teo Macero shortly before leaving on a tour of Australia: "It seems like all these projects have dragged on for years . . . I will feel very defeated and disappointed if you won't take one good, long, hard day of editing (at the very most) and finish these projects—I don't function well as a person or a musician when too many things are left undone."[133] By March, the two parties had reached an impasse, signaled by the company president's willingness to consider cutting Brubeck loose, in the wake of a fraught and "lengthy conversation [between their respective attorneys] regarding the status of Brubeck's outstanding contract."[134] The lawyers

129 Walter L. Dean (Columbia Records) to Mike Maloney [cc: Glancy and Macero], February 24, 1964 (Macero Collection, box 7, folder 20).
130 Office Communication, Columbia Records, Walter L. Dean to Clive Davis [cc: Beulike, Glancy and Macero], June 18, 1964 (Macero Collection, box 7, folder 20).
131 Walter L. Dean to Mike Maloney [cc: Davis, Drosnes, Glancy and Macero], August 17, 1964 (Macero Collection, box 7, folder 20).
132 Office Communication, Columbia Records, Walter L. Dean to Ken Glancy [cc: Lieberson, Davis, Gallagher and Macero], December 29, 1964 (Macero Collection, box 7, folder 20).
133 Dave Brubeck to Teo Macero, February 16, 1965 (Macero Collection, box 7, folder 21).
134 Office Communication, Columbia Records, Walter L. Dean to Ken Glancy [cc: Lieberson, Gallagher, Macero and Davis], March 11, 1965; Office Communication, Columbia Records, Goddard Lieberson to Walter Dean [cc: Glancy, Gallagher, Macero, Davis], March 19, 1965 (Macero Collection, box 7, folder 21).

met in person in May, and apparently were able to clear the logjam.[135] By September 1965, fourteen months after the previous one had expired, Brubeck's new (and final) term contract with Columbia Records finally was executed.[136]

It is just as well that this was Brubeck's last record contract, because he was growing increasingly weary from the stresses and strains of his career. Although there had been rumors of the Quartet's demise in the past, by September 1967 it was a sure enough thing that a major trade publication was able to announce, "The Dave Brubeck Quartet, which has been in existence for sixteen years, will fade from the scene with the end of 1967."[137] The group played its last concert on December 26, and an article in the *New York Times,* published on Christmas Eve, shone a spotlight on the problem Brubeck sought to escape: "The fact that Tuesday is the day after Christmas exemplifies part of Brubeck's reason for abandoning a group whose record of extended, consistent success is almost unparalleled in jazz. 'It's typical of what always happens to us,' Brubeck exclaimed in exasperation a few days ago. 'The kids are coming home from their schools . . . and we wanted to be together with them at Christmas. But instead, I have to go to Pittsburgh and play a concert.' "[138]

No one could have known or suspected at that time that Brubeck would remain active and productive for another forty-five years, until his death on December 5, 2012, one day short of his ninety-second birthday. Heading the long list of accomplishments in his *New York Times* obituary is, fittingly and unsurprisingly, the very project that has occupied us here. Above all, Dave Brubeck is remembered as "the pianist and composer who helped make jazz popular again in the 1950s and '60s with recordings like *Time Out,* the first jazz album to sell a million copies, and 'Take Five,' the still instantly recognizable hit single that was that album's centerpiece."[139]

135   Walter L. Dean to Jim Bancroft (Brubeck's attorney) [cc: Lieberson, Glancy and Macero], May 10, 1965 (Macero Collection, box 7, folder 21).

136   Office Communication, Columbia Records, Walter R. Yetnikoff to Teo Macero [cc: Gallagher, Davis and Dean], September 13, 1965 (Macero Collection, box 7, folder 21).

137   "Brubeck Quartet to Fade Away," *Melody Maker,* September 9, 1967.

138   John S. Wilson, "Brubeck: He's Breaking Up That Old Gang of His," *New York Times,* December 24, 1967.

139   Ben Ratliff, "Dave Brubeck, Whose Distinctive Sound Gave Jazz New Pop, Dies at 91," *New York Times,* December 5, 2012.

BIBLIOGRAPHY

Adedeji, Moses. "Crossing the Colorline: Three Decades of the United Packinghouse Workers of America's Crusade against Racism in the Trans-Mississippi West, 1936–1968." PhD diss., North Texas State University, 1978.

Adelt, Ulrich. *Blues Music in the Sixties: A Story in Black and White*. New Brunswick, NJ: Rutgers University Press, 2010.

"Dave Brubeck Pointer to New Jazz Form." *The Age* [Melbourne, Australia], March 11–17, 1960.

Angeletti, Norberto, and Alberto Oliva. *"TIME": The Illustrated History of the World's Most Influential Magazine*. New York: Rizzoli, 2010.

Balliett, Whitney. "An Insouciant Sound." In *American Musicians II: Seventy-Two Portraits in Jazz*, 433–441. New York: Oxford University Press, 1996.

Baraka, Amiri. *Blues People: Negro Music in White America*. New York: Morrow, 1963.

Barrett, Samuel. *"Kind of Blue* and the Economy of Modal Jazz." *Popular Music* 25 (2006): 185–200.

Barrett, Sam. "Classical Music, Modal Jazz and the Making of *Kind of Blue*." *Dutch Journal of Music Theory/Tijdschrift voor Muziektheorie* 16 (2011): 53–63.

Bass, Milton R. "The Brubeck Septet." *Berkshire Eagle*, July 25, 1959.

Bates, Eliot. *Music in Turkey: Experiencing Music, Expressing Culture*. New York: Oxford University Press, 2011.

Berman, Jonah. "Legendary Brubeck Album *Jazz at Oberlin* Marks 50 Years." *Oberlin Conservatory Magazine* (2003). http://www2.oberlin.edu/con/connews/2003/ofnote.html#9 (accessed March 16, 2018).

Billboard. "Col Rampant with Every Type of Jazz." September 10, 1955.

Birtwistle, Andy. "Marking Time and Sounding Difference: Brubeck, Temporality and Modernity." *Popular Music* 29 (2010): 351–371.

Bordowitz, Hank. *Billy Joel: The Life and Times of an Angry Young Man*. Rev. ed. Milwaukee, WI: Backbeat Books, 2011.

Bourne, Michael. "Dave Brubeck at 70." *Down Beat* 58, no. 3 (March 1991): 19–21.

Bourne, Michael. "Classic Time: Dave Brubeck's Tireless Journey as a Global Jazz Ambassador." *Down Beat* 70, no. 9 (September 2003): 42–47.

Bowen, José A. "The History of Remembered Innovation: Tradition and Its Role in the Relationship between Musical Works and Their Performances." *Journal of Musicology* 11 (1993): 139–173.

Bowen, José Antonio. "Who Plays the Tune in 'Body and Soul'? A Performance History Using Recorded Sources." *Journal of the Society for American Music* 9 (2015): 259–292.

Brubeck, Darius. "Jazz 1959: The Beginning of Beyond." MA thesis, University of Nottingham, 2002.

Brubeck, Darius. "1959: The Beginning of Beyond." In *The Cambridge Companion to Jazz*, edited by Mervyn Cooke and David Horn, 177–201, 351–352. Cambridge: Cambridge University Press, 2002.

Brubeck, Dave. "The Beat Heard 'Round the World." *New York Times Magazine* (June 15, 1958): 14, 31–32.

Brubeck, Dave. *Themes from Eurasia*, edited by Howard Brubeck. Delaware Water Gap, PA: Shawnee Press, 1960.

Brubeck, Dave. "A Long Partnership in Life and Music." An oral history conducted in 1999 and 2001 by Caroline C. Crawford, Regional Oral History Office, The Bancroft Library, University of California, Berkeley, 2006.

Burton, Richard F. *Supplemental Nights to the Book of the Thousand Nights and a Night.* 7 vols. N.p.: Printed by the Burton Club for private subscribers only, c. 1886–1888.

Carr, David. "Can White Men Play the Blues? Music, Learning Theory, and Performance Knowledge." *Philosophy of Music Education Review* 9 (2001): 23–31.

Chambers, Jack. "Bravo, Brubeck!" [Review of *The Dave Brubeck Collection* on Columbia.] *Coda* 285 (May 1999): 30–32.

Cooke, Mervyn. *The Chronicle of Jazz.* Rev. ed. New York: Oxford University Press, 2013.

Crist, Stephen A. "The Role and Meaning of the Bach Chorale in the Music of Dave Brubeck." In *Bach in America*, edited by Stephen A. Crist, 179–215. Bach Perspectives 5. Urbana and Chicago: University of Illinois Press, 2003.

Crist, Stephen A. "Jazz as Democracy? Dave Brubeck and Cold War Politics." *Journal of Musicology* 26 (2009): 133–174.

Cvetkov, Vasil. "Dave Brubeck's Definitive 'Jazzanians.'" *Journal of Jazz Studies* 9 (2013): 53–93.

Daley, Mike. "'Why Do Whites Sing Black?': The Blues, Whiteness, and Early Histories of Rock." *Popular Music and Society* 26 (2003): 161–167.

Dave Brubeck Anthology, Volume One: Song Book. Miami Beach, FL: Hansen House, 1979.

Davis, Francis. *Like Young: Jazz and Pop, Youth and Middle Age.* Cambridge, MA: Da Capo Press, 2001.

Dove, Ian. "Nobody Wanted to Know about 'Take Five' in London, Says Dave Brubeck." *New Record Mirror,* November 1961.

Elisofon, Eliot. "New Life for U.S. Jazz." *Life* 38, no. 3 (January 17, 1955): 42–49.

Elworth, Steven B. "Jazz in Crisis, 1948–1958: Ideology and Representation." In *Jazz among the Discourses*, edited by Krin Gabbard, 57–75. Durham, NC: Duke University Press, 1995.

Endress, Gudrun, and Ulrich Roth. "Zwischen Jazzclub und Kirche: Dave Brubeck." *Jazz Podium* 39 (February 1990): 4, 6–7.

Faulkner, Robert R., and Howard S. Becker. *"Do You Know . . . ?" The Jazz Repertoire in Action.* Chicago: University of Chicago Press, 2009.

Feather, Leonard G. Review of *The Real Ambassadors. Down Beat* 29, no. 27 (October 25, 1962): 35–36.

Feather, Leonard. "Dave Brubeck, Composer." *Down Beat* 33, no. 13 (June 30, 1966): 18–20.

Feather, Leonard. "The End of an Era in Modern Jazz." *Los Angeles Times*, July 30, 1967.

FitzGerald, Cathy. "The Magic Carpet Flight Manual." *BBC World Service*, originally broadcast on September 24, 2010. http://www.bbc.co.uk/programmes/po2sbwtq (accessed March 14, 2018).

Fosler-Lussier, Danielle. *Music in America's Cold War Diplomacy.* Oakland: University of California Press, 2015.

Fowler, Susanne. "Young Jazz Musicians Find a Niche in Istanbul." *International Herald Tribune*, February 17, 2011.

Freeman, Don. "Dave Brubeck Answers His Critics." *Down Beat* 22, no. 16 (August 10, 1955): 7.

Gallo, Denise. "Lyricist Iola Brubeck" (April 10, 2008 interview, 39 minutes). http://www.loc.gov/today/cyberlc/feature_wdesc.php?rec=4797 (accessed March 16, 2018).

Garabedian, Steven P. "The Blues Image in the White Mind: Blues Historiography and White Romantic Racialism." *Popular Music and Society* 37 (2014): 476–494.

Gavin, James. "A Free-Spirited Survivor Lands on Her Feet." *New York Times*, October 3, 1993.

Giddins, Gary. "A Quartet of Five (Dave Brubeck)." In *Weather Bird: Jazz at the Dawn of Its Second Century*, 333–339. New York: Oxford University Press, 2004.

Gioia, Ted. *West Coast Jazz: Modern Jazz in California, 1945–1960.* Berkeley: University of California Press, 1998.

Gioia, Ted. *The Jazz Standards: A Guide to the Repertoire.* New York: Oxford University Press, 2012.

Gitler, Ira. Review of *Time Out. Down Beat* 27, no. 9 (April 28, 1960): 37–38. Reprinted in *Down Beat* 72, no. 1 (2005): 83.

Glackin, William C. "The Bigger Brubeck: Dave Has Fine Time with Symphony." *Sacramento Bee*, June 21, 1964.

Gleason, Ralph J. "Brubeck Adds a Bassoonist." *Down Beat* 18, no. 19 (September 21, 1951): 13.

Gleason, Ralph J. "Perspectives." *Down Beat* 22, no. 7 (April 6, 1955): 18.

Gleason, Ralph J. "Perspectives." *Down Beat* 23, no. 16 (August 8, 1956): 39.

Gleason, Ralph J. "Brubeck: For the First Time, Read How Dave Thinks, Works, Believes, and How He Reacts to Critics." *Down Beat* 24, no. 15 (July 25, 1957): 13–14, 54.

Gleason, Ralph J. "'They Said I Was Too Far Out.'" *Down Beat* 24, no. 16 (August 8, 1957): 17–19, 39.

Gleason, Ralph J. "Brubeck: 'I Did Do Some Things First.'" *Down Beat* 24, no. 18 (September 5, 1957): 14–16, 35.

Gleason, Ralph J. "Racial Issue 'Kills' Brubeck Jazz Tour of the South." *San Francisco Chronicle*, January 12, 1960.

Gleason, Ralph J. "Competition Will Weed Inferior Talent, Says Kenton." *Boston Globe*, January 31, 1960.

Gleason, Ralph J. "An Appeal from Dave Brubeck." *Down Beat* 27, no. 4 (February 18, 1960): 12–13.

Gleason, Ralph J. "Perspectives." *Down Beat* 27, no. 6 (March 17, 1960): 43.

Gleason, Ralph J. "A Symbolic Finale at Monterey." *San Francisco Chronicle*, September 24, 1962.

Gleason, Ralph J. "Brubecks' 'Ambassadors' Wows 'Em as Monterey Jazz Fest Pulls 87½G." *Variety*, September 26, 1962.

Gleason, Ralph J. "Can the White Man Sing the Blues?" *Jazz & Pop* 7, no. 8 (August 1968): 28–29.

Goldsmith, Owen. "Dave Brubeck." *Contemporary Keyboard* 3, no. 12 (December 1977): 26–42.

Granz, Norman. "The Brubeck Stand: A Divergent View." *Down Beat* 27, no. 15 (July 21, 1960): 24.

Hall, Fred M. *It's about Time: The Dave Brubeck Story*. Fayetteville: University of Arkansas Press, 1996.

Hallum, Rosemary. "The Best of Times for Dave Brubeck." *Clavier* 35, no. 4 (April 1996): 8–12.

Hancock, Herbie. "Dave Brubeck." *Time* 180, no. 27 (December 31, 2012/January 7, 2013): 136.

[Harman, Carter.] "Subconscious Pianist." *Time* 60, no. 20 (November 10, 1952): 94.

[Harman, Carter.] "The Man on Cloud No. 7." *Time* 64, no. 19 (November 8, 1954): 67–76.

[Harman, Carter.] "Mood Indigo & Beyond." *Time* 68, no. 8 (August 20, 1956): 54–63.

Harris, June. "I Don't Want to Go Commercial, Says Dave Brubeck." *Disc*, November 25, 1961.

Hatschek, Keith. "The Impact of American Jazz Diplomacy in Poland during the Cold War Era." *Jazz Perspectives* 4 (2010): 253–300.

Hentoff, Nat. "Jazz Reviews." *Down Beat* 21, no. 21 (October 20, 1954): 14.

Hentoff, Nat. "What's Happening to Jazz." *Harper's Magazine* 216, no. 1295 (April 1958): 25–32.

Holly, Hal. "New Dave Brubeck Combo Scores Solid Hit in L.A." *Down Beat* 18, no. 21 (October 19, 1951): 9.

Honolulu Star-Bulletin. "Isle Progressive Jazz Fans Welcome Brubeck at Shell." March 23, 1962.

Horricks, Raymond. *These Jazzmen of Our Time*. London: Victor Gollancz, 1959.

Houston, Bob. "Dave Brubeck: Such a Long Time over This Matter of Time." *Melody Maker*, November 5, 1966.

Huff, Christopher A. "Roy V. Harris (1895–1985)." *New Georgia Encyclopedia* (January 10, 2014). http://www.georgiaencyclopedia.org/articles/history-archaeology/roy-v-harris-1895-1985 (accessed March 14, 2018).

Isenberg, Barbara. *State of the Arts: California Artists Talk about Their Work*. New York: William Morrow, 2000.

Jet. "Lambert, Hendricks Add Ceylonese Beauty to Trio." Vol. 22, no. 6 (May 31, 1962): 65.

Kahn, Ashley. *"Kind of Blue": The Making of the Miles Davis Masterpiece*. New York: Da Capo Press, 2000.

Kaplan, Fred. *1959: The Year Everything Changed*. Hoboken, NJ: John Wiley & Sons, 2009.

Keepnews, Peter. "Iola Brubeck, Collaborator and Wife of Jazz Pianist, Dies at 90." *New York Times,* March 14, 2014.

Kernfeld, Barry. "II. History of Jazz Recording, 7. The Effects of Technological Change." In "Recording," by Gordon Mumma, Howard Rye, Barry Kernfeld, and Chris Sheridan. *Grove Music Online.* http://www.oxfordmusiconline.com/grovemusic/view/10.1093/gmo/9781561592630.001.0001/omo-9781561592630-e-2000371600 (accessed March 15, 2018).

Klotz, Kelsey. "Racial Ideologies in 1950s Cool Jazz." PhD diss., Washington University in St. Louis, 2016.

Koch, Ed. "His Music Will Be Missed" [obituary]. *Las Vegas Sun,* February 15, 2006.

Korall, Burt. "Dave Brubeck: Ambassador of Jazz." *BMI MusicWorld* (Winter 1989): 16–19.

Lamb, Evelyn. "Uncommon Time: What Makes Dave Brubeck's Unorthodox Jazz Stylings So Appealing?" *Scientific American,* December 11, 2012. http://www.scientificamerican.com/article/uncommon-time-dave-brubeck/ (accessed March 14, 2018).

Larkin, Philip. *All What Jazz: A Record Diary 1961–1971.* Rev ed. London: Faber & Faber, 1985. First published 1964.

Leach, Brenda Lynne. *Looking and Listening: Conversations between Modern Art and Music.* Lanham, MD: Rowman & Littlefield, 2015.

Lee, David. *The Battle of the Five Spot: Ornette Coleman and the New York Jazz Field.* Toronto: Mercury Press, 2006.

Lee, Iara. Interview with Teo Macero, September 1997. *Perfect Sound Forever* (online music magazine). www.furious.com/perfect/teomacero.html (accessed March 14, 2018).

Leigh, Spencer. "When It Comes to Songwriting, There's a Fine Line between Inspiration and Plagiarism." *Independent,* July 7, 2010. http://independent.co.uk/arts-entertainment/music/features/when-it-comes-to-songwriting-theres-a-fine-line-between-inspiration-and-plagiarism-2021199.html (accessed March 16, 2018).

Lewis, George E. *A Power Stronger Than Itself: The AACM and American Experimental Music.* Chicago and London: University of Chicago Press, 2008.

Lewis, Joel. "Dave Brubeck: Jazz Journeyman." *New Jersey Performing Arts Center* (October 2002).

Lewis, Thomas P., ed. *Something about the Music 2: Anthology of Critical Opinions.* White Plains, NY: Pro/Am Music Resources; London: Kahn & Averill, 1990.

London, Justin. *Hearing in Time: Psychological Aspects of Musical Meter.* 2nd ed. New York: Oxford University Press, 2012.

London, Justin, ed. "Musical Rhythm across Cultures." *Empirical Musicology Review* 10, no. 4 (2015). http://dx.doi.org/10.18061/emr.v10i4 (accessed April 22, 2019).

Lopes, Paul. *The Rise of a Jazz Art World.* Cambridge: Cambridge University Press, 2002.

Mach, Elyse. "With Dave Brubeck the Music Never Stops." *Clavier* 40, no. 5 (May 2001): 6–20.

Madura, Patrice D. "A Response to David Carr." *Philosophy of Music Education Review* 9 (2001): 60–62.

Martin, Henry. *Enjoying Jazz.* New York: Schirmer Books, 1986.

McElfresh, Dave. "Paul Desmond: Still Waters Run Deep." *Coda* 264 (November 1995): 7–11.

McFarland, Mark. "Dave Brubeck and Polytonal Jazz." *Jazz Perspectives* 3 (2009): 153–176.

McLellan, Dennis. "Russell Garcia Dies at 95; Arranger, Composer and Conductor." *Los Angeles Times*, November 24, 2011.

McPartland, Marian. *Marian McPartland's Jazz World: All in Good Time.* Urbana and Chicago: University of Illinois Press, 2003.

Meadows, Eddie S. *Bebop to Cool: Context, Ideology, and Musical Identity.* Westport, CT: Praeger, 2003.

Mehegan, John. "Jazz Pianists: 2." *Down Beat* 24, no. 13 (June 27, 1957): 17.

Melody Maker. "'Brubeck Deserves Success.'" February 6, 1965.

Melody Maker. "Brubeck Quartet to Fade Away." September 9, 1967.

Merriam, Alan P. Review of LP reissue of *The Belgian Congo Records: Primitive African Music, Stirring Rhythms and Unusual Melodic Tunes as Played and Sung by the People of the Great Equatorial Forest*, Denis-Roosevelt Expedition 1935–1936. *Ethnomusicology* 7 (1963): 57–58.

Monson, Ingrid. *Freedom Sounds: Civil Rights Call Out to Jazz and Africa.* New York: Oxford University Press, 2007.

Montparker, Carol. "Taking Five with Dave Brubeck." *Clavier* 26, no. 2 (February 1987): 6–11.

Myers, Marc. "Ranching's Loss, Jazz's Gain." *Wall Street Journal*, December 1, 2010.

Myers, Marc. "Sounds of Suspense: Cultural Conversation with Lalo Schifrin." *Wall Street Journal*, November 12, 2012.

Naden, Corinne J. *The Golden Age of American Musical Theatre, 1943–1965.* Lanham, MD: Scarecrow Press, 2011.

Neumann, Michael. "Distributive History: Did Whites Rip-Off the Blues?" In *Blues— Philosophy for Everyone: Thinking Deep about Feeling Low*, edited by Jesse R. Steinberg and Abrol Fairweather, 176–190. Chichester, UK: Wiley-Blackwell, 2012.

New York Post. "Why Brubeck's Band Won't Play in Georgia." February 24, 1959.

New York Times. "Louis Armstrong, Barring Soviet Tour, Denounces Eisenhower and Gov. Faubus." September 19, 1957.

New York Times. "Musician Backs Move: Armstrong Lauds Eisenhower for Little Rock Action." September 26, 1957.

New York Times. "Ivory Joe Hunter, Blues Pianist, 63: Song Writer Who Had Two Gold Records Is Dead." November 10, 1974.

Nicholls, Brian. "Dave Brubeck." *Jazz Journal* 9, no. 9 (September 1956): 1, 4.

Nisenson, Eric. *The Making of "Kind of Blue": Miles Davis and His Masterpiece.* New York: St. Martin's Press, 2000.

Oakland Tribune. "'Matter of Money' Cancels Brubeck." January 13, 1960.

O'Brian, Jack. "More Courage Than Cohesion." *New York Journal-American*, February 19, 1962.

Oklahoma Eagle. "Jazz Pianist Brubeck Turns Down $17,000 from S. Africa." October 30, 1958.

Olshausen, Ulrich. "Swingender Akademiker: Dave Brubeck—Zwischen Kritik und Anerkennung." *Musik + Medizin* 3 (1979): 44, 46–47.

Pitts, George E. "Give Brubeck Credit for a Slap at Bias." *Pittsburgh Courier*, February 13, 1960.

Porter, Eric. *What Is This Thing Called Jazz? African American Musicians as Artists, Critics, and Activists.* Berkeley: University of California Press, 2002.

PR Newswire. "Dave Brubeck's 1959 Jazz Masterpiece *Time Out* Certified Double Platinum by RIAA." December 6, 2011.

Punch. "Brubeck on Jazz" (May 13, 1964): 709–712.

Quigg, Doc. "Symphony, Plus Brubeck, Is Cool, Man." *Oakland Tribune,* December 11, 1959.

Race, Steve. "Analysing Brubeck: Bags of Ballyhoo—Little Technique." *Melody Maker* 28, no. 958 (January 26, 1952): 4.

Race, Steve. "Brubeck." *Melody Maker* 31, no. 1121 (March 12, 1955): 3–4.

Race, Steve. "Brubeck and the Future." *Melody Maker* 32, no. 1222 (April 6, 1957): 6.

Race, Steve, Tony Brown, and Bob Dawbarn. "Brubeck in 3D." *Melody Maker* 33, no. 1267 (February 15, 1958): 10–11.

Radano, Ronald M. *New Musical Figurations: Anthony Braxton's Cultural Critique.* Chicago and London: University of Chicago Press, 1993.

"Ralph J. Gleason's Jazz Casual: Dave Brubeck, Featuring Paul Desmond." Los Angeles: Rhino Home Video, 2003. Originally aired on KQED, San Francisco, on October 17, 1961.

Ramsey, Doug. "Dave Brubeck: A Life in American Music." In booklet for four-CD compilation, *Dave Brubeck: Time Signatures: A Career Retrospective,* 26–72. New York: Columbia/Legacy, 1992.

Ramsey, Doug. *Take Five: The Public and Private Lives of Paul Desmond.* Seattle: Parkside Publications, 2005.

Ratliff, Ben. "Barry Ulanov, 82, a Scholar of Jazz, Art, and Catholicism" [obituary]. *New York Times,* May 7, 2000.

Ratliff, Ben. "Dave Brubeck, Whose Distinctive Sound Gave Jazz New Pop, Dies at 91." *New York Times,* December 5, 2012.

Reich, Howard. "Brubeck: Going Full Tilt at 70, He Still Likes to Take Five." *Chicago Tribune,* March 25, 1990.

Reinhard, Kurt, Martin Stokes, and Ursula Reinhard. "Turkey." *Grove Music Online.* http://www.oxfordmusiconline.com/grovemusic/view/10.1093/gmo/9781561592630.001.0001/omo-9781561592630-e-0000044912 (accessed March 16, 2018).

Rhomberg, Chris. *No There There: Race, Class, and Political Community in Oakland.* Berkeley and Los Angeles: University of California Press, 2004.

Rice, Robert. "The Cleanup Man." *New Yorker* 37, no. 16 (June 3, 1961): 41–89.

Rogers, Ethan L. "Convergent Styles: A Study of Dave Brubeck's *Points on Jazz.*" DMA thesis, Louisiana State University, 2017.

Rudinow, Joel. "Race, Ethnicity, Expressive Authenticity: Can White People Sing the Blues?" *Journal of Aesthetics and Art Criticism* 52 (1994): 127–137.

Sales, Grover. *Jazz: America's Classical Music.* New York: Da Capo Press, 1992. First published 1984 by Prentice-Hall (Englewood Cliffs, NJ).

Salmon, John. "What Brubeck Got from Milhaud." *American Music Teacher* 41, no. 4 (February–March 1992): 26–29, 76.

Schmelz, Peter J. "'Shostakovich' Fights the Cold War: Reflections from Great to Small." *Journal of Musicological Research* 34 (2015): 91–140.

Shipton, Alyn. *A New History of Jazz.* Rev. ed. New York: Continuum, 2007.

Simon, Alissa. "Film Review: 'Jazz in Turkey.'" *Variety,* May 12, 2014. http://variety.com/2014/film/reviews/film-review-jazz-in-turkey-1201178822/ (accessed March 14, 2018).

The film may be viewed at https://www.youtube.com/watch?v=ohJ38Es2P-c (accessed March 14, 2018).

Smith, Arnold Jay. "The Dave Brubeck Quartet: A Quarter of a Century Young." *Down Beat* 43, no. 6 (March 25, 1976): 18–20, 45–46.

Smolko, Tim. *Jethro Tull's "Thick as a Brick" and "A Passion Play": Inside Two Long Songs.* Bloomington: Indiana University Press, 2013.

Soeder, John. "Brubeck's Still Calling His Own Tune." *Cleveland Plain Dealer,* May 31, 2009.

Spencer, Michael T. "Pacific Standard Time: Modernism and the Making of West Coast Jazz." PhD diss., Michigan State University, 2011.

Spencer, Michael. "'Jazz-Mad Collegiennes': Dave Brubeck, Cultural Convergence, and the College Jazz Renaissance in California." *Jazz Perspectives* 6 (2012): 337–353.

Sprague, David. "Brubeck's Timeless 'Time Out.'" *Daily Variety* 302, no. 26 (February 6, 2009): A4.

Starr, Kevin. *Golden Dreams: California in an Age of Abundance, 1950–1963.* New York: Oxford University Press, 2009.

Storb, Ilse, and Klaus-Gotthard Fischer. *Dave Brubeck, Improvisations and Compositions: The Idea of Cultural Exchange.* Translated by Bert Thompson. New York: Peter Lang, 1994.

Suskin, Steven. *The Sound of Broadway Music: A Book of Orchestrators and Orchestrations.* New York: Oxford University Press, 2009.

Suther, Kathryn Hallgrimson. "Two Sides of William O. 'Bill' Smith." *Clarinet* 24, no. 4 (July–August 1997): 40–45; 25, no. 1 (November–December 1997): 42–48.

Taylor, Michael. "Joe Kennedy Jr." [obituary]. *Richmond Times-Dispatch,* February 1, 2002.

Thomas, Ralph. "Brubeck vs. Schuller: Two Approaches to Modern Music." *Toronto Sun,* 1964.

Time. "Louis the First." Vol. 53, no. 8 (February 21, 1949): 54–59.

Time. "Symphonic Jam Session." Vol. 68, no. 7 (August 13, 1956): 45.

Time. "An Island of Jazz." Vol. 74, no. 10 (September 7, 1959): 56.

Time Out, The Dave Brubeck Quartet, 50th Anniversary Edition, Piano Solos. Van Nuys, CA: Alfred Music Publishing Co., 2009.

Tirro, Frank. *"The Birth of the Cool" of Miles Davis and His Associates.* Hillsdale, NY: Pendragon, 2009.

Tom Magazine. Interview with Ian Anderson. October 7, 2014. http://www.tommagazine.com.au/2014/10/07/ian-anderson/ (accessed March 15, 2018).

Tommasini, Anthony. "Charles Jones, a Composer, 86" [obituary]. *New York Times,* June 10, 1997.

Totusek, Martin A. "Dave Brubeck: Interview." *Cadence* 20, no. 12 (December 1994): 5–17.

[Tracy], Jack. "Coronation Ceremonies Nearing for Brubeck." *Down Beat* 20, no. 3 (February 11, 1953): 3.

Ulanov, Barry. "Dave Brubeck." *Metronome* 68, no. 3 (March 1952): 16–17.

Ulanov, Barry. "A Talk with Dave Brubeck." *Metronome* 69, no. 4 (April 1953): 13, 29–30.

Vitello, Paul. "Dwike Mitchell, Zealous Jazz Pianist, Dies at 83." *New York Times,* April 18, 2013.

Von Eschen, Penny M. "*The Real Ambassadors*." In *Uptown Conversation: The New Jazz Studies*, edited by Robert G. O'Meally, Brent Hayes Edwards, and Farah Jasmine Griffin, 189–203. New York: Columbia University Press, 2004.

Von Eschen, Penny M. *Satchmo Blows Up the World: Jazz Ambassadors Play the Cold War.* Cambridge, MA: Harvard University Press, 2004.

Wein, George. "Unique Concert by Brubeck at Symphony Hall March 10." *Boston Sunday Herald,* February 24, 1957.

White, Stanley H. "Dave Brubeck." *Jazz Journal* 11, no. 2 (February 1958): 3–4.

Whitehead, Kevin. *Why Jazz? A Concise Guide.* New York: Oxford University Press, 2011.

Williams, Martin. *Jazz Heritage.* New York: Oxford University Press, 1985.

Williams, R. John. "'I Like Machines': Boris Artzybasheff's Machine Aesthetic and the Ends of Cyborg Culture." *Interdisciplinary Humanities* 24 (2007): 120–142.

Williams, Richard. *The Blue Moment: Miles Davis's "Kind of Blue" and the Remaking of Modern Music.* New York: W. W. Norton, 2010.

Wilson, John S. "Brubeck: He's Breaking Up That Old Gang of His." *New York Times,* December 24, 1967.

Wilson, John S. "Paul Desmond, Alto Saxophonist with Dave Brubeck Quartet, Dies." *New York Times,* May 31, 1977.

Wilson, Russ. "Brubeck Makes Jazz History with New Rhythm Patterns." *Oakland Tribune,* June 13, 1959.

Yanow, Scott. "Dave Brubeck: A 75th Birthday Celebration." *Coda* 264 (November 1995): 20–23.

Yanow, Scott. *Jazz on Film: The Complete Story of the Musicians & Music Onscreen.* San Francisco: Backbeat Books, 2004.

Yardley, William. "John McClure Dies at 84; Produced Classic Records." *New York Times,* June 24, 2014.

Young, H. G., III. "The Sacred Choral Music of Dave Brubeck: A Historical, Analytical, and Critical Examination." PhD diss., University of Florida, 1995.

Yudkin, Jeremy. *The Lenox School of Jazz: A Vital Chapter in the History of American Music and Race Relations.* South Egremont, MA: Farshaw Publishing, 2006.

Yudkin, Jeremy. "The Naming of Names: *Flamenco Sketches* or *All Blues?* Identifying the Last Two Tracks on Miles Davis's Classic Album *Kind of Blue*." *Musical Quarterly* 95 (2012): 15–35.

Zollo, Paul. *Songwriters on Songwriting.* 4th ed. Cambridge, MA: Da Capo Press, 2003.

INDEX